D1244591

Reformers, Corporations, and the Electorate

Reformers, Corporations, and the Electorate

An Analysis of Arizona's Age of Reform

David R. Berman

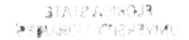
University Press of Colorado

Copyright © 1992 by the University Press of Colorado
P.O. Box 849
Niwot, Colorado 80544

The University Press of Colorado is a cooperative publishing enterprise supported, in part, by Adams State College, Colorado State University, Fort Lewis College, Mesa State College, Metropolitan State College of Denver, University of Colorado, University of Northern Colorado, University of Southern Colorado, and Western State College.

Library of Congress Cataloging-in-Publication Data

Berman, David R.
    Reformers, corporations, and the electorate: and analysis of Arizona's age of reform / David R. Berman.
        p.   cm.
    Includes bibliographical references and index.
    ISBN 0-87081-249-1 (cloth)
    1. Elections — Arizona — History. 2. Voting — Arizona — History. 3. Political parties — Arizona — History. 4. Arizona — Politics and government — To 1950.   I. Title.
JK8292.B47   1992
324'.09791 — dc20   92-365
                                                       CIP

The paper used in this publication meets the minimum requirements of the American National Standard for Information Sciences — Permanence of Paper for Printed Library Materials. ANSI Z39.48-1984

∞

10 9 8 7 6 5 4 3 2 1

CONTENTS

PREFACE

This book is about political reform. It offers a detailed history of reform activity in the territory and state of Arizona from the 1880s to when the United States entered World War I in 1917. It also offers observations about the goals and the career of the anticorporate reform effort, the characteristics of the Populist and Progressive movements as they appeared in the Mountain West, and the electoral dimensions of reform. Specifically, the study asks who in the electorate favored or opposed various reform candidates and causes; what factors account for these positions; and what the effect of the electoral activity was.

This book culminates a long-term research project. Some of the themes advanced in the pages that follow were developed, in part, from a series of journal articles I wrote, which are listed in the references. This study, however, represents a fresh attempt to examine the reform period in Arizona, the characteristics of the anticorporate and other reform efforts, and the electoral dimensions of reform.

The research presented here owes much to county recorders in Arizona who helped supply voting information, and to librarians throughout the state. I am especially appreciative of the help I received from the Arizona Collection and Arizona Historical Foundation at Arizona State University. I also would like to acknowledge my debt to the staff at the Western Collection, University of Colorado, for their help in gathering materials from the archives of the Western Federation of Miners. A grant from the National Endowment for the Humanities helped finance travel to examine this material. Other travel expenses were financed by an Arts/Social Sciences/Humanities (ASH) grant from

Arizona State University, 1990–1991, and a research grant from the College of Liberal Arts and Sciences, Arizona State University, 1987.

This book has benefited greatly from the constructive criticism and advice offered by several people over the years. Some of these individuals critiqued papers I gave at professional conferences. Others reviewed proposed journal articles and drafts of the book-length manuscript on an anonymous basis. Those whose assistance I am able to acknowledge are Herbert Asher, William Childs, Robert Erikson, Lewis Gould, James Kuklinski, David Levy, Harvey Tucker, Gary Moncrief, David Olson, Jim McBride, Bill Phillips, Brian Gratton, John Stookey, George Watson, Pat Kinney, Ruth Jones, and Pat McGowan.

DAVID R. BERMAN

INTRODUCTION

The "age of reform" in American politics from the 1890s through the first decade and a half of the twentieth century was the result of a wide variety of forces. Scholars have quarreled over the nature of various reform efforts, the relationships among them, and, indeed, over whether there was a single Populist or Progressive movement.[1]

Political reform efforts are collective actions that explicitly indict the status quo and demand changes in public policy. Such efforts have an ideological component, that is, ideas that specify grievances, prescribe solutions, and justify change. Reform efforts have formal associations with specific programs and objectives. They also have a base of support in the broader society. Voting is one way of expressing this support.[2]

In tracing the career of a political reform effort through its electoral stages, we look for objective and subjective situations conducive to reform, evidence of general discontent, the emergence of formal associations to articulate grievances, adjustments in the party system such as changes in platforms or the creation of new parties, the rise of reformers to power, alterations in public policy, and factors influencing the decline of reform activity.

The anticorporate reform effort examined in this book represented an attack on the political and economic influence of organized wealth. This was a central theme of the Populist-Progressive period nationally.[3] The anticorporate reform effort in Arizona took root in the 1880s in response to the emergence of large corporations, especially railroad and mining enterprises. Reformers called for the democratization of the political system (especially through the initiative, referendum, and recall)

ix

to ward off corporate control of the political process, increased corporate taxation and regulation in the public interest, and extension of governmental protections to working people or, more broadly, "the producers" from their employers.

Third parties (the Populists, Socialists, Laborites, Bull Moose Progressives, and, to some extent, the Prohibitionists) and the reform wing of the Democratic party advocated these reforms over the period from 1890 to 1916. Reform Democrats came to power in Arizona for a brief period from 1910 to 1916 under the leadership of Governor George W.P. Hunt. Progressives and socialists throughout the nation knew of Hunt. His acquaintances included William Jennings Bryan, Mother Jones, and Upton Sinclair.

Pursuing similar goals during the era of reform in Arizona was an emerging labor movement that was particularly strong in mining areas. Out of these places came the radical Western Federation of Miners that, in turn, helped give birth to the even more radical Industrial Workers of the World. Overlapping the activity of the anticorporate reformers and complicating their task were several other causes of which free silver, statehood, woman suffrage, prohibition, nativism, and penal reform proved to be the most important.

Exploration of the electoral dimensions of reform raises several questions about the appeal and role of reform-minded third parties. Who, in the electorate, supported these parties? Did they appeal to the same type of voter? What was the basis for this support? Was electoral support for these third parties such that they were important forces in placing reform on the public and governmental agendas? How did the major parties adjust to the electoral threat, if any, posed by third parties?

Understanding the electoral dimensions of reform also requires an examination of the rise of those reformers who actually took control of government and their subsequent fall from public favor. How did the reformers, principally George W.P. Hunt and his associates, manage to win office? What factors appear to account for changes in electoral support for the reformers and for their later fall (or near-fall) from power?

The Arizona electorate involved in the political struggle over reform, like that in much of the Mountain West, was a highly diverse one. Arizona was a "meeting place" for people with a variety of cultural backgrounds and occupational interests.[4] Few contrasts were as striking in terms of life-styles, values, and philosophy as those between the stable, family-centered, pietistic Mormon farming communities and the highly unstable, male-dominated, and "spiritually feeble" mining communities. Miners in the 1890s, with changes in the nature of the industry, found themselves in what Rodman Paul describes as isolated "industrial islands."[5] Some gravitated into a class-conscious political movement. Labor-management conflict in mining areas steadily intensified throughout the 1890s and first two decades of the twentieth century. It formed a major element in the history of reform politics during that era.

Like other states in the region, Arizona's population was highly fluid. Much of the change resulted from migration. Yet control of Arizona politics was in the hands of the native- and foreign-born Anglos who made the "first effective settlement" of the area and who continued to pour into the territory and state as it developed.[6] Less well-integrated into the system were Hispanics (especially after the period of rapid development), Chinese, blacks, and Europeans from the southern or eastern part of the Continent.

The economic interests of most people in Arizona during the period under review centered on mining activities. "The mining industry," as a state report concluded in 1915, "is that about which all other industries are grouped, and upon which their existence depends."[7] Mines, from this perspective, stood at the beginning of the developmental chain: "the mines bring capital; capital brings labor; labor means increased population; increased population means a greater market for other products; and the creation of a market means more population in other lines."[8]

While mining was the key to development and growth, particularly in the early years, it was also the key to economic hard times. When prices for precious metals fell, general prosperity suffered. The effects were widespread because mining was a statewide activity. Arizona's essentially "one-crop" economy brought considerable political instability. Changes in the health of the mining industry brought widespread dislocations, conflict, and relatively rapid shifts in political allegiances and policy demands.

Furthering the instability in Arizona politics toward the end of the period under review was the influx of citizens to farms (especially after the initiation of large-scale irrigation projects in 1910–1915) and to economically diversified cities. As the economy became more diversified, the political dominance of mining regions became less secure. The struggle among economic interests — mining, farming, mixed activities in cities and towns — also became part of the environment in which reform politics took place.

What happened in Arizona during the period under review was of direct interest to Presidents Grover Cleveland, Theodore Roosevelt, William Howard Taft, and Woodrow Wilson and to national politicians like William Jennings Bryan and Eugene V. Debs. These figures are part of the story that follows.

Concentrating on Arizona provides an opportunity to examine several social forces and conflicts that emerged in the relatively unstudied Mountain West and nationally in the Populist-Progressive era. Direct measures of citizen opinion on important issues debated around the country are possible because of the frequent use of the initiative and referendum in Arizona during this period. Issues voted upon ranged from suffrage and prohibition to rail regulation and labor protection. From a group perspective, this study offers insights into the roles played by Europeans, Hispanics, Mormons, recently enfranchised women, and an emerging class of industrial wage miners in reform politics.

Throughout the book we shall examine election returns in light of the partisan, ethnocultural, and occupational characteristics of the voters. Decisions made on initiative and referendum measures in the 1912, 1914, and 1916 elections also make it possible to analyze support for various candidates in terms of how voters felt about various issues. Women in Arizona received the right to vote by a constitutional amendment adopted in 1912. Voter registration material allows us to estimate the effects of this change on voting for candidates and proposition measures in the 1914 and 1916 elections.

In describing relationships this study relies on correlational analysis. This technique gives us some idea of the association between, for example, the vote for a candidate or proposition and a particular variable such as gender. The analysis also relies on regression techniques. Regression models allow us to estimate both the relative importance of particular variables and the combined importance of the variables entered into an equation in explaining election results. Appended to this study is an account of the theory, data, and methods used to examine election returns. Also appended are tables showing results by counties, findings from the analysis of election returns, and political trend material.

Chapters 1–6 consider the career of the anticorporate reform effort as part of the general history of reform activity. In Chapter 7 we concentrate on the unique character of this reform effort and its historical relationship to other causes or movements.

Reformers, Corporations, and the Electorate

1

PROMOTION, GROWTH, AND DISLOCATION

President James Buchanan in 1858 called the attention of Congress to "the unhappy conditions of affairs" in Arizona, then in the New Mexico Territory. The thousands of poor souls out there in the middle of nowhere were, in the opinion of the chief executive, "practically without a government, without laws, and without any regular administration of justice."[1] Throughout his administration (1857–1861) Buchanan urged Congress to give Arizona separate territorial status. This was not to come, however, until 1863.

With territorial status, increased private investment, and considerable help from the federal government, the territory began to grow. In the 1880s and 1890s Arizonans focused on attaining statehood and obtaining favorable federal policies on silver production. They also looked at social uplift issues, long-term problems growing out of economic development, and short-term problems affecting the health of various sectors of the economy.

Early Settlement and Political Patterns

What is now the state of Arizona existed as part of the New Mexico Territory from 1850 to 1863. The capital of the territory, Santa Fe, was over five hundred miles away from the Tucson area. Most of the Anglos in Arizona lived in Tucson. "Our citizens cry aloud for protection," declared a Tucson citizens' group in 1860. The government in Santa Fe had done nothing to protect persons and property in Tucson from crime and hostile Indians. It had provided "only scorn and neglect."[2]

Several members of Congress felt they had an obligation to protect and advance the interests of constituents, some rich, some not so rich, who had invested in territorial mining ventures. Ohio Representative John A. Gurley, for example, noted that many people in his district had sacrificed considerable time and money in opening silver, copper, and other mines in Arizona. The federal government, Gurley told his colleagues, had a special obligation to protect these investors by giving them a better government.[3]

Congress approved separate territorial status for Arizona in spite of objections that it did not have enough settlers to justify a new government. The exact population of the new territory in 1863 was a matter of some dispute. Some used the figure of 6,482, excluding Indians, during the congressional debate. A census taken in 1864, however, showed only some 4,000 Hispanics and Anglos. These people lived in isolated mining, farming, and ranching communities scattered around the territory. Between these settlements were some 30,000 American Indians.

Census figures for 1870 showed a total non-Indian population of 9,581. Nearly 60 percent of these people resided in Pima County in southern Arizona. Tucson, the largest city in Pima County and in the entire territory, had a population of 3,224. In the north, 683 people lived in Prescott (Yavapai County). Another 1,142 resided in Arizona City (Yuma County) in the southern corner along the California border. The Salt River Valley district was in the middle of the state. Including Phoenix, it had a grand total population of 246 people. The most prominent occupations throughout Arizona in 1870 were soldiering, mining, and farming. Federal military installations provided much of the business of the territory.

Arizona in 1870 was almost entirely a land of migrants. Only 13 percent of the residents had been born in the territory. Most of these people were Hispanic. Over 60 percent of the residents had been born in other nations. About 15 percent came from Europe. England, Ireland, and Germany were the leading sources of European migrants. Mexico, however, was by far the largest contributor to the Arizona population. Forty-five percent of the total population came from this country. Compared to later years, Hispanics played active roles in the territory's early public and political life, often holding prominent positions.[4]

The territory drew 12 percent of its population from eastern states, 7 percent each from midwestern and southern states, and about 3 percent from other western states or territories. Yankee migrants were particularly prominent in northern Arizona. Many of those who migrated to the southern part of the state, on the other hand, came from Texas and other southern states. The ranks of southerners swelled after the war when many ex-Confederate soldiers and other displaced persons from that region migrated to the territory. Most southerners engaged in farming or ranching activities.

During the first few years of separate territorial status, however, northerners and people identified with mining activities were in control. An examination of the backgrounds of those in the first three territorial legislatures shows, for example, that about half of the members were from the East. New York was the most common native state. Close to half of the members were miners or associated with the mining industry.

The governmental system operative in Arizona up to 1912 was much like that originally set up by Congress in 1787 to provide for the gradual admission of new states. Formal control over affairs was in the hands of a governor, a secretary, and other officials appointed by the president. The governor had to meet with an elected two-house legislature — an upper house (called the "Council") and a lower house (called the "House of Representatives" or "Assembly"). After 1868 the legislature convened only every other year. Originally, the legislature consisted of nine council members and eighteen assembly members. This changed to a council of twelve and house of twenty-four in 1881. The number of legislators from a particular county depended on the size of its population, excluding Indians and soldiers.[5]

3

As a territory of the United States, Arizona sent an elected nonvoting delegate to Congress. Politicians desired this position, in part, because it allowed the holder to return to a more comfortable environment than found in Arizona. The appeal of the office was strong enough, according to pioneer Charles D. Poston, that the first batch of federal officials appointed to govern Arizona "quarreled all the way across the plains about who should be the first delegate to Congress from a territory they had never seen."[6] Local newspapers condemned "colonizing politicians" who "have come here at government expense to lord it over the people of the territory, and lay plans for going back to Washington as Delegate from Arizona."[7]

To most Arizonans the territorial government in the 1860s and 1870s probably was nothing much more than a local arm of the national government. Local newspapers, noting that real power resided in Washington, expressed contempt for the "body of men styling themselves as the 'Legislature of Arizona.' "[8] The federal government played a dominant role in territorial affairs. It conditioned the authority of the territorial government, controlled the governmental purse strings, and provided the troops necessary to protect settlers from hostile Indians (and vice versa). Territorial officials, whether appointed or locally elected, worried about placating Washington officials and avoiding federal investigations.[9]

Apathy, contempt, and the lack of convenient transportation meant that early legislatures often had a problem securing a quorum.[10] Over time, however, legislators realized that sessions were worth attending. This was largely because the legislature made important decisions on the level and distribution of public projects. Legislators were anxious to get what they could for their districts. They distributed roads, bridges, hospitals, prisons, colleges, and other facilities among various regions of the territory through a logrolling process of mutual support.[11]

Serious problems emerged when there was competition for a single prize. Several cities, for example, competed for the prestige and economic benefits of being the territorial capital. In the early years of territorial status, the capital moved from Prescott in the north, to Tucson in the south, to Prescott again, and finally to Phoenix, located between Prescott and Tucson. Bribes to key legislators facilitated the various moves.

Promotion and Development

Arizona in the 1860s and 1870s was far from economically developed. Progress made in the 1850s was undone by the withdrawal of federal troops in the Civil War period and subsequent Indian difficulties. While labor and resources were in relatively large supply, the territory lacked capital and, mainly because of Indian wars, the conditions of law and order necessary for economic growth. It needed all kinds of help from Washington and considerable financial assistance from eastern and European investors.

Political life in the first decades of territorial status featured regional disputes and factional infighting among political leaders. There was, however, a general consensus on the need for unity in overcoming, if not eliminating, hostile Indians, securing various forms of aid from the federal government, improving transportation (especially establishing a railroad system), and attracting private capital to develop the territory's natural resources.

A clique of appointed federal officials and prominent Arizona pioneers known as the "Federal Ring" provided unity and direction during the early territorial period. Arizona's first three governors (John N. Goodwin, Richard McCormick, and A.P.K. Safford) assumed leadership of the ring. All three governors were Republicans. Their emphasis on nonpartisanship and their ability to secure needed assistance from the federal government, however, soothed relations with the large segment of the population that had its roots in the South and strong ties to the Democratic party.

The problem of hostile Indians, particularly subtribes of Apaches, was the most pressing one facing the ring. These Indians had taken advantage of federal troop withdrawals from Arizona at the beginning of the Civil War to wage war on settlers and miners. As territorial officials discovered upon their arrival in the territory, these outrages were uppermost in the minds of Arizonans. Joseph Pratt Allyn, a native of Connecticut appointed by President Lincoln to the first Supreme Court of Arizona, noted shortly after his arrival in the territory: "a miner seems to regard an Indian as he would a rattlesnake."[12]

Governor Goodwin told a meeting of the territorial legislature in 1864 that the Apache "is a murderer by hereditary descent." If it were not for the Apache, the governor maintained, "mines would be worked, innumerable sheep and cattle would cover these plains, and some of the bravest and most energetic men that were ever the pioneers of a new country, and who now fill bloody and unmarked graves, would be living to see their brightest anticipations realized."[13]

Pioneer Arizonans condemned the federal government for abandoning the area during the Civil War and leaving settlers in peril. During the Indian depredations of the 1870s, they again criticized the federal government for failing to use enough force to bring an end to the conflict.[14]

In Arizona, as elsewhere in the period of rapid industrialization that occurred after the Civil War, people viewed government as an instrument of material progress. As historian Samuel P. Hays has noted about the period in general: "No doctrinaire view prevailed as to the proper role of government in economic life. There was only the pragmatic assumption that the business of America was to create wealth and that government at all levels should contribute to this task."[15]

Arizona's wealth rested in its mineral resources. To the pioneers much of the responsibility for developing this wealth belonged to the national government. A principal duty of the nonvoting delegate to Congress was to make sure the federal government assumed this responsibility. As the single pledge in the platform of the successful candidate for the delegate seat in 1868 and 1870 stated: "If elected I will vigorously labor to procure from Congress and the Departments those measures of assistance to which the people are entitled and which are essential to the speedy and successful development of the rich resources of the Territory."[16]

The first territorial assembly set the tone for legislatures to come by requesting aid from the federal government for help against the Indians, improved mail service, and better transportation facilities. Lawmakers gave considerable attention to the development of the area's mineral wealth, principally silver. Toward this end they prescribed a low, virtually nonexistent, level of corporate taxation, increased protection of private property rights, and greater provision of transportation services. The legislature chartered railroads and, being unable to directly finance road construction, granted franchises to toll-road companies, which could charge whatever rates the market would bear.

Newspapers joined the promotional effort in the 1860s and 1870s. At that time Arizona journalists largely wrote for newspaper subscribers in the States or in foreign countries. Newspapers produced a continuous stream of information about the territory's economic potential. Several promotional books were also written for consumption by investors in other parts of the United States and abroad.[17] Much of the information was of dubious quality. As an editor in the Globe area complained: "Whenever a mine is discovered in Pima County, the newspapers of Tucson publish exaggerated accounts of its richness and predict it will be the biggest bonanza ever discovered."[18] Exaggerated claims led to disappointment for both investors and workers attracted to such areas.

Territorial boosters, in print or in person, strove to overcome the image of Arizona as a dangerous place to live. Leaders of the territory's immigration movement working in the nation's capital in the late 1870s, for example, met the challenge head on by telling meeting halls filled with potential colonists that "the Indians are perfectly quiet now, and human life is as secure" in Arizona "as on the streets in Washington."[19]

By the late 1870s the territory began to prosper. Thanks in large part to federal troops, Indians were, by the 1880s, no longer a major military threat. By 1884 two transcontinental railways — the Santa Fe and the Southern Pacific — moved across the territory, and several lesser companies provided services to passengers and shippers. Meanwhile, capital necessary for deep mining operations began flowing in from the eastern United States and Europe.[20]

Prospectors and, later, large-scale development companies found gold, silver, and copper throughout the territory except in the northern counties of Apache, Coconino, and Navajo. Gold was the initial attraction. Changes in market conditions from the 1870s to the mid–1880s turned attention to silver. After the price of silver declined, investors returned to gold. Small companies and even individuals could profitably mine and transport gold and silver.

Development of the territory's copper resources, however, was more difficult and awaited the railroads and large infusions of capital. By the 1890s copper mines were in production at Clifton, Bisbee, Jerome, Globe, and other parts of the territory. Outside investors had supplied the capital. A major investor was the Phelps Dodge Corporation, which was headquartered in New York. The company, in 1881, began buying up claims in the process of cornering a large segment of the territory's mineral wealth. Phelps Dodge first invested in Arizona mines at Morenci and Bisbee, acting upon the advice of Dr. James Douglas, a Canadian metallurgist. Douglas later directed the company's mining operations in Arizona. Another entrepreneur was William A. Clark, at one time a U.S. senator from Montana, who developed the ore at Jerome through the United Verde Company.[21]

By the last decades of the nineteenth century, placer mining in Arizona had begun to give way to deep shaft mining. The changing character of mining in Arizona was comparable to that which had already occurred in California: from an occupation described as one that offered "to all the world the chance to be one's own master" and "an equal opportunity for wealth" to one whose "attractions were only those of an eastern factory town."[22]

With the development of mining, the population of the territory increased dramatically. From under 10,000 in 1870 the population grew to 40,400 in 1880, an increase of around 319 percent. Population more than doubled over the next decade to 88,243. By 1900 there were 122,931 persons according to the official federal census count for the territory of Arizona. Most of these people, some 87 percent in 1880, had been born outside the territory.

From the 1880s through the 1890s Hispanics, some of whom were native to the territory and some of whom were immigrants, constituted some 20 percent of the population. In 1870 Hispanics represented 45 percent of the territory's population. Territorial growth brought a flood of Anglo-American and European immigrants that overwhelmed the Hispanic population. Many of these newcomers demonstrated an anti-Hispanic bias. With the new influx of people, Hispanic representation in the territorial legislature diminished.[23]

Hispanics lived throughout the territory at the turn of the twentieth century, although more commonly in counties near the southern border. Most were laborers in railway, agricultural, and mining activities. Usually, Hispanic laborers stayed out of direct competition with what some called "white labor."[24]

Some Hispanics reacted with violence to the erosion of their political and economic status and to threats against their culture. More accommodated themselves to Anglo society. Others sought to assimilate into that society entirely. Starting in Tucson in the early 1890s Hispanic community leaders organized mutual benefit and protection societies to fight discrimination. Some of these groups also sought to elect more Hispanics to governmental positions.[25]

European-born migrants made up around 14 percent of the population in 1880. The percentage fell steadily down to around 9 percent in 1900, largely because of an increase in the number of native-born Arizonans and migration from other parts of the United States. Chief among the earliest European migrants were people from England, Ireland, and Germany. Included in the European group were the Cornish or "Cousin Jacks" who, in the 1870s, began to drift into parts of the territory, like Globe in Gila County, where they used their knowledge of deep shaft mining. Eventually, they became a dominant ethnic group in the major mining areas.[26] The territory experienced a major influx of southern and eastern Europeans, many of whom found work in the mines at the turn of the century.

The most common source of domestic migration in the early 1890s and early 1900s was the Midwest, especially Ohio, Indiana, Illinois, Iowa, Missouri, Kansas, and Nebraska. On occasion there were also relatively large movements from other western mining states. From 1890 to 1900, for example, miners came into the territory from several Mountain States, particularly Colorado, where labor disturbances had induced them to seek employment elsewhere.[27] Migration of miners also occurred on a seasonal basis. "Snowbird" itinerant miners moved to mining areas in the southern part of Arizona such as Bisbee in the winter and went north to Utah, Nevada, Idaho, and Montana for the summer.[28]

The movement of Mormons from Utah into the Arizona territory, which began in the late 1870s, was another significant migration. Church leaders organized the migration to create a chain of Mormon communities that would extend into Mexico. Mormons created several settlements as they moved south along the eastern Arizona border. By one count, in 1893 there were sixteen Mormon churches in Arizona with a combined membership of 8,190 people.[29] This figure amounted to about 15 percent of the population. Other estimates are that by the late 1890s the Mormon share of the population came to 20 percent.[30] Mormons were a majority of the population in two of the territory's eleven counties, Apache and Graham. They were also present in particularly large numbers in parts of Maricopa and Navajo counties.

The Mormon migration greatly advanced farming in the territory. Mormons were efficient in reclaiming land through irrigation projects.[31] Farming, however, developed at only a gradual pace. Rapid change awaited large-scale reclamation projects financed by the federal government.

Population growth brought considerable heterogeneity and tension. Anglo farmers scorned the Hispanics they found in the Salt River Valley.[32] The clannish Cornish found it difficult to relate to either the Mormons or the Spanish-speaking "greasers."[33] Nearly everyone turned on the Chinese brought in by the railroads. The Chinese were willing to work for less than any other group. The number of Chinese in Arizona was small compared to those in other western states. It reached a height of some 1,400 in the 1900 census. They, like Hispanics and blacks (also a small percentage of the population), were victims of social, economic, and political exclusionary practices.

With the lessening of the need for unity, Arizona in the 1880s and 1890s became the scene of considerable partisan activity. Democrats began to organize on a territorywide basis in the 1870s. Party members serving in the legislature spearheaded the organizational effort. Democrats were confident they had more than enough popular support to dominate territorial politics. Republican leaders quickly followed the Democrats' example. By the 1880s both parties conducted territorywide campaigns.

The change from a regime without parties to one with parties gave ordinary citizens something more than a choice among notables, the type of system under the Federal Ring. It gave them, in essence, a choice among "great spiritual families."[34] Yet while the ensuing two-party competition was often intense, to a certain extent it failed to reflect opinions and issues that divided the public. The Democrats and Republicans who organized the government promoted development and distributed projects around the territory. They had difficulty, however, in meeting demands that came in reaction to development and in resolving conflicts among emerging economic and social classes.

Statehood, Silver, and Social Uplift

Many Arizonans looked upon favorable economic and population trends in the 1880s and 1890s as proof that the territory was ready to make the transition to statehood. Statehood meant self-government, a step upward in status, and full participation in national politics. For many citizens, however, perhaps its chief value was in getting away from carpetbag rule.

Contempt for carpetbag government reached the surface in the 1870s. Much of the scorn focused on the performance of appointed officials from the East. Many of these officials spent far more time advancing their financial interests, particularly through mining ventures, than they did dealing with territorial affairs. Those who, for one reason or another, had to impose taxes made enemies. As a newspaper editor expressed it in 1897: "As long as Arizona is the political dumping ground for the riff-raff of eastern ward heelers, aided by the scattering local scum of the earth, so long will the home maker and the property holder be burdened with taxes and more taxes until he becomes manacled to his possessions which are an ever increasing burden instead of a profit to him."[35] A considerable number of Arizonans appear to have believed that officials at the territorial and county levels had fallen in with racketeers and criminals such as cattle rustlers.[36]

Throughout the territorial experience governors were the principal symbols of outside control. As the drive for statehood became more intense, Arizonans became more outspoken in their criticism that governors were often easterners and, in contrast to the partisan attachment of a majority of residents, Republicans. To some, the legislature became the champion of people against colonial rule. Yet, reformers were to argue, the legislature also was corrupt and undependable without the safeguards of the initiative, referendum, and recall.

Protest of carpetbag rule reflected, in part, resentment over outsiders coming in to govern. It also reflected the belief that offices should go to citizens of Arizona who needed the jobs rather than politicians from other states.[37] In more practical terms, rallying against the territory's colonial status and carpetbag rule also reflected the belief that there were votes to be gained by doing so.

Statehood had a positive appeal to reformers who saw it as a means, if granted under the right constitution, by which the people could harness the influence of mining and railroad interests. Others saw statehood as a key to further economic development.[38] On the negative side were Republican leaders who worried about a loss of jobs and control over territorial affairs. Railroad and mining interests also worried about a loss of political influence. From a more general segment of the population came the fear that the result would be higher taxes or fewer services because the territory lacked population and a large enough economic base to go it on its own.[39]

Arizonans supportive of statehood tried to prompt action by going ahead and writing a constitution without the customary permission of Congress. Such a gathering took place in Phoenix in the fall of 1891. Democrats dominated the convention. The constitution produced indicates the strong populist sentiment already evident in the state. It provided for several types of business regulation and placed streams under control of the government.

The framers of the 1891 document went so far as to call for establishing silver as legal tender in the payment of debts, whether private or public, incurred in the state. Delegates declared: "free silver coinage is the demand of people everywhere." In addition to its merits, the silver provision went into the constitution for strategic reasons. Framers hoped the provision would both encourage miners in Arizona to vote for the constitution and help secure the support of silver senators in Congress for statehood.[40]

Arizona voters approved the proposed constitution, described by one historian as the "acme of constitutional atrocities," by a vote of 5,440 to 2,280.[41] It did well in mining as well as nonmining counties. All of this activity, however, was to no avail in impressing Congress. Indeed, if anything, the exercise set back the cause of statehood by making Arizona look even more radical than it was.

With rapid population growth statehood became more creditable. Yet the effort continued to face serious obstacles. One problem was that many of the territory's most prominent citizens, politicians, and office holders qualified as radicals because they favored bimetallism and progressive reforms such as the initiative, referendum, and recall. Another problem from the Republican point of view was that Arizona as a state was sure to send two Democratic senators to Congress.

Free silver was a major theme of Arizona politicians during the 1890s. It served as the favorite rallying cry of Republicans, Democrats, and Populists alike. Although the demonetization of silver in 1873 may have had little actual effect on the territory's mining economy (most of the silver mines closed before the effects of demonetization set in), many Arizonans clung stubbornly to the 16 to 1 theory as the cure for a variety of evils.[42]

The admission of several western states (the Dakotas, Idaho, Montana, Washington, and Wyoming) in 1889–1890 strengthened the free silver lobby in Congress. Easterners, however, continued to control that body. The radical populism they saw in the Plains and western states alarmed them. Thus, while Populist leader Mary E. Lease of Kansas marched up and down the state telling farmers to "raise less corn and more hell," the *New York Evening Post* declared: "We don't want any more states until we can civilize Kansas."[43]

The desire for statehood also encouraged reformers in the 1880s to find ways of improving the social image of Arizona and its quality of life. One area of reform was increasing financial support for public education. This cause was spearheaded by Governor Safford, who placed considerable emphasis on the importance of schools in assimilating Hispanic children. Another focus consisted of an attack on drinking, gambling, and prostitution. Many found these practices objectionable on religious and moral grounds. In addition, Arizona reformers viewed social change as a necessary evolutionary step up from "our earlier and ruder days" when single men dominated the territory to an environment suitable for women and children.[44] On a more practical basis, doing what could be done to improve the image of Arizona was good for the statehood drive.

Leadership of various social reform causes came from territorial governors during the early 1880s. Prominent among them was Louis C. Hughes, a pioneer newspaperman and editor of the *Tucson Star,* appointed governor by President Cleveland in 1893. Hughes sought antigambling legislation, prohibition, woman suffrage, and greater "purity in elections." In the latter regard he recommended that all candidates for office file sworn statements concerning their election finances. He also called attention to the "pernicious practice" whereby candidates for office deposited money in saloons for free drinks. This custom, to the governor, was "no less than a bribe to the saloon keepers and the electors for political support."[45]

Alcohol was a major problem. Hughes reported to the secretary of interior in 1895 that three-fourths of the inmates in the territorial prison and more than half of those in the territorial asylum were the victims of strong drink. In addition, the governor contended, the selling of whiskey to Indians had led many of them to a life of crime and impeded their "progress towards civilization and independent tax-paying citizens."[46]

Aiding Hughes in the struggle for prohibition were branches of the Woman's Christian Temperance Union (WCTU). These sprang up in Tucson, Prescott, Phoenix, and other places in Arizona shortly after a visit of Frances Willard to the territory in 1884. Nothing of consequence developed out of these efforts, however, because the saloon interests exerted considerable influence in the territorial legislature.[47]

Woman suffrage also gained saliency as an issue in the 1880s and 1890s. This reform cut across several dimensions. Suffrage, proponents argued, would help advertise the territory and encourage the immigration of more women. This, in turn, would help rebuild Arizona society in matters of deportment and improve chances of statehood.

More important in political terms was the link both proponents and opponents of suffrage saw between it and prohibition. Prohibition forces, such as the WCTU and various church groups, also were ardent supporters of woman suffrage, in part, because they saw women favorably disposed toward the cause of prohibition. The belief that if women could vote they would vote dry, on the other hand, made liquor and saloon interests unremitting opponents of woman suffrage. These interests prevailed during the drafting of the proposed constitution in 1891. Delegates rejected equal suffrage even though many agreed that women had done more than men to civilize Arizona and that suffrage was simply a matter of justice to them.[48]

The National American Woman Suffrage Association joined local suffrage leaders in pressing for passage of an equal suffrage measure in 1899. A key contact person was Morris Goldwater, president of the council. Writing to Goldwater, Mrs. L. C. Hughes, the governor's wife, noted that as a Democrat, he would undoubtedly agree that their party should have the credit for securing suffrage. "As you know," she went on, "the Mormon vote is very large in this territory and they every one demand suffrage."[49] The measure failed despite whatever weight this incentive carried. According to a report later written by suffrage leaders Carrie Chapman Catt and Nettie Rogers Shuler, the defeat resulted from "the barter and sale of senatorial votes to the proprietors of the prosperous saloons" of the territory.[50]

Considerations similar to those that underlie the suffrage movement — moral objections, profamily sentiment, and the desire to impress Congress — help explain the intense crusade against polygamy that reached its height in the 1880s. Also behind this activity was a more general anti-Mormon feeling based on economic considerations and on the fear that this group was trying to politically dominate various counties, if not the entire territory. Contemporary observers noted that Mormon colonies established years earlier in other states like Idaho were now exerting considerable political influence.

Mormons were the victims of considerable harassment in Arizona during the early 1880s. They risked arrest and conviction for the crime of unlawful cohabitation. Some paid fines, while others went to prison for violating this law. The territorial legislature added to this harassment by attempting to disfranchise not only those who engaged in polygamy but those who simply believed in polygamy. Under law, those who wished to vote had to first swear they did not believe in polygamy. The test oath idea had the support of Republican governors. Governor Conrad Meyer Zulick, a Democrat, came to the rescue of the Mormons in 1887 by warmly defending the group and leading a campaign that resulted in the repeal of the oath legislation. Officials had not enforced the act rigorously. Its repeal, however, came as an important symbolic victory for the Mormons.

The issue of polygamy surfaced again during the framing of the 1891 constitution when the Democratic majority refused to accept proposals condemning it as a crime and calling for the test oath. Republican papers charged that by these actions the Democrats were encouraging Mormons to migrate from Utah and join the some 12,000 Mormons already in Arizona to take control of the territory.[51] Arizona Republicans were quite willing to state their belief that "the influences of the Mormon Church upon the progress of Western civilization, and their effect socially and morally, are vexatious."[52] Such attacks solidified the Democrats' support in Mormon communities.

After the Church softened its position on polygamy, Republicans contended for the Mormon vote. They assumed that Mormons shared a belief in protectionism and other basic GOP policies.[53] In 1891 Mormon Church leader Joseph F. Smith encouraged Arizona Mormons to more evenly distribute their support between the two parties, as a way of protecting themselves from hostile action.[54] Mormons in Arizona, however, remained largely Democratic.

Railroads, Mines, and Workers

Along with the agitation over statehood, silver, and social issues in the 1880s and 1890s came controversy resulting from economic change. Governors, legislators, and delegates to Washington were successful in encouraging transcontinental railways to extend their tracks through the territory and in attracting capital for large-scale mining ventures. Once established in Arizona, however, the railroads and large mining companies became, in the eyes of reformers, the outside "money interests" who were exploiting Arizona's wealth, taking far more out of the territory than they put in it. In addition, critics charged the giant corporations with mistreating workers, farmers, and small businesspeople and with corrupting the political system.

The Santa Fe and the Southern Pacific and several lesser companies were providing services to passengers and shippers throughout the territory by the late 1880s. In Arizona, as elsewhere in the West, governments made special inducements to stimulate railroad building. Counties issued railroad bonds for rail construction, thereby creating debts that the territorial government often assumed. Territorial assemblies helped by granting property tax exemptions to railroad companies.

Reformers in the 1880s and 1890s questioned the validity of preferential credit and tax treatment for the railroads. They also complained that rail companies hoarded land given to them by the federal government, were partial to particular shippers through kickbacks and preferential shipping allotments, and charged excessively high rates.

Phoenix papers contended in the early 1880s that rail rates had soared so high they were causing a business slowdown. Only rate-limiting legislation, editors argued, could remedy the situation.[55] Similar complaints came from newspapers and businesspeople in Prescott. In this city merchants resorted to a boycott against the railroads to bring down freight rates.[56] From the shippers' point of view an equally, if not more, vexing problem was gross favoritism in freight charges.[57]

Despite these complaints, railroad companies had no reason to worry about effective governmental regulation. The giants of the industry, the Santa Fe and Southern Pacific, and their affiliated lines were quick to flex their political muscle when the occasion required action. Sometimes they simply paid off troublesome territorial officials.

One account has it that when Safford was governor the president of the Southern Pacific Railroad gave him $25,000 to influence members of the legislature in the railway's interests. Safford, reportedly, found that he only had to spend $5,000 to achieve the objective. He returned the rest of the money to the railroad president with a note explaining that he overestimated how much it would cost to "fix" the legislature.[58]

A more routine method employed by the railroads to curry the support of politicians was to give them railroad passes. As an Arizona historian has noted, in the 1880s "it had come to the point where the annual transportation given by the Southern Pacific and Santa Fe had become considered a part of the legislator's legitimate emoluments of office."[59] While the free pass was a relatively petty evil, it did raise the question of why some citizens rode free while others had to pay. As Peter Lyon has noted about the practice elsewhere: "The fact that those who rode deadhead were the politicians and the newspaper editors and the legislators and the judges served only to confirm the general suspicion of an invisible government, of the control exerted by the railroads over public officials and public opinion."[60]

Railroad owners, if not outright crooked, were "scrupulously dishonest" and, in the eyes of contemporary critics, powerful.[61] Reform-minded Governor Hughes suggested in 1895 that the industry-dominated Board of Railroad Commissioners either have new powers, comparable to those of agencies in other states, or be abolished.[62] Meaningful steps toward rail regulation, however, were years away.

Continued mineral development, meanwhile, fed complaints that the mine owners were not paying their share of the tax burden. Governor

Safford, who had worked diligently in bringing eastern and foreign capital to the territory, was among the first to contend that the mines had to begin paying their fair share of taxes to support education and local government. Responding to a recommendation of the governor, the eighth legislature on January 11, 1877, passed a net proceeds tax on the profits of mines. An accommodating eleventh territorial assembly in 1881, however, repealed this Bullion Mine Tax Law. This action, defended on the grounds it would attract more investors, reportedly cost the mining companies some $26,000 in bribery money.[63]

Following repeal of the bullion tax, the legislature decided to assess and tax mines on an ad valorem basis, just like other property. Local assessors, who handled these duties, were subject to considerable political pressure. As a consequence, they underassessed the value of mine property. Governor Hughes in 1893 complained to the legislature that because of the underassessment, the tax rolls, which should have shown a total value of $80 million, showed only $28 million.[64]

Another major spillover from economic development was conflict between labor and management. To the extent one can speak of a working class in Arizona during the last decades of the nineteenth century, it consisted of native-born Anglos, Hispanics, and European-born immigrants who found employment in farming, mining, and transportation, especially with the railroads. Native-born and European Anglos held the skilled and semiskilled positions. Much of the unskilled work was done by Hispanics.[65] Workers divided not only on the basis of skilled–unskilled differentials, but by language and ethnic background.

The most skilled workers were first to organize to protect and advance their economic status. Much of the labor activity occurred in areas influenced heavily by railroad and mining activities. By the early 1880s railroad brotherhoods for engineers, firemen, conductors, trainmen, and switchmen existed throughout the territory and were strong enough to force operators to bargain on demands for greater job safety, security, and compensation. These labor organizations, however, had little of the militancy or radicalism of Eugene Debs's old American

Railway Union (ARU), which had been broken after the Pullman strike in 1894. Former members of the ARU found it difficult to secure jobs in Arizona and elsewhere because of blacklisting.

More intense labor–management conflicts developed in mining areas. In the transition from placer mining to deep shaft mining, the occupational status of Arizona miners turned from self-reliant prospectors who stood a chance of striking it rich to industrial workers or wage miners dependent on absentee owners of large corporations for their livelihood. Miners, both new and old, often found employment in isolated company towns where virtually everything, including the homes in which they lived, belonged to the mining companies. Miners in some camps received script redeemable only at expensive company stores as pay.[66]

Absentee ownership made conditions worse in that it brought an end to the rather close relationship that had existed between employee and employer in locally owned mining companies.[67] With absentee ownership, employees discovered that employers were more difficult to reach and owners found it easier to ignore workers' grievances. Critics charged that local managers were incompetent, especially in personnel matters, and too eager to please owners with bottom line results.[68]

Within the mining communities, tension escalated because those who had grown wealthy from the mining activities — company officials, leading merchants, and professional people — began to separate themselves from the less successful. As Duane A. Smith has noted, class consciousness came early to the new industrial communities.[69]

The composition of the mining population continued to be generally native born. There was, however, a large influx of European-born and highly skilled hardrock miners. Hispanics, the original miners in many camps, were "relegated to the lowest place on the social ladder and disparagingly referred to as Greasers and Cholos."[70]

Miners in Arizona during the 1880s and 1890s lagged considerably behind railroad workers in terms of organization and, thus, economic and political influence. Individual miners were often able to find employment with mine owners they knew. If they were unhappy with their wages, they could often find a new camp where employers were willing to pay more. Problems, however, were beginning to emerge because increased immigration and the introduction of machinery were beginning to produce surplus labor. Organization became necessary to protect wages from those who were willing to work for less, if for no other reason.[71]

As early as 1884 there was evidence of considerable worker discontent in the industrial mining areas of Arizona. In that year a strike occurred in Tombstone after workers refused to accept a cut of wages from $4 to $3 a day — a move defended by the mining company because of rising costs and a decline in the quality of ore mined. Workers formed a union in Tombstone that, for a time, drew upon the support of unions in Virginia City, Nevada, Bodie, California, and elsewhere.[72]

During the 1890s Globe became a center of labor agitation in Arizona.[73] Globe began in the late 1870s with an influx of immigrants attracted by silver. Later wages, employment levels, and the intensity of labor-management conflict in Globe rose and fell with the price of copper. As in Butte, Montana, Lead, South Dakota, and Leadville and Aspen, Colorado, corporate mining came to the forefront in Globe and the ensuing tension led to union activity.[74]

Following some relatively minor disturbances, a serious strike occurred at Globe in 1896 in reaction to the decision of the Old Dominion Mining and Smelter Company to cut wages and hire Hispanic miners who would work for lower wages. The strike led to the creation of a miners' union that voted to join the Western Federation of Miners (WFM), which had been formed three years earlier in Butte, Montana. Other local unions in various parts of the Arizona territory followed Globe's in joining the WFM lead as working conditions worsened.

The immediate cause of many conflicts in mining camps was the refusal of owners to bargain with unions or anyone other than individual workers. Other disputes, as evidenced in Globe, grew out of the desire of mine owners to bring in Hispanics or Chinese as low-paid workers or strike breakers. Such conflicts, to Anglo miners, were struggles to maintain "the white man's wage" and to ensure that the place where they lived remained a "white man's town."[75]

Setbacks and Disillusionment

While growth and prosperity characterized the Arizona economy during the 1870s and 1880s, by the 1890s hard times had set in. Adverse economic conditions affecting the health of major segments of the Arizona economy were due, in part, to the nationwide depression of 1893. In Arizona, as elsewhere, this lowered farm prices, caused mines to close, and forced banks and stores out of business.

A large increase in the number of tramps passing through the territory illustrated the unemployment problem. Anson Smith, editor of a paper in Kingman, located in the silver-mining county of Mohave, noted on August 12, 1893: "More tramps have passed through Kingman the past week than in any like time in the history of the town."[76] Smith, a true believer in the free silver cause, blamed these adverse conditions on the failure in Washington on the silver issue. He warned: "A government that will make paupers of its workingmen will not long hold together and our national government is doing its best to arrive at this stage."[77]

Within Arizona unemployment conditions were especially bad in mining communities. "Arizona mining camps," Smith noted, "are crowded with idle men and the towns are filled with idle workmen."[78] Indeed, over the decade 1880–1890 mining activity fell off throughout the territory — the loss of mining population being particularly noticeable in Cochise and Gila counties, where silver mining had declined because of the low price of silver bullion.[79]

Offsetting the loss of mining population was the growth of cities, particularly Phoenix, and agricultural areas. Some miners and smelter workers turned to farming because of depressed conditions in their industry.[80] Yet although their numbers were on the increase, farmers in Arizona were not an altogether prosperous or contented group. Many faced declining prices. Many also were unhappy with the prices and services of railroads and irrigation companies. Charles T. Hayden, the father of future Congressman Carl Hayden, was among those displeased with the latter. Speaking to a meeting of farmers, fruit growers, and stockmen, Hayden declared "that the water belonged to the people and under no circumstances or conditions was subject to sale and the control of any corporation."[81]

Governor Hughes in his 1895 address to the legislature attempted to remedy a common complaint by recommending "a more stringent law requiring irrigation companies to supply water sold or paid for, or in default of such supply, to reimburse the purchaser thereof."[82] Farmer discontent over water and other issues facilitated the efforts of Farmer Alliance organizers in Arizona.[83]

Additional problems were apparent during the 1890s in the sheep and cattle industries. Both cattle and sheep came in large numbers to the territory shortly after the Civil War. By the early 1880s and into the 1890s there was considerable contention between cattle and sheep owners over open range grazing lands. These competing interests also had their own particular problems. A dramatic drop in the price of wool in the early 1890s hit Arizona's sheep ranchers hard. The Arizona Sheep Breeders and Wool Growers Association spent much of the decade seeking ways to cope with declining profits, for example, through lower shipping rates and reduced tax assessments.[84] On the national level, sheep owners favored the Republican stand for a protective tariff on wool.

Cattle ranchers, meanwhile, struggled with problems caused by overgrazing and drought.[85] Like other shippers, they became increasingly unhappy over the rates charged by the railroads.[86] Turning to government, an association of cattle ranchers was able to secure some help. This included a quarantine law to prevent the introduction of Texas fever (carried by ticks), a Livestock Sanitary Board, and the Arizona Rangers to protect against cattle-rustling. Cattle ranchers, however, were unable to get much relief on rail rates.

The considerable discontent evident in the territory in the 1880s and 1890s strained the party system. Out of this, as the following chapter indicates, came the populist protest.

2

THE POPULIST PROTEST

Writing in 1896, Joseph H. Kibbey, a Republican party leader in Arizona, noted that political life in the territory was in flux. Since the late 1880s, Kibbey contended, more and more people had become interested in politics and more and more people had become willing to experiment with radical changes in governmental functions. The people, Kibbey concluded, "are thinking hard, are thinking rapidly, and more than ever are less disposed to adopt party policy simply from mere party adherence."[1]

William "Buckey" O'Neill, leader of the Arizona Populist party, agreed with this observation. O'Neill argued that the decline in allegiance to the older parties resulted from their failure to address major problems. Democrats and Republicans had failed, in the Populist's view, because of their "subserviency to the plutocratic power of the nation." Government under the major parties, O'Neill asserted, had come to mean the "rule of the masses by a privileged class — a class whose only claim to recognition is their wealth."[2]

Arizona was a remote and sparsely settled territory of about 100,000 Anglos and Hispanics at the time Kibbey and O'Neill wrote. It was, however, by no means isolated from national reform politics. Kibbey, in accounting for the present stir of activity in Arizona, pointed to an increased role played by newspapers and periodicals in quickly diffusing knowledge throughout the country. Also keeping Arizona in the stream of current thinking was a steady flow of migrants from other states and countries.

The ideas of the national Populist movement were not, however, simply imported into Arizona. Rather, these ideas were adapted and applied to local problems. Arizona was ripe for reform. Changes in the party system over the 1880–1896 period reflected this pressure.

Reform and the Two-Party System

Territorial Governor Louis C. Hughes in his 1893 report to the secretary of the interior contended that political parties in Arizona were less well defined than in the more settled part of the nation. Arizonans were "independent in thought as well as action" and, thus, not likely to form attachments to any particular party.[3] Hughes wrote when political attachments in the territory were in a state of change. The Populist party had appeared on the ballot and was challenging voters to question their allegiance to the major parties. Yet when one considers the electoral history of the territory, it is misleading to suggest that the bulk of voters had a natural tendency toward independent action.

Hughes was a proponent of statehood. He may have emphasized the independence of Arizona voters to offset the fear of Republicans in Congress that Arizona, if granted statehood, would be a one-party Democratic state. Hughes, himself a Democrat, could take considerable pride in the Democrats' domination of territorial elections over the previous decade. From 1880, when partisan politics began on a serious basis in the territory, to 1892 the Democrats won six of the seven contests for the delegate office and usually controlled the territorial legislature.

People with strong attachments to the major political parties filled the territory during the 1880s and 1890s. As Arizona historian Will Robinson once noted, beginning in the 1880s, "party allegiance rather than personal liking of the voters" became the dominating influence at the polls.[4] This is not to say that the personal touch became altogether irrelevant to campaigning. Frontier conditions encouraged candidates of all parties to employ a hand-grabbing, "friends and neighbors" approach. In some counties it was highly desirable to buy a round or so in local bars. This was done, however, in the understanding that much of the audience had already decided to vote in a certain partisan direction.[5]

The Democratic party had a broad base of support in the 1880s. Democratic votes came from farming, ranching, and mining areas. Democrats also did particularly well among Anglos with roots in southern states, who brought their partisan loyalties with them, and among Mormons.[6] The latter, as noted earlier, turned to the Democratic party because of harassment from GOP leaders over the polygamy issue.

Republicans did their best in northern counties that had a relatively large number of Yankee settlers. Hispanics were also largely Republican, although perhaps only a small percentage of this group voted on a regular basis.[7] The tendency of Hispanics to vote Republican reflected, in part, appreciation of that party's concern with the civil rights and welfare of minorities. Hispanic leaders were especially appreciative of Republican Governor Safford's attempts to improve the educational opportunities for the Spanish speaking.[8] Also involved was the perception on the part of Hispanics of the GOP as the party closer to employers and, thus, the party more likely to provide jobs, although low paying, to minority workers. In New Mexico during the same period the Hispanic elite accepted the tenets of the Republican party and as patrons were able to influence large numbers of Hispanics to vote that way.[9] To some extent, a similar situation existed in Arizona.

Some contemporary observers credited much of the success of the Democratic party to an energetic and vigilant Democratic press. From this viewpoint editors working for Democrats offset the influence of the monied interests — the large irrigation, mining, cattle, and banking concerns — which were solidly behind the Republicans.[10] An alternative view, and one that reformers grew to favor, was that the corporate interests really did not have to combat the Democratic press because they had no more reason to fear Democratic office holders than they did Republican office holders.

The Democratic party of the 1880s and 1890s was considerably divided. The Civil War continued as northerners and southerners struggled over control of party affairs. This struggle was particularly clear in the effort, ultimately successful, of southerners to oust Governor Hughes from his position.[11] On issues, one found disagreement within the party over what to do about the liquor industry and, although the goldbugs were a very small minority, over the monetary question.[12] In the 1890s Democrats also began to disagree on economic-political reform issues involving the corporations.

Democrat Marcus Aurelius Smith was the most visible political personality in Arizona from the 1880s until the early 1900s. Smith moved to Arizona in 1881 shortly after earning a law degree in his native state of Kentucky. He won election as district attorney of Cochise County in southern Arizona. From this he moved up to become the territory's delegate to Congress for a total of sixteen years, starting in 1886. Other than on the silver issue, Smith was, in neither word nor deed, a reformer. He led the "Corporation Democrats."[13] Smith kept in close touch with mining and railroad executives and his conservative constituents, many of whom were from the South. The more liberal Bryanites and labor-oriented members of the Democratic party criticized Smith on the issues.

Slowly rising as the leader of this wing of the Democratic party in the 1880s was George W.P. Hunt. Like nearly everyone else in the territory, Hunt, in the 1880s, was a newcomer. He had left his native state of Missouri at the age of eighteen. After wandering through Colorado and New Mexico prospecting for gold, he arrived in Arizona in 1881. Settling in Globe, Hunt went through a variety of jobs. Initially, these were low-status and low-paying positions (dishwasher, waiter, mine mucker, and store clerk). Ultimately, he became a successful businessman as the head of a merchandising firm. Hunt, as his diary shows, never forgot his humble origins. In particular, his brief experience as a copper mine worker created a lifelong empathy for the working class.[14]

Entering politics in the 1880s, Hunt first won election to several local offices, including that of mayor of Globe. He went on in 1893 to represent Gila County, which included Globe within its boundaries, in the territorial legislature as a member of the House. Globe was at the center of reform activity during this period. Hunt was the nominee of both the Democratic and the People's (Populist) parties in some of his campaigns. Hunt refused the offer of a railroad pass as a member of the legislature. On this grounds alone, he was not a "regular feller." He sponsored a variety of reform measures regarding social uplift (drinking and gambling), corporate regulation, worker protection, and direct democracy.

Both major parties during Hunt's early career had their anticorporate reform elements. Conservatives, however, dominated both parties. It may well have occurred to many citizens that the dominant elements in both major parties were unwilling or unable to respond to problems growing out of changing economic and social conditions. At campaign time, differences between Democrats and Republicans appeared more related to long-standing conflicts that divided people nationally, such as the tariff (the GOP calling for protection, the Democrats demanding tariffs for revenue only), rather than local issues brought on by development.

On the territorial level it was exceedingly difficult to get anything out of the legislature in the late 1880s and early 1890s that would regulate effectively the railroads, tax the mines, or protect the interests of labor. These failures, to many, reflected the influence exercised by the large corporate interests over both major parties. To the 1890 reformer like George Hunt the major obstacle to progress in the territorial legislature was the "big four" — two copper companies, the United Verde located in the north and the Copper Queen located in the south, and two railroads, the Santa Fe and the Southern Pacific — which had shown their ability to work together to block any legislation that adversely affected any of their interests.[15]

The corporations, at times, simply bribed public officials to secure their ends. Corruption was nothing new in the territory. In the pre-development years, however, it had largely taken the form of pilfering from the treasury, although it was common practice to take payments from outsiders for special favors like moving the capital. Development brought with it the additional problem of the wholesale purchase of officials by out-of-state investors.

The existence of corruption was hardly a secret. Acting Governor John Gosper openly noted in his 1881 report to the secretary of interior that "many of the men who become candidates for seats in our legislative bodies do so with the secret purpose and expectation of securing from some source, honorable or otherwise, a reasonable compensation for their services."[16] Gosper added that by increasing the pay levels above the current rate of $4 a day plus mileage, the federal government could bring a more honest, intelligent, and industrious class of citizens into the territorial legislature.

Arizonans had reason to be unhappy with the two major parties on national as well as local issues. The national parties in the 1890s appeared particularly unreliable on an issue of prime importance to Arizonans: the free coinage of silver. Both local Democrats and Republicans throughout the 1880s and early 1890s claimed that they were the true and only champions of the silver cause. Being on the wrong side of the silver issue was political suicide. Arizona newspaper editors warned in the 1890s: "None but men square on the silver question need apply for office."[17]

Arizona partisans, however, had to live with the fact that many nationally prominent Republicans and Democrats did not share their views on this issue. Leaders of the national Republican party clearly were not in favor of a silver or bimetallic standard. By the mid-1890s even local Republicans appeared to waver on the issue. In 1895 the Republican delegate to Congress, Nathan O. Murphy, faced severe criticism for testifying in Washington that the people of Arizona were really not extremists on the silver issue. This statement, intended at least in part to advance statehood, provoked the following editorial response: "Mr. Murphy's assertion is entirely gratuitous and unwarranted and is an affront to his party in Arizona. The debasement of silver was a crime, and, in Arizona, the evil effect of that conspiracy will continue until silver is restored as a money metal to a parity with gold, at the former ratio of 16 to 1."[18] In 1896, in spite of these feelings, the Arizona GOP officially abandoned silver.

Arizona Democrats maintained their devotion to silver throughout the 1890s but were, nevertheless, often embarrassed by their national party. The silver Democrats of Arizona were particularly defensive about their ties with Grover Cleveland. The president was not only a goldbug but, partly because of the sentiments of Arizonans on the silver issue, was far less than enthusiastic about statehood for the territory.

As an editorial writer obviously unsympathetic to the plight of Arizona's Democrats put it: "Grover Cleveland opposes statehood for Arizona and free coinage of silver, yet the democrats (of Arizona) declare in favor of statehood and silver, and endorse Grover Cleveland personally and officially. This is what might be termed political hash."[19] Additional discomfort came to local Democrats because Democratic governors appointed by Cleveland, L. C. Hughes and Benjamin Franklin, openly favored the gold standard.

Coming into the 1890s, the Democratic and Republican parties were vulnerable on the statehood and silver issues. They also suffered because they offered little to entice voter interest. As the *Arizona Silver Belt* saw it in 1890, the platforms of both major parties were "not only tiresome as to quantity, but equally fatiguing in quality." Excessive length and meaningless flourishes could not hide the fact, the editor concluded, that the differences between the two parties "are in substance the same that have existed for a quarter of a century."[20]

During the 1880s and early 1890s both major parties stood for statehood, free silver, and continued economic development. General issues involving dislocations from economic development did sometimes surface, although most often in references to events elsewhere. Discussion of these issues also occurred within the limits imposed by the commitment to local development. Thus, while newspapers might acknowledge labor unrest as a problem, they never acknowledged it to be so much of a problem that investors should worry about pouring money into the territory.

Along with minimizing economic dislocation issues, both parties strove to avoid the highly controversial subjects of woman suffrage and prohibition. Perhaps the most heated issue involving territorial affairs centered around the attack of Republicans on the Mormon practice of polygamy. While Democrats did not defend polygamy, they did oppose Republican efforts to disfranchise anyone who believed in this practice.

The more typical debates, especially in the congressional races, centered on traditional national issues and over which party could achieve statehood. The Republican party supplied most of the territorial governors sent into the territory. The GOP had to fight off the label of "Carpetbag party." With more national significance, the Democrats also designated Republicans the "Monopoly party," the "Grab party," and the "Dishonest party."[21]

Frequently, the best argument Republican candidates for the congressional seat could muster was that a Republican would be able to accomplish much more in Washington than any Democrat because the job involved working with a Republican administration. The GOP, however, received little support from Arizona voters. It relied on federal patronage for its survival. Even this proved to be a mixed blessing because squabbles over who should fill the various federal offices divided the party into warring factions.[22] To resolve the conflict among rival local applicants for the office of governor, Arizona Republicans sometimes urged that a presidential appointee come from outside the territory.[23]

The local Democratic press often praised the national Democratic party for battling against the monied power and being in favor of the laboring and producing classes.[24] The same sources found Republicans guilty of siding with employers and "trying to pauperize American labor."[25] After reviewing the Homestead matter, Anson H. Smith, the fire-eating editor of a Democratic paper in Mohave County, a thinly populated mining area, went on to ask (and answer): "Why is it that so many manufacturers are Republican, if politics does not cut a big figure in the manufacturing industries? The Democratic party is the party of the masses, the Republican, the party of the classes. The classes propose to rule by whatever methods circumstances suggest."[26]

Smith, however, did not say whether or, if so, ho, the classes were influential in Arizona. Like other partisan editors, he was content to view Republican–Democratic differences from a national perspective. Given the inactivity of the legislature, however, local citizens may have well wondered if more than a small number of Arizona Democrats were really friends of the working class. This minority, represented by Hunt and other anti–Marcus Smith Democrats, was one outlet for protest. Another, and for a time more vocal, outlet was the People's party.

Enter the Populists

The national Populist, or People's, party, formed in 1891, represented the culmination of farmer and worker protests. Also on hand at the founding were former Greenbackers, Socialists, Prohibitionists, urban reformers, members of free-silver clubs, single-taxers, and others who, for one reason or another, were unhappy with how the economic, social, and political systems were evolving in the last decades of the nineteenth century.

Populists offered a broad-ranging reform program that called for, among other matters, increasing the money supply (through more currency and the production of silver coins), a graduated income tax, and reclamation of alien land holdings and lands held by the railroads in excess of their needs. The Populists saw the need for governmental ownership of the railroads and other growing monopolies like telephone and telegraph companies.

For labor the Populists demanded recognition of the right to organize, an end to the Pinkerton system of industrial armies, and an eight-hour day. The Populists also campaigned for several measures intended to protect the political system against special interests. Included among these were the secret ballot, popular election of U.S. senators, the initiative, and the referendum.

Free coinage of silver was far less central to most Populists than other planks such as the subtreasury plan to obtain easy credit. The silver issue, however, took on great importance in the direction of the party. Throughout the 1890s Populist orators found free silver to be their best "talking point."[27] Free silver was attractive to debtors, especially farmers in the South and the West, who believed free coinage of silver would lead to a cheaper dollar with which they could pay off their debts. In the

West it was additionally popular because it would revitalize mining activity.

At the Omaha convention in 1892 the People's party nominated James B. Weaver of Iowa as its presidential candidate. Weaver, a former Republican and general in the Union Army, had carried the standard of the Greenback party in 1880. The basic theme of the party according to its 1892 nominee was simply: "Equal rights for all and special privileges for none."[28] Although portrayed as a lunatic by the major parties, Weaver secured more than a million votes in 1892, some 9 percent of the total cast. He carried Colorado, Idaho, Kansas, Nevada, and North Dakota. Populists in 1892 also elected several state and local officials, especially in Kansas, Nebraska, North Dakota, Minnesota, and Colorado.

National events in 1893 and 1894 helped build further support for the new party. An economic depression set off by the panic of 1893 brought considerable hardship and, coming on the heels of booming prosperity, much disillusionment. Drawing upon this, the Populist party in 1894 gathered some 1.5 million votes in off-year elections.[29] The Populists wound up, after a bitter internal fight, nominating William Jennings Bryan, the Democratic candidate, for president in 1896. In fusing with the Democratic party the Populists also chose to place the silver issue at the center of the reform movement. Following Bryan's failure, a disgusted Populist leader, Ignatius Donnelly, concluded: "We had a splendid candidate and he had made a gigantic campaign; the elements of reform were fairly united; and the depression of business universal, and yet, in spite of it all the bankrupt millions voted to keep the yoke on their own necks!"[30]

The Arizona People's (Populist) party first nominated candidates for office in 1892. The party at that time, by the admission of its own leaders, was only a little club "burning for liberty." It received little attention from the electorate.[31] The press, most of which sided with one of the two major parties, was, likewise, not impressed by the new party.

One reporter, covering a Populist convention in Phoenix attended by some one hundred people on a Sunday in October 1892, noted that following an inconclusive discussion over whether the party should nominate candidates or simply endorse the nominees of other parties, "the feeble pulse beat of the convention ceased, and those present carefully tiptoed down the stairs."[32]

The Phoenix organization emerged out of the Farmers' Alliance and Industrial Union created in 1890 with about thirty members on the west side of that city.[33] Better organized in 1892 was the People's party in Globe.[34]

By 1894, the Populists in general started to receive more attention. Buckey O'Neill became the most prominent Arizona Populist. O'Neill was born in Ireland in 1860 and came to Arizona in 1879. He first settled in Phoenix, where he made his living as a typesetter and printer. In 1881 O'Neill moved to Prescott, where he started a livestock newspaper. Entering politics, he became a probate judge and, later, sheriff. O'Neill had been a Republican before accepting the Populist nomination for Congress in 1894 and 1896.[35]

According to one source, O'Neill became a Populist because he objected to Republican attacks on Mormons.[36] This explanation, while perhaps at least partially accurate, also had its strategic value. It surfaced in political campaigns as part of O'Neill's effort to attract Mormon voters.

Other accounts of O'Neill's initial dissatisfaction with the Republican party point to a disagreement over policies on railroads. As tax assessor of Yavapai County, a job that came along with that of sheriff, O'Neill billed the Atlantic and Pacific Railroad at $1.25 an acre for property it owned in the county. The County Board of Equalization overruled his action. The board determined that the railroad's offer to pay thirty cents an acre was a reasonable assessment. Shortly after this event, local political bosses offered O'Neill the Republican nomination for delegate to Congress in 1894, but only on the condition that he "lay off" the railroads. O'Neill rejected the offer and ran instead as a Populist.[37]

The Populist party in O'Neill's view owed its existence to the failure of the major parties to eradicate "corruption and evils in public affairs."[38] The major parties had fallen: the Democratic party was no longer the party of Jefferson and the Republican party had ceased to be the party of Lincoln. Both of these parties now belonged to "the power of organized money." Their policies, moreover, "have been and are now dividing the people into two classes — a pauper class, who are laborers and producers, the workers in the field and the mines, and a moneyed aristocracy who are drones in our body public."[39]

Arizona Populists endorsed the platforms adopted by the National People's party at Omaha in 1892 and at Saint Louis in 1896.[40] With particular reference to the Arizona situation, the Populists called for the elimination of the "system of extortion, peculation, jobbery, corruption, and bribery" operating in the territorial and various county governments; the initiative and referendum as means by which the people could prevent "the sale of their interests to corporations, millionaires, and syndicates"; and an end to the method of taxation under which banks, railroads, and other corporations had been able to escape paying their just share of governmental expenses.

While others argued that the latter policies were a valid means of encouraging growth, the Populists argued that exemptions simply created a "privileged class of taxpayers."[41] Also included among the privileged class were the owners of water monopolies, who had "systematically robbed" the farmers and, through them, all others for years.[42] The *Arizona Populist*, a party paper, accused the water monopolies of charging farmers for water they did not receive. The paper declared: "Wake up you grangers" and "kick out the water monopoly!"[43] O'Neill called for government reclamation and irrigation programs and for public control over irrigation and canal companies, that is, to have them regulated as common carriers.[44] O'Neill concluded: "Under Democratic and Republican rule the public waters of Arizona — the very life-blood of our people — have passed into the hands of non-resident individuals and corporations, who control the water that should belong to the people, for the interest and profit of themselves."[45]

O'Neill and other Populists took care to articulate the grievances of labor. The two major parties, O'Neill argued, woefully ignored this group. With the Homestead and Pullman strikes in mind, O'Neill reminded the voters that they had "seen the wives of Homestead made widows and their children orphans by the bullets of Pinkerton thugs in order that this man Carnegie might add to his wealth at the expense of American labor."[46] Pinkerton thugs, court injunctions, and federal troops frustrated labor's legitimate efforts to organize.

Turning to the local scene, O'Neill contended that workers in Arizona had been "blacklisted and driven like outlaws from the Territory, simply because they dared to organize for mutual protection."[47] O'Neill asked his opponents to "think of the wives and children of these men sitting in the houses of desolation and want, while the husband and father is a fugitive from the fierce wrath of the little gods who control railroad corporations."[48]

In regard to the control of property and wealth, O'Neill noted that the actual residents of Arizona controlled less than half of the $28 million of assessed property value. Wealth was in the hands of the relatively few nonresidents who owned the railroads, canals, and big cattle companies.[49]

Populists pulled no punches on the local economic-political problems. They moved more cautiously when it came to woman suffrage. Although O'Neill favored the reform, the dominant theme of the local Populists was that the question of equal suffrage go to a vote of the people (men) as soon as practicable.[50]

On matters affecting Arizona that required national action, Populists, like other local politicians, sought two major objectives: statehood and the free coinage of silver. To the Populists free silver was every bit as important as statehood, if not more important. Those who used the territory's commitment to the cause of silver against statehood angered the Populists. The People's party of Maricopa County declared: "We urge the immediate admission of Arizona as a state and denounce as un-American the policy which has opposed its admission, simply because many of its citizens are the supporters of a financial system which does not find favor with the money-lenders and money traffickers of America and Europe."[51]

Populists claimed the goldbug conspiracy was a major failure of the two dominant parties. It also was a central factor behind declines in prices for cattle, wheat, copper, wool, and other products. To O'Neill "the deification of gold" simply meant "the enrichment of the money owning classes, and the impoverishment and debasement of the masses."[52] With gold as the standard, the man who lends money will receive a higher rate of interest and will acquire "that power and control over his fellow citizens that has never failed to result in the peonage of those whose only crime is poverty."[53]

Looking around him, O'Neill concluded:

If you would realize to the fullest what the depreciation in values of all classes of property, through the demonetization of silver has cost Arizona, look at the assessment roll of the Territory, which has declined over 25 per cent; look at the dead mining camps; look at the increased and growing indebtedness owed by our citizens, and the constant and steady decrease in wages.[54]

If, O'Neill asserted, the Republicans and Democrats were actually champions of free silver, "they could long ago have passed a free silver bill" to eliminate these problems.[55]

The Elections of 1894 and 1896

O'Neill surprised most observers by polling 22 percent of the vote in 1894. He carried Mohave and Gila counties and several mining camps. He received 61 percent of the vote in Globe. O'Neill finished a strong third behind the Democratic candidate John C. Herndon, who had 36 percent, and the Republican candidate Nathan O. Murphy, who had 42 percent of the ballots cast. Herndon, like O'Neill, was from Prescott. He represented Yavapai County as a councilmember of the sixteenth legislative assembly (1891–1892). Murphy moved up from territorial secretary to governor in 1892. The Maine native had been in Arizona since 1883 when he arrived to engage in mining activities with his brother, Frank M. Murphy, who became president of the Santa Fe, Prescott, and Phoenix railroad company and a leading behind-the-scenes force in Arizona politics.

Although he turned aside Republican challengers in 1886, 1888, 1890, and 1892, Marcus Smith decided not to run in 1894 because he felt it would be a bad year for Democrats.[56] Smith's prediction was accurate. In 1894 the GOP won with Murphy and did well in other territorial elections. It elected a majority in both territorial legislative bodies and captured many county offices.

The only other territorywide vote in 1894 was for a seat as councilmember at large in the territorial legislature. This contest went to a Republican who received around 42 percent of the vote. The Populist candidate for this position, G. W. Woy, did less well than O'Neill — pulling a total vote of 1,531 (14%), compared to 2,596 (22%) for O'Neill. Contemporary observers unsympathetic to Populism contended that Woy's vote was far more indicative of the strength of the new party than was O'Neill's.

One paper argued: "Mr. Woy is a new comer to the territory, a stranger to her people and a regular populistic demagogue who is full of the talk and blow of the man he aspires to pattern after, Waite of Colorado, and those of the citizens of Arizona who voted for him, undoubtedly did so because they believed in the principles of populism."[57] Woy, although doing less well than O'Neill, drew his support from the same segments of the electorate (the Woy and O'Neill votes correlate at .9).

Compared to Woy and other Populists, O'Neill received good press treatment. Perhaps typical of newspaper reaction to O'Neill's effort in 1894 was the sentiment expressed by the *Prescott Weekly Courier:* "Buckey lost the race, but he is a royal good fellow and an able man."[58] To this the *Arizona Gazette* chipped in: "Populistically, we cannot but feel with sorrow that Buckey has got off somehow radically wrong. He will reform and become a good democrat in good season."[59]

Some papers attributed O'Neill's relative success with the press to his background as a newspaperman. "The press gang," one editor wrote, "as a rule stick together as close as a bunch of burdock in a bellwether's fleece." Otherwise, the editor concluded, the Populist candidate for Congress would have been "skinned, quartered, roasted and toasted."[60] Rather than attack O'Neill, many editors chose to ignore him in their coverage.

While Buckey may have fared better than expected with the press, he did not escape criticism. Critics from the right considered him a radical. O'Neill, to some of those on the left, was an opportunist, a Johnny-come-lately on free silver, rail regulation, labor protection, and other issues.[61]

Liberal Democratic newspapers such as Anson Smith's *Mohave County Miner* found little fault in the Populist platform, but argued that the Populists had not made the case that their party, one "composed of malcontents," could do any better than the Democrats. Indeed, when it came to the congressional delegate position, it was ludicrous to think that a Populist could do more for the territory than a Democrat or Republican. Their party status would give them some allies, while the Populist would have to work virtually alone. Smith also took issue with the "holier than thou" approach of the Populists, claiming that they had no monopoly on virtue and, indeed, once in office were as likely to be as corrupt as any official from any other party.[62]

O'Neill took satisfaction in the performance of the Populist party in 1894, given its newness and the limitations on its financial resources. The party, O'Neill wrote for a popular magazine, "was young and unorganized; its members were hardly known to one another in their own communities." The party also suffered from a lack of funds. This condition was "doubly irksome on account of its candidates being men of small means."[63]

The Populists had only a handful of supporters in the press. One Populist editor was Kean St. Charles, a native of Virginia, who later became a prominent Bryan Democrat and a member of the territorial legislature. Back in the 1890s St. Charles's paper, *Our Mineral Wealth*, regularly took the corporate Democrats to task. Marcus Smith was described, for example, as a leading practitioner of the "Do Nothing Take It Easy After You Get in Congress Element" whose "purpose is to roll in idle luxury at the expense of the people whom they represent."[64]

In 1896 O'Neill increased his percentage of the vote to 28 although he again finished third. This time the winner was Democrat Marcus Smith, who received 43 percent of the vote and ousted Murphy from office. Newspapers attributed both O'Neill's increase and the Democratic reversal of the 1894 outcome to the Arizona Republican party's decision to declare in favor of a single gold standard.

This decision sent the *Arizona Republican,* a party organ, into shock. Just a few weeks before the official change on the silver issue, the paper had editorialized: "No man today need say that he is not a Republican simply because he is for the free coinage of silver. . . . The fact that you are for the free coinage of silver shows you to be a better Republican than he who dares your fealty."[65]

After the local GOP's change in policy, the editor declared the party "sold out to the gold-bugs for a mess of pottage — for the federal offices — but this newspaper is still the friend of silver and for being so is none the less Republican in politics." The editor also noted that silver was the leading industry of Arizona and that probably 95 percent of the voters in the territory favored free silver.[66] The paper's criticism of the GOP subsided after October 14, 1896, when, through purchase, it fell under the control of conservative Republican activist Frank M. Murphy.[67]

Democrats joined the Populists in jumping all over the Republicans on the silver issue. Smith wasted little time in sending a telegram to a rally of the Bryan-Sewell Club in which he re-endorsed free silver. Henry M. Willis, chair of the Maricopa Central Committee, followed up by telling a Democratic rally that the Republicans' reversal on the issue was a matter of backsliding in the interest of receiving patronage from McKinley. This "brought with it the righteous condemnation of all true Americans."[68] The Populists, meanwhile, received criticism because they threatened to split the free silver vote and thereby aid (deliberately, Democrats suggested) the goldbugs.[69]

The Democrats went into the campaign with a solid front as Smith was easily chosen the nominee at the territorial convention. The Republican party went into the campaign split wide open over the free silver issue. The chair of the 1896 GOP campaign later remarked: "The silver mining interests of the Territory left no stone unturned to put their pet scheme over. When the votes were counted, Arizona showed herself strong for the 16 to 1 idea."[70] Arizona voters also lined up solidly behind Marcus Smith and the Democratic party.

The appearance of Populists on the ballot in 1894 and 1896 brought about some pronounced shifts in voting behavior. Up until 1894 Democrats and Republicans in the electorate divided along ethnocultural lines. Southerners and Mormons gravitated toward the Democrats; Yankees and non-Mormons were particularly numerous in the Republican party. In 1894 and 1896 these divisions did not altogether disappear, but the electorate additionally divided up on the basis of economic characteristics in voting for the candidates of particular parties. The advent of the Populists reflected and encouraged divisions among people in mining, farming, and other economic activities.[71]

On a partisan level the emergence of the Populists in 1894 did not greatly disturb the pattern of Republican voting. The GOP attracted the regular party vote and showed signs of additional strength among Hispanic voters and in economically mixed cities and towns. The party was not popular in mining areas in 1894 and, partially because of its stand on silver, even less popular there in 1896.

Democrats in 1894 and 1896 held their own among Mormons and southerners but, compared to the past, did poorly in mining areas. Many Democrats defected to the Populists, especially to O'Neill.[72] Democrats feared this would happen. In 1892, when the Populists first appeared, the Democratic press declared the new party was "a wing of the Republican party" trying to woo voters away from the Democrats.[73] O'Neill's entry in 1894 probably drew enough Democratic votes away from the Democratic candidate to throw the election to the Republican.

While drawing well with past Democratic voters, more important to the strength of the Populists was the party's attraction in mining communities. Despite their campaign efforts the Populists did not do particularly well with farmers — a sharp contrast to the Populist experience in other states — or with Mormons in either of these elections. Mormons may have felt particularly uncomfortable in a party such as the Populist that, as a major part of its program, attempted to attract alienated miners and labor agitators.[74] Memories of the conflict between Mormon farmers and non-Mormon miners may well have been part of the cultural baggage Mormons had brought with them from Utah.[75] The general farm vote and the Mormon vote in 1894 and 1896 remained largely Democratic. Populists did even more poorly in emerging cities and towns. The poor showing of the Populists with people in these areas also occurred in other states during the Populist era.[76] Like villagers in Nebraska, many residents of growing cities and towns in Arizona appear to have accepted an outlook toward growth favored by the business elite in their settlements. Populists, to these people, in some direct or indirect fashion, threatened continued economic development.

In Arizona, as elsewhere, progrowth and anti-Populist sentiments appear to have been particularly strong among Republicans. As Robert Cherny notes about Nebraska, the "calamity howling" of the Populists "ran contrary to Republican boosterism, threatening the GOP image of unfettered growth and prosperity."[77] Republicans were relatively numerous in Arizona's cities and small towns.

This is not to say that all or even most Populists in Arizona were, in fact, antigrowth. Their more direct concerns were with how growth occurred and with who was gaining and who was losing by economic development. At times, Arizona Populists took positions that were dear to the heart of the business community. For example, the People's party in Gila County stressed that county salaries were too high (largely because of unnecessary officials and offices) and that the rate of taxation "was burdensome and oppressive, deterring capital from investment and retarding the development of the natural resources of the county."[78] Likewise, the *Arizona Populist,* a party paper, came out for "the fostering of every legitimate industry," although it was quick to add "and the abolishment of all manner of injurious combinations oppressive to labor."[79]

Yet whatever the real intent of the local Populists, the two-party press did all it could to portray them as economic radicals who would scare off investors. As one editor lectured:

Opposition to corporations is one of the cardinal principles of the People's party. Their denunciation is entirely too sweeping, and serves

43

to inflame an unreasonable prejudice. Corporations and aggregations of capital are necessary to the development and prosperity of our country and its industries, without them the West would be a wilderness. The interests of capital and labor are largely mutual and they must remain dependent upon each other.[80]

Populists cast a wide net, hoping to attract all types of groups to their party. In the end, the strongest element in their support was the vote from mining communities. Populists certainly hoped for this support, but it is difficult to tell from the literature of the period whether the new party made any special effort to recruit miners (as the Socialists most certainly did in later years). The party may have benefited, in large part, from an automatic and unanticipated response. In Idaho during the same period the Populist party also made a significant showing in mining areas even though it made little special effort to organize or convert the miners.[81]

Populist success in mining areas rested, in part, on economic stress and the popularity of the silver issue. One should note, however, that mining areas were not the only ones experiencing economic difficulty (farm and ranching areas also faced downturns) and that Populists had to contend with other parties, especially the Democrats, on the silver issue. Economic distress and the silver issue were, perhaps, necessary but not sufficient factors leading to Populist support.

What appears a more important factor in the support of Populists was the appeal the party had to an emerging class of industrial miners. The major parties all but ignored this group. The Populists stood virtually alone in critically critiquing the effects, if not the goal, of economic development, and in offering aid to the new breed of miners.

One observer, writing in 1893, may well have had the hardrock miners in mind when he contended that the Populist party in Arizona "largely voices the sentiments of people who are not wealthy and have lost the hope of ever being so" and "of those who have suffered from the soulless grind of corporations."[82] The feelings tapped in mining areas by Populists in Arizona, as elsewhere in the West, were not so much of economic distress as they were of class consciousness.[83]

Aftermath and Legacy

O'Neill remained active after the 1896 election on several reform projects. He was a leader in the territory's home rule movement. This had the goal of making territorial officials elected as a precondition for full statehood.[84] In 1897 O'Neill won election as mayor of Prescott. He took pride in presiding over the first city to adopt a law that put the principles of the single tax into operation and the first city to adopt the initiative and referendum.[85] O'Neill also took a leading role in helping to secure a short-lived law allowing women to vote in municipal elections.[86]

As another reform focus, O'Neill criticized the practice of Governor Myron McCord of contracting out prison labor to private corporations. McCord, perhaps anxious to get rid of a critic, commissioned O'Neill as captain of a troop of Rough Riders. O'Neill died in 1898 while fighting in the Spanish-American War.

The People's party disappeared from the Arizona scene before the 1898 election. A similar fate befell Populist parties in other parts of the country as the surge for reform began to decline on a national basis. Sentiment for reform declined with the swelling of national pride in the victory over Spain in 1898 and with the revival of national prosperity.

A more immediate cause of decline in Arizona, however, was O'Neill's death. Contemporary observers were quick to conclude that the Populists had little chance without O'Neill's name at the top of the ticket.[87] Developments in states where Populists had gained control also damaged the hopes of Arizona Populists. They applauded victories in Kansas and Colorado and elsewhere in the 1890s. Yet the performance of Populists in these states, particularly as interpreted by the corporate press, helped label the new party as wild-eyed, controversial, and crankish.[88]

Even though the Populists were critical of the two major older parties, certain county leaders calculated that third-party prosperity, if not survival, necessitated fusion with the Democrats. This was done in 1896, for example, when George W.P. Hunt secured a nomination along with others on a fusion ticket that proudly declared: "The Populists, Silver and Democratic parties represent the best interest of the great mass of people, while the present Republican party stands for the plutocrats and the shylocks."[89] In 1898, with O'Neill no longer around, Populist leaders tried to fuse their party with Democrats and silver Republicans. These attempts failed and the People's party regressed to the status of a politically isolated small club.[90]

Meanwhile, in 1898 the Democrats rode to victory once again under the banner of free silver and a highly populistic-sounding program. John F. Wilson, the Democratic nominee, was the "silver candidate" for Congress and the author of a platform that, in words reminiscent of the fusion ticket discussed above, advocated "the cause of the people as against the shylocks who would subvert their personal ends by increasing the already heavy burden resting upon the taxpayers of the territory."[91]

Papers reported that the Democrats' victory would have been greater but some 350 Populists in Maricopa County voted Republican out of pique because the Democrats had refused to fuse in the county convention.[92] Analysis suggests, however, that, in general, the Populist vote tended to gravitate back to the Democratic party.

The Populist party was first to call attention to the adverse consequences of development and to offer an explanation for the dislocations and hardships apparent in the territory during the 1890s. The Populists spoke out of concern for those no longer in the territory, "men who have been driven from Arizona with their wives and children," and things past, especially "the deserted mining camps of Arizona — those silent graveyards of human effort and industry."[93] The Populists also articulated the grievances of a new breed of industrial miners and assembled a wide-ranging reform program for the future. In later years many of the reforms championed by the Populists found their way into platforms advanced by Democrats, Progressives (growing out of the Republican party), and Socialists.

3

REFORM AND RADICAL POLITICS

The first decade of the twentieth century was one of continued growth and turmoil in Arizona. In the early 1900s the drive for statehood became more intense. Territorial politics, meanwhile, often pitted Republican governors against Democratic legislatures. At times, conflict was as great within the parties as it was between them.

President Theodore Roosevelt added fuel to the fire in Arizona by appointing governors who, like himself, enjoyed taking swings at the "malefactors of great wealth." These appointments angered old-line Arizona Republicans.[1] Within the Arizona Democratic party, the ranks of the progressive anti–Marcus Smith wing grew after 1896 because of an infusion of Populist activists.[2] This group took aim at "old-line" Democrats who were close to the rail and mining corporations and who skirted taking stands on working-class legislation and direct democracy. Reform Democrats like George Hunt, president of the council from 1905 to 1909, drew closer to the emerging forces of organized labor over the decade. By 1908, with labor's help, Hunt Democrats took charge of the legislature.

On the electoral level during this period, the Populist reform spirit funneled not only into the Hunt wing of the Democratic party but also into the Arizona branch of the Socialist Party of America.

47

Statehood, Uplift, and Exclusion

Arizona's population grew from about 123,000 in 1900 to over 204,000 in 1910. This increase amounted to some 66 percent. In the same period the population of the United States increased by only 21 percent. Much of Arizona's population in 1910 resided in two diversified urban centers, Tucson (13,193) and Phoenix (11,134). Another segment lived in communities built on a thriving mining industry. Among these were Bisbee (9,019), Douglas (6,437), Globe (7,083), Jerome (2,393), and Clifton (4,874).

A good part of the territory's growth from 1900 to 1910 resulted from immigration. Migrants came from the Midwest and from other mining states where operations had stalled, sometimes because of labor-management conflicts. Thousands of Hispanics came to work on the railroads as section hands and as laborers in and around the mines. Also arriving in Arizona were immigrants from various places in Europe. Relatively prominent among these were people from eastern and southern Europe. Chief among the occupations were miner and general laborer. Many of those in the latter group headed toward work in mining communities.

With population and economic growth Arizona politicians became increasingly critical of the "infamous territorial system," which subjected citizens to the "whim and caprice of politicians" and "a government of carpetbag rule."[3] Arizona leaders compared the plight of territorial citizens to that of colonists before the American Revolution and to that of white southerners prior to "redemption" (the end of Reconstruction).

During the early 1900s, as in the 1890s, statehood appealed to both anticorporate reformers and the large economic interests. The former looked at statehood, with direct democracy, as a means of reducing the influence of the large railroads and mining companies. The latter looked at statehood as a way of securing greater investment, growth, and profits.[4]

Statehood advocates, however, continued to face an uphill fight. The partisan implications of statehood were particularly salient in minds of Washington decision makers. This was true of Albert J. Beveridge, Republican from Indiana, who chaired the Senate Committee on

Territories. Beveridge's committee in 1902 considered an omnibus statehood bill, already approved by the House, which provided for the immediate admission of Oklahoma, Arizona, and New Mexico. Territorial delegate Marcus Smith was a leading architect of the measure. Beveridge feared that, in one stroke, the bill would wipe out the GOP majority in the Senate.[5]

Beveridge received several letters from corporations with interests in Arizona and from prominent Republicans in the territory urging approval of the bill. Many of those writing from the territory, including Nathan Murphy who now was governor, argued that the admission of Arizona would produce two more Republican senators.

The GOP was weak in the territory, Murphy asserted, because the officials of the Santa Fe and Southern Pacific and the leaders of the large mining corporations were apathetic. These corporations controlled the legislature without much difficulty and, thus, had no motive for participating in electoral politics. With statehood, however, the stakes, including two senatorial positions, would become greater. Seeing this, Murphy concluded, the corporations would become active on the part of the GOP and ensure its success.[6]

Beveridge dismissed these arguments. He became suspicious over the eagerness of the large corporate interests in Arizona for statehood. He blocked action on the bill. Later, Beveridge and other senators made an on-the-spot investigation of Arizona and New Mexico (the Arizona portion took but three days). On return, they concluded that neither territory was ready for statehood. Arizona, the committee concluded, had too few people, high rates of illiteracy, little civic excellence (because, for example, gambling houses and saloons ran day and night), and an economy dependent on mining activity that could not support future generations.[7]

With the omnibus bill stalled, attention turned to a proposal favored by Beveridge to reunite Arizona and New Mexico and enter the two into the Union as one state. New Mexico was heavily Republican. Because New Mexico was far more populous than Arizona (some 300,000 people compared to 123,000), Republicans would dominate the politics of the new state.[8] Not surprisingly, Arizona politicians fought joint statehood as "only men fight when about to die."[9] Democrats obviously had the most to lose. Yet opposition came from Arizona Republicans as well as Democrats. Arizona Republicans did not want to compete with New Mexico Republicans for the new offices.

Politicians from both major parties warned that the Spanish-speaking population of New Mexico would dominate the new state. Marcus Smith and others publicly shuddered at the thought of mixing "a pure American strain" with Spanish stock or, in the words used by Smith, the "greasers" of New Mexico. Opponents warned that if jointure came about, Spanish would replace English in schools and judicial proceedings.[10] Opponents also contended jointure would bring back the days when Arizona was a neglected part of the New Mexico Territory.

The negative reaction of the territorial legislature came in a 1905 resolution adopted unanimously in both houses. The resolution condemned the joint statehood bill for fastening upon the citizens "a government that would be neither of, by, nor for the people of Arizona." The bill "humiliates our pride, violates our tradition and would subject us to the domination of another commonwealth of different traditions, customs, and aspirations." The memorial concluded: "With the most kindly feelings toward the people of New Mexico, we must protest against this proposed union and would rather remain forever a territory than to accept statehood under such conditions."[11]

Railroad and mining interests joined the opposition to jointure. They contended "union with the Territory of New Mexico would make property insecure and progress impossible in Arizona."[12] More directly, they worried about losing taxation and other advantages in a larger territory in which agriculture was the dominant activity. Indeed, breaking the hold of the corporate interests on Arizona politics was one of the goals of Beveridge and other congressional supporters of joint statehood.[13]

Beveridge persuaded President Roosevelt to support joint statehood in his annual message. The measure, however, had trouble in the Senate. Arizona corporations, organized behind Frank M. Murphy, president of the Santa Fe, Prescott, and Phoenix Railroad and one of the territory's leading mine owners, lobbied in Washington against jointure. The Arizona lobby and Marcus Smith were able to get a provision inserted in the legislation that required that voters in both territories had to approve joint statehood.[14]

Roosevelt encouraged Arizona voters to take advantage of the opportunity to join the Union and thereby escape the "tutelage" of territorial status. The extent to which Arizonans suffered under territorial rule is difficult to determine. It is clear, however, that they did not want statehood at any price. On November 6, 1906, Arizona voters over-whelmingly rejected the proposal. Out of 32,788 registered voters, 19,406 voted on the proposition, and, of these, 16,265 or around 84 percent cast their ballots against jointure. Joint statehood lost in every county. New Mexico, on the other hand, approved of joint statehood by a vote of 26,195 to 14,735.

Returns indicate that the proposal had its greatest support in Arizona counties with relatively large numbers of Hispanics, Mormons, and farmers. Contemporary observers argued that Hispanics in Arizona were anxious to join with their fellow Spanish-speaking citizens in New Mexico so they could control the new state. Mormons, rumor had it, received instructions from the Church to vote for joint statehood. Mormons were farmers and may have expected greater benefits under the new arrangement.[15]

Beveridge credited the "corrupt influences" — the mining compa-nies, the railroads, the gamblers, the cattle barons, and the politicians — for defeat of the measure. According to his biographer, "the statehood fight marked the first step in Beveridge's shift from standpattism to progressivism." Up to the statehood battle he had extolled business statesmanship as a remedy for the nation's ills. The statehood battle changed his mind. "I don't want anybody ever again to talk to me about the high moral tone of wealthy men when their pocketbook is touched," he said angrily of the Arizona lobby.[16]

The virtually universal condemnation of the jointure proposal by Arizona corporations, politicians, and newspapers, no doubt, greatly influenced the public. Opponents of jointure appealed to feelings of state pride. They also attempted to tap anti-Hispanic sentiment that, by all accounts, was considerable at the time. This bias existed in part because Hispanics, being willing to work for low wages, were taking jobs away from Anglos. Hispanics also suffered because they were Catholics. As one observer notes, in Arizona during this period "anti-Catholic and anti-foreign sentiments did not lurk, but stalked."[17]

With the Spanish-American War, Hispanics faced the additional burden of having their loyalty questioned. During the war one paper contended, for example: "Many of the Mexican population of Southern Arizona are in hearty sympathy with Spain and are not slow in voicing their sentiments. A necktie party is liable to result from a too excessive use of their mouth."[18] Also stirring anti-Hispanic sentiment in 1904–1905 was a well-publicized controversy involving the adoption of Anglo children by Hispanic parents.[19]

Agitation for statehood continued until 1910, when Arizona finally received the right to frame a constitution. Meanwhile, territorial officials grappled with several issues left over from the 1890s. On one remaining social uplift issue, prohibition, a milestone came in 1901 when the legislature agreed to allow local option on the question. The law, however, required a two-thirds yes vote in a county or town before the jurisdiction could go dry. The two-thirds rule confined prohibition successes to rural areas where there was virtually a consensus for the reform. After 1909, when the law changed so only a majority vote could bring about prohibition, several more localities also chose to go dry.

In the meantime, Councilman W. P. Hunt was among the leaders in the successful effort in 1907 to enact a high license bill. This measure, in effect, abolished low-level saloons or dives commonly found in small mining camps and the tougher parts of towns by requiring owners to pay a license fee of $300 per year. In related moves, the legislature also, with the support of Hunt and like-minded reform Democrats, decided to ban prostitution and gambling in the territory. Advocates of social legislation defended the changes, in part, as a way of improving the image of the territory and, thus, improving the chances for statehood.

Woman suffrage was another long-standing reform demand in the early 1900s. Suffragists lost in the territorial legislature to the liquor lobby in 1899. The liquor lobby saw suffrage leading to prohibition. Two years later a newspaper editor, noting continued agitation for suffrage, complained: "Most folks do not appreciate that the work for female suffrage is nothing more than an entering wedge for a booze law such as Bleeding Kansas is at present afflicted with."[20] The existence of this connection did not escape notice by the legislators. In 1901–1903, however, many were willing to go on record as favoring equal suffrage as well as prohibition.

The Democratic legislature passed an equal suffrage bill in 1903. Republican Governor Alexander O. Brodie vetoed the measure, ostensibly on constitutional grounds. The politics of the situation is somewhat unclear. Democrats may have hoped to claim credit for passage of a suffrage bill and, later, claim their just reward from the new voters. On the other hand, being the majority party, the Democrats had the most to lose by expanding the suffrage base. Anticipating that Brodie would veto the measure, the Democrats perhaps hoped to make the Republicans take the blame for rejecting a reform that they (the Democrats) really were not all that enthusiastic about themselves.[21]

On the broader issue, conventional wisdom, as reflected in newspaper editorials, appears to have been heading toward the conclusion that suffrage expansion would not make much difference. For one reason, women were not likely turn out in large numbers. Those who would vote, moreover, were likely to vote the same way as their husbands, fathers, brothers, or closest male friends. These lessons, editors contended, came from western states where women had the vote.[22] Suffragists, for strategic reasons, were content with this conventional wisdom. They assumed that by downplaying the significance of suffrage extension, the reform would be more acceptable to male voters.

Assurances of continued male domination of political affairs, however, were not enough to silence opponents. The suffrage question involved several unknowns. Politicians were uncertain as to which, if any, party would benefit. The issue also raised questions regarding prohibition. In the sexist thinking that characterized the era, some people worried that the addition of women would bring an infusion of "sentiment rather than reason" into the political system, which would make elections unpredictable.

Of particular importance in Arizona, editors also suggested that the experience in Utah showed that Mormon women voted as directed by the Church.[23] Given the relatively large female population in Mormon communities, the expansion of suffrage in Arizona could increase dramatically the power of the Church in territorial politics.

Overall, the territorial government in its declining days did little to advance the cause of democracy. The legislature in 1909 approved a measure calling for direct primaries, but a proposal introduced by Hunt and favored by labor, calling for what some considered the radical initiative and referendum processes, passed the council only to die in the lower house. In 1909 the Democratic-controlled legislature, acting on the belief that Hispanics tended to vote Republican, secured passage of a measure over the veto of Republican Governor Joseph H. Kibbey providing for a literacy test in English as a condition of voting.

Earlier, a Democratic legislature had passed and a Republican governor had signed a law requiring a poll tax of $2.50. The law caused liberal papers to object: "If a state or territory has the right to impose a license tax of two dollars upon the voter, what is to hinder it from passing a law taxing him fifty, one hundred or a thousand dollars, all of which would mean the disfranchisement of all save wealthy and privileged classes."[24]

Exclusionary sentiments led to the passage of the territory's first segregation law in 1909. This act, supported by Hunt among others, passed over the objections of Governor Kibbey. The law required segregation of "students of the African race" from white students when a majority of a school district's residents required segregation. The vote was perhaps largely symbolic, reflecting long-standing viewpoints about race. Blacks constituted less than 2 percent of the territory's population.[25]

Combating the Corporations

During the early 1900s the railroads and mines were still able to promote their interests and defend themselves from attack.[26] Democratic-controlled legislative bodies in this period continued to give railroads exemptions from taxation. This was done in violation of the party's platform commitments. One paper chided: "Railroad exemption bills are now in evidence and the democrats will vote for them like little men. Exemptions of this kind are all right and aid in building up the territory, but the democrats, if we remember rightly, are pledged against everything that savors of exemption."[27]

About 30 percent of the nearly two thousand miles of railroad in the territory in 1905 were exempt from taxation.[28] In his case against statehood, Beveridge took time to note that the history of the territory clearly indicated that railroads were likely to receive an exemption any time they requested one.[29] In regard to property taxation, railroads in Arizona paid about $137 per mile of line in 1900, compared to a national average of around $255 per mile of line. Ten years later, at the end of the territorial period, taxes increased a bit to $158 per mile, but Arizona was even farther beneath the national average, which stood at $431.[30]

Complaints frequently surfaced in the early 1900s not only over railway taxes but also over rates, services, and the free pass evil. Examples of discontent over rates and services are not difficult to find. A strong response to high rates came in a letter from William E. Brooks (we introduce Brooks a bit later) to his mother in 1904. Having noted that a round trip from Solomonville, Arizona, to Boston, Massachusetts, would cost $150, he exclaimed:

> Just think of it! All except about twenty five dollars is clear profit to the owners of the railroads. When the people come to themselves and get a little sense these roads will be run for the public and not for speculators. At such rates, there is no telling when I can come east. I would rather walk than squander money and add to the piles of millionaires in such a manner.[31]

As for rail service, one paper noted the same year: "The M&P train was eight hours late today, arriving shortly after noon." This, however, was not unusual or unexpected. Indeed, "the only time the train has ever been on time, there were no busses or cars at the depot to take the passengers."[32] Although the free pass situation had improved from the 1890s, critics still found it bad enough "to in many cases defeat the ends of justice, and to allow some of our big corporations to avoid the payment of their just proportion of the taxes."[33]

The territorial legislature in the 1907 session considered proposals to end the free pass problem and to strengthen rail regulation. Some legislators called for a strong railroad commission. Others wanted to directly mandate a three cent passenger fare. Finally, in 1909, the legislature took action against free passes and unregulated rates and services by creating the Arizona Railway Commission.[34] The commission, however, in the eyes of its critics, soon fell under the control of the railroads.[35]

Territorial governors (Democrat Benjamin Franklin and Roosevelt appointees Alexander O. Brodie and Joseph H. Kibbey) continued in the late 1890s and early 1900s to provide leadership in the crusade to force the mines to pick up a greater share of the tax load. The notion of shifting more of the financial burden to the mines played well in the diversified cities and ranching and farming regions, the last of these somewhat contemptuously called the "alfalfa" counties. Spokespeople for the mines looked elsewhere for revenue. They suggested, among other measures, increased taxation of railroad property.[36] On this, of course, the "corporate interests" disagreed.

Franklin's proposal to tax the net proceeds of mines failed when, according to the governor, lobbyists for mining companies bribed nine members of the legislature.[37] In fending off increased taxation, the mining companies acknowledged they were enjoying an increase in profits, but this meant simply that they enjoyed a reward for the risks they had taken. Mine officials warned the legislators: "Knock the copper mines and you knock Arizona."[38]

Eventually, the legislature adopted a tax measure agreed to by the mine companies. This measure, the Bullion Tax Law of 1907, valued each mine at 25 percent of the value of its annual output. It raised total valuation of mining property from $14 million to $20 million. Governor Hughes in the 1890s valued considerably less mining property at $28 million. Even those who had worked hard for the reform saw the act as only a small step in the right direction.[39]

The early 1900s also brought some gains for organized labor. Among the best organized workers were the relatively safe and sane railway brotherhoods. These organizations already had the reputation of being "the aristocrats" of the labor movement. Their views were not working-class radical.[40] Socialist leader Eugene Debs complained in 1908 that "railroad employees as a rule are densely ignorant of the real spirit and purpose of the trade union movement. They know very little concerning the traditions and principles of unionism and absolutely nothing of its history. Of economics they are as guiltless of knowledge as babes."[41] Making a possible exception for the Switchmen's Union, Debs complained that "each of the railroad organizations is run on the theory that the interest of labor and capital are identical."[42]

The lack of radicalism partially reflected the effect of federal legislation adopted in 1898, the Erdman Act, which provided for arbitration of railway labor disputes and banned blacklisting by railroad corporations engaged in interstate commerce. Although the U.S. Supreme Court voided the blacklisting prohibition in 1908, these reforms momentarily stifled the intensity of the union cause.[43]

In contrast, the Western Federation of Miners in the early 1900s became increasingly radicalized by employer and state resistance to miners' demands. Violent strikes, such as the one in the Coeur d'Alene in Idaho, converted indifferent WFM members "into radical militants and confirmed radicals in their beliefs."[44] The official journal of the Western Federation of Miners, the *Miner's Magazine,* pledged the organization "to the advocacy of the miner's cause" and, more broadly, "to the cause of the producing masses, regardless of religion, nationality or race, with the object of arousing them from the lethargy into which they have sunk, and which makes them willing to live in squalor, while their masters revel in the wealth stolen from labor."[45]

This editorial, written in 1900 by WFM president Edward Boyce, also noted that the union's enemies, "those who believe in upholding the present robber system of oppression and greed," were hiding behind patriotism "in denouncing the WFM as a band of agitators, foreigners, socialists, and anarchists."[46] Boyce's magazine recognized a kinship with former Arizona Populist Buckey O'Neill who, it declared, never received credit as a leader of the Rough Riders because he had championed the cause of workers.[47]

The WFM under Boyce was a "union of factions and fractious locals."[48] Boyce, a Socialist, was unable to get the WFM to formally endorse the Socialist Party of America, although there was a strong faction in support of such action.[49] Nor did the WFM follow through on his suggestion that locals form rifle clubs so workers would be in a better position to protect their interests. Boyce also called for the WFM to buy its own mines. As an employer, it could give workers control of the means of production. The WFM did not do this either.[50]

Boyce was, however, able to forge the WFM into a radical-looking organization. It was frightening enough so mine owners in Colorado, Idaho, Arizona, and elsewhere marshaled their forces against it. For the WFM leadership it became increasingly important over the decade that it be active on the political as well as industrial field. Leaders reasoned that the capitalist class could not win on the industrial field without the aid of government. As a WFM report declared: "It is the union of these economic powers with the powers of government, city, state and nation which so often results in disastrous defeat in our struggles on the economic field."[51] To avert these defeats, concerted political action was needed to "wrench from capitalism the control of government."[52] The acquired taste for political activity led the WFM to become involved in Arizona politics, most notably, in influencing the framing of the state constitution.

The WFM, in 1905, helped create the even more militant Industrial Workers of the World (IWW). Both the WFM and the IWW recognized the class struggle and the folly in believing there could be any lasting peace between workers and capitalists. In later years the WFM was to moderate its position. The IWW remained radical.[53]

The WFM during the early 1900s represented "isolated bands of workingmen trying to improve their lives."[54] At any given time during this period WFM locals existed in a score of mining towns scattered around the Arizona territory. Some miners in the WFM locals had bitter experiences in other mining states and had fled to Arizona, sometimes under assumed names, to find employment. Some locals such as in Globe and McCabe were dominant influences in their communities. In the latter the WFM local had been able to require that virtually all goods sold in the town carry the union label.[55]

The local WFM in Jerome was less well integrated into the community. Having aroused some suspicion, the miners' union decided to do away with the secrecy that commonly had characterized its meetings. Members hoped the move would put the spotters and private detectives who infiltrated the meetings out of work. The main purpose of the open meetings, however, was so "the outside public, whose minds have been poisoned by the capitalistic press, will learn that we are organized solely for the emancipation of our class."[56]

Throughout the early 1900s the major labor needs of the territory were in the mines. Immigration from Europe filled some of this need. Some observers, however, pointed with alarm to the "growing menace" of an influx of "the lowest type of Europeans" from Austria-Hungary, Italy, Russia, and other places into mining areas. The editor of a Globe newspaper complained that most of these people were "ignorant of our language, of our customs and of our laws" and, as a rule, were far too clannish to be good citizens.

On the economic level, the editor continued, the new immigrants "contribute little or nothing to the support of government, and the greater part of the money they earn is sent abroad to support families in foreign countries, or to be hoarded until such time when, having saved a competence, they can return to their native land and live in unmeasurable comfort."[57] Others came to similar if not harsher conclusions about

Hispanics who also moved into mining areas. Both groups had reason to feel uncomfortable in their communities.

For Hispanics in mining towns like Morenci and Metcalf, some of the more egregious abuses came from local officials, especially those in the system of justice. Noting these conditions, a Spanish-language news-paper contended that the only remedy was that Hispanics who live in mining camps become citizens and, through their vote, "give their due to the multitude of greedy Pilates who today live off the toiling miners."[58] WFM organizers in Arizona largely passed up the opportunity to organize Hispanic workers, although there was some dissension over this policy.

WFM organizers often found that the new immigrants from eastern and southern Europe were right off the land. They knew nothing about organization. The industrial world was new to them. Compared to native-born miners and those from western Europe, the new immigrants were more anxious to establish homes and, because of this, more willing to accept harsh working conditions, although there were limits to their endurance. What union organizers thought of as "American miners," the English-speaking natives or western European born – immigrants, were more likely than others to become "hobo miners." These miners objected to conditions. They organized, soon found themselves blacklisted, and roamed the country in search of work. Miners who decided to stick to their jobs had to worry about pay cuts and, increasingly important, safety conditions and the quality of company hospitals. As one organizer concluded: "We make hobo miners of those we don't cripple, and we make cripples of those we don't make hobo miners."[59]

At the turn of the century, magazines aimed at investors portrayed Arizona as remarkably tranquil in regard to labor problems in mining camps, especially when considering the violent strikes occurring in adjoining states.[60] The principal exception to this occurred after the passage of the Eight Hour Bill signed into law by Governor Brodie in 1903. The new law prohibited more than eight hours of work under-ground in the mines. Some companies reacted by reducing wages. Companies in the Clifton-Morenci area switched to an hourly rate and offered underground miners nine hours of pay for eight hours of work.

The new plan discriminated against those (largely Hispanics and southern Europeans) who worked in above-ground unskilled positions. Those who worked below ground received an average of $4 for eight hours of work. Those who worked above ground received an average of $2 for ten hours of work.[61]

Workers in the Clifton-Morenci area went on strike rather than accept the new pay system. Eighty percent of the strikers were Hispanic. The remaining strikers were mostly eastern and southern Europeans, particularly Italians and Slavonians. Both groups demanded wages equal to that given native-born Anglos and western Europeans who worked underground.

Acting governor Issac Stoddard considered the strike serious enough to justify sending territorial troops, the Arizona Rangers, into the district to protect the property of the mine owners. Stoddard also asked President Roosevelt to send federal troops to the area. Roosevelt complied with the request. Judges helped out the mine owners by restraining strikers from interfering with mine operations. Strike leaders who defied the court found themselves under arrest. Some leaders were confined in the territorial prison. Newspapers made much of the "Mexican Affair" at Clifton.[62]

Governor Brodie, however, gave little attention to the event. He simply attributed the problem to "a foreign element among the miners."[63] Most of his report painted a favorable picture of the territory's labor force and conditions. The *Engineering and Mining Journal,* a year later, also commented upon the good labor conditions prevailing in Arizona. One editor commented that Morenci and Bisbee were model mining camps, "both as regards the character and general morale of the miners, and the provisions made by the companies for their health and entertainment." The writer concluded that because of excellent employee relations, unions never had much appeal in Bisbee, although the Western Federation of Miners had tried to organize the miners on several occasions.[64]

These viewpoints partially reflected the desire to encourage investment. They were, however, off the mark. At the turn of the century a radical labor movement was well under way in Arizona and labor disturbances occurred in nearly every large copper camp in the territory.[65] Strikes over working conditions occurred in 1906 and 1907 in Bisbee, Morenci, Globe, and other camps around the territory. These were largely unsuccessful. Failure came, in part, because the panic of 1907 destroyed the copper market and, thus, reduced the pressure on employers. It also failed because the miners' organizations could not keep the strikers out long enough to realize their objectives. In Bisbee the companies simply shut down the mines, thus breaking the strike.

By 1906 the battle to organize Bisbee had been going on for over a quarter of a century. The mining companies united in opposition to the WFM or any other labor organization. The WFM, on the other hand, focused on organizing Bisbee because it was an open camp for scabs and thus had a detrimental effect on mining camps throughout the Southwest and into California. Organizing was also worth the effort because Bisbee had a potential membership of some five thousand to six thousand members. WFM organizers liked to think that the words "Western Federation of Miners" in Bisbee constituted a "bugaboo" that haunted the dreams of corporate managers.[66]

WFM organizers in 1907 were able to sign up 1,224 members in Bisbee but the companies retaliated by firing 1,500 men. Among these were people whose only crime was that, in the opinion of their employer, they might have joined the WFM. The WFM called a strike "for principle," that is, for the right of workers to belong to unions. Corporate-owned papers condemned the strikers. Those on strike found their ranks infiltrated with spies. Many faced threats of violence. As time went on, they found little alternative but to stand by as the companies brought in nonunion workers. The chief WFM organizer, Joseph D. Cannon, concluded: "It is a pretty hard proposition to be a union man when your life is at stake, when your job is at stake and when your family is at stake."[67]

Following the disturbances in Bisbee and elsewhere in 1906–1907 came what labor officials considered to be "a ruthless campaign of blacklisting" against the workers who had participated in the strikes. Prospective workers had to give detailed histories of their lives, in some cases, of their families, as a precondition of employment. The result of blacklisting was that miners who had joined the WFM moved from camp to camp to secure employment. As a labor official described the process: "A union man would secure a few days work, attend a union meeting and a detective would report him, with the result he would soon be on the tramp again."[68]

Throughout the early 1900, employer reaction to labor discontent included several techniques and strategies. To increase their influence in the legislature and in dealing with employees, mine owners banded together into mining associations. They also hired strike breakers ("scab labor") who would work for reduced wages. The availability of nonunion labor was a central factor in company resistance to strikes. Operations closest to the southern border had a distinct advantage because Hispanic workers provided the greatest pool of strike breakers. This practice, of course, simply heightened the antipathy Anglo workers felt toward Hispanics.

Among other means of resistance employed by mine owners and managers were hiring labor spies supplied by detective services, closing down operations until workers got hungry and gave up their demands, and circulating blacklists of those suspected of being union troublemakers to keep such people from employment. Mine owners in Arizona found judges, such as Richard E. Sloan, who became territorial governor, quite willing to issue injunctions prohibiting interference with the peaceful operation of mines. When all else failed, the local police or sheriff, state troops, and, with presidential approval, federal troops came in to protect strike breakers and the property of the owners.

While there was considerable agitation in mining areas, the farm labor scene was tranquil. Farm labor in Arizona was fairly abundant at the turn of the century, according to a report emanating from the experiment station at the University of Arizona. Farm workers came mostly from three classes: Anglos (many of whom were from southern states), Hispanics, and Indians.

Anglos, according to the report, were "an industrious and efficient class of men." As for the others: "The Mexican laborers are fairly good men at routine work, especially in irrigating. They make little provision for the future, depending upon day wages for their support. Men with families must receive their pay every Saturday evening. The Indians are found to be serviceable for some kinds of farm work, but as a whole are not very efficient."[69]

No one in the labor movement paid much attention to the farm workers until the IWW came along in 1905. This organization also tried to reach out to Hispanics and others in mining communities. The WFM neglected these workers, despite its claim of interest in the working class regardless of race or nationality.

Joining the WFM and the railway brotherhoods in the ranks of organized labor in the early 1900s were people in skilled occupations ranging from barbers to boilermakers and typographers. The growth of the labor movement encouraged Democratic leaders in Arizona, as elsewhere, to move closer to labor goals. As a result of their increasing influence, labor organizations enjoyed some success on legislative matters directly affecting their interests. In 1903, for example, the Arizona railway brotherhoods secured passage of a measure through the twenty-second legislature that forbade working train crew members for more than sixteen consecutive hours. As indicated earlier, mining unions, several of which affiliated with the Western Mining Federation, successfully sponsored a measure prohibiting more than eight hours of underground work per day in the mines (the standard had been ten hours) and another practice of paying wages with tokens.

The legislature in 1909 passed more labor-inspired reforms. These included the abolition of the Arizona Rangers, an organization with a history of intervening on the side of management in labor disturbances. Among the failures during the last years of territorial government for the miners, however, were an "anti-pluck-me store bill" aimed at company stores, mine safety legislation, and, of considerable importance to workers, anti-blacklisting legislation. Labor's greatest gains were yet to come.

Electoral Politics and the Rising Tide

Democrats dominated electoral politics in Arizona during the first decade of the twentieth century. Democrats controlled the territorial legislature. Democrat Marcus Smith won the congressional seat in 1900, 1904, and 1906. His rival within the Democratic party, John F. Wilson, won in 1902. Smith based most of his campaigns on the statehood cause.

Joint statehood was the chief issue of Smith's 1906 campaign. As one reporter described a typical Smith campaign speech: "Not a word did he say against the opposing candidate, not a word against the opposing party, not a word in favor of his own party, and scarcely a word in favor of himself. The whole of his talk was against the one great issue of jointure."[70] Smith won the contest with 11,101 votes, compared to 8,909 for his Republican challenger, who also opposed jointure. C. F. Ainsworth, who ran as a joint statehood candidate, received only 508 votes. In 1908, however, Smith lost to Republican Ralph Cameron, a prominent mine owner and businessman, who campaigned on the theme that, after several years of trying, Smith had shown that he did not have what it took to secure statehood.

Democrats during the early 1900s had a highly populistic-sounding platform and, especially toward the end of the decade, one in which labor issues played a prominent role.[71] The party was not, however, always able (or willing) to deliver on its promises. Democrats in the legislature faced criticism for being untrue to their articulated principles by, for example, voting against working-class legislation on blacklisting, mine inspection, eight-hour days, *boletas* (tokens used as payment), and other bills.[72] By 1909 Democrats had only partially made up for these failures.

Many citizens, probably, had learned early on that the major party platforms were not serious statements. One disgusted editor suggested that both major parties in Arizona "would probably gain in the respect of voters if they would throw away their platforms and confess that the emoluments and pull to be gained from office-holding are the chief, if not the only issues."[73] Platform or no platform, members of both parties in the legislature could be, and often were, depicted by leading newspapers as "subservient to the wishes of the railroads and other corporations."[74]

From another angle, criticism of the legislature and members of both parties centered on wasteful spending and excessive taxation. These came as a result of trying to come "to the relief of everything and everybody."

After reviewing the performance of a hectic and expensive territorial assembly, one editor concluded: "The Legislature has adjourned and the people of Arizona now feel safe."[75]

The political system as a whole was more responsive to various demands, especially in 1908–1909, than it had been in the populist years. Yet the performance (or lack of performance) of the major parties left some room for third-party agitation.

Prohibitionists, frustrated over the lack of progress nationally and in the territorial legislature in the 1890s, decided to exert additional pressure by forming their own political party. They nominated their own candidate for Congress in 1900. Hoping to draw upon a broader populistic vote, the party not only condemned drinking and gambling but called for adoption of the devices of direct democracy and for government ownership of public utilities. The Prohibition candidate drew only 292 votes out of the some 16,000 cast. The effort, though, may have had something to do with the decision made by the legislature in 1901 to try a local option plan.

The Socialist Party of America (SPA) played the role of third-party advocate in the Populist tradition more consistently during the early 1900s. This party nationally grew out of a meeting in Indianapolis in 1901 called by Eugene V. Debs and attended by representatives of various radical groups.[76] National organizers visited the Arizona territory on several occasions between 1901 and 1904. On each occasion they found an active interest in the new party.[77] By the early 1900s Socialist organizations existed throughout the territory.

During the early 1900s Socialist groups met in Phoenix, Globe, Safford, and even in company towns like Bisbee and Jerome where law enforcement officials tried to discourage such associations.[78] In the cities Socialists were active in the cause of municipal reform and in the rural areas they gave attention to the plight of the farmer.[79]

Socialists also made some inroads among the Mormon population. The Mormon cooperative tradition may have drawn its members in that direction. In Arizona during the early 1900s, however, the Church's drift toward capitalism appears to have been well under way. As one leading

Mormon socialist wrote during this period: "So effectively have the great money kings done their work of deception among the people that even the Church of Christ is permeated with its pernicious doctrines. The idea being that those who have the ability to corner the world's wealth and appropriate it to themselves are entitled to it even though it means the enslavement of the masses and the destruction of humanity."[80]

The Mormon position on capitalism and, more particularly, its negative view of unions, made it a central target of Socialist scorn and attack. In various Arizona counties Socialist candidates were a threat to the power of the Mormons.[81] In this respect Arizona Socialists may have had something in common with their comrades in Utah. Socialism in Utah during this period was "more a mood than a theory, and an important part of that mood was anti-Mormonism."[82]

By all accounts Socialists were most prominent in mining communities and, particularly, where there were active WFM locals. Socialist organizers came to mining camps in the Mountain West, including Arizona, in the early 1900s.[83] Debs, deeply concerned over the struggles of western miners, was perhaps the most effective agitator in raising the class consciousness of this group.[84] Debs regularly toured western mining camps to build support for the Socialist party and gather votes for his bid for the presidency.[85]

Socialists acted on the principle "every strike is a socialist opportunity." Debs and other socialist organizers routinely went into strike areas to take advantage of worker discontent.[86] Because of the high level of labor discontent in western mining camps during the first decade of the twentieth century, these places figured to be particularly fruitful sources of new party members.

One of the nationally most prominent radical miners' unions was the WFM local in Globe. Indeed, national organizers considered Globe Miners' Union #60 to be "the most revolutionary in the Southwest." WFM organizers looked at the leaders and most of the members of this local as deeply "class-conscious wage workers."[87] They were more than willing to financially support workers on strike in other states.[88]

Members of the Globe local were not afraid to display their political sentiments. On Labor Day in 1902, for example, they marched, carrying banners declaring "The Toilers are the Producers of All Wealth." They cheered the loudest in response to a speech by an orator brought in from Colorado who gave an address described by a critical reporter as "of the calamity type of labor speakers who pose as hostile to employers and capitalists in general" and who wound up with a plea for socialism.[89]

WFM members in Globe also took local politics seriously. They were, for example, behind the "free ride" out of town on a railroad given to a member of the legislature from the Globe area who voted wrong on the Eight Hour Bill.[90]

Although the miners' union had a strong influence in Globe, from time to time it met with resistance from conservative groups. The Globe Merchants Association, for example, withdrew its advertising from the official organ of the miners' union, the *Globe Times,* because "it had been radical in its expression on matters of local concern, has upheld unlawful acts committed in our midst and by almost continual agitation has disturbed the peace and well-being of our community."[91] The miners' union, in turn, blacklisted and boycotted the merchants. In the end, however, the *Times* closed down. Critics attributed this fate to "too much socialism, too much miners' union, too much rot."[92]

Among those living in Globe during the early 1900s was William E. Brooks. Brooks, born in Alabama, had practiced law in Arizona from 1903 in various mining communities. He was later to represent Gila County in the state legislature as a Democrat. In 1904, however, Brooks wrote his mother: "At present the party that comes nearest to my ideas of right political progress in the country is the Socialist. I do not feel that any hope is held out by either of the old political parties that they care or will make any effort to stem the tide of gigantic corporations in public life."[93] Brooks had been heading in a socialistic direction since first hearing Eugene Debs in 1897. According to his correspondence, however, Socialist principles and programs did not make much of an impression on him until he came to Arizona and saw the actual conditions.

Questions concerning giant corporations, the distribution of wealth, and the rights of labor bothered Brooks. He particularly felt for the masses whose "labor is bought and sold in the market without any regard to the fact that they are human" and who get virtually nothing out of their jobs but small pay checks. As Brooks saw it: "They don't get pleasure or happiness out of their work, for they leave it at the first opportunity and it is their great desire to have their children escape it."[94]

Brooks may well have participated in the various Socialist meetings regularly held in Globe. Another prominent resident of Globe during this period, George W.P. Hunt, was later rumored to have been among those to enroll in the Socialist Club in Globe.[95]

By the early 1900s the Socialist party in Arizona had taken the place of the People's party as the major third-party alternative. Socialist candidates for the congressional seat represented a radical alternative to Marcus Smith and his Republican opponents. The platform of the SPA in the first decade of the twentieth century was a compromise between revolutionary and evolutionary socialism. Socialists sought a wide audience. Beyond a call for the attainment of general principles (for example, the abolition of the wage system), the party made several immediate demands.

Among the immediate demands were the initiative, referendum, and recall, equal rights for women, a direct primary, corrupt practices acts, a federal department of labor, an eight-hour day for all industries, a system of social insurance for workers, abolition of child labor, public works for the unemployed, the reduction of working hours in proportion to the increased use of machines, public ownership of major industries (including railroads and mines), and a graduated income tax.[96]

While strong on enthusiasm, Socialist candidates did not make anywhere near the showing in Arizona that O'Neill had for the Populists. The Socialist candidate for Congress in 1902 could get on the ballot in only a few counties and wound up receiving just 510 votes that year. By 1904 the party had improved its organization. However, it lacked a well-financed journal to advance its platform and candidates and, therefore, had to rely, in large part, on the willingness of the regular press to convey its message.

In 1904 the party began to receive some limited coverage, particularly in liberal Democratic papers. One of these, the *Arizona Daily Star,* predicted in August 1904: "The socialists are in the field for business. They are in to make a record. They have organized their party to stay, and to work out some social and political problems neither of the old parties will recognize in their platforms. The socialists will make a strong showing this trip."[97] Socialists, to reform-minded Democratic papers like the *Star,* were a threat because the public identified them with popular and "sound" ideas like the initiative, referendum, and recall.[98]

One of the most popular Socialist orators who traveled around the territory extolling the virtues of direct democracy was Albinus A. Worsley. Worsley, a Wisconsin native, joined the direct legislation movement in his youth and, at the age of twenty-four, headed the Labor and Populist ticket for governor of Wisconsin. A lawyer by trade, he moved to Arizona in 1904. Like Brooks, he later became a prominent Democrat.

Direct legislation, Worsley told his audiences, was necessary simply because the emergence of "mighty combines of capital seeking special privileges" had corrupted the system of lawmaking by representatives.[99] The real problem was not so much in the method of electing representatives, but in what happened to people after their election. It was after the election that the "temptations and seductions of the mighty combinations of capital" came before the legislator. "If then he prove true we are fortunate indeed, but if he prove false he is beyond our control, he is the master and we are the servant."[100] Direct legislation, Worsley instructed the crowds, was the only way they, the people, could control officials after election and protect themselves from bad legislation.

To the Socialists, devices of direct democracy were worthy ends in themselves. They were also of considerable importance as issues in attracting voters to the Socialist party. In addition, socialists valued the initiative and referendum because they provided a new basis for independent political action. They would help "educate the masses and prepare them for socialism" and "help identify the socialists with popular causes or reforms which could be adopted over the heads of the old party politicians." With the referendum the Socialist party could "constitute itself a permanent vigilance committee that would promptly call a popular veto on every bill which is hostile to the interests of the working class."[101]

Socialist gains in Arizona, even with the direct democracy issue, were not spectacular. They did, however, increase their vote total to 1,304 in 1904 and to 2,078 in 1906. The 1906 candidate, Joseph D. Cannon, a former underground miner who participated in the unsuccessful WFM struggle to unionize Bisbee miners, did the best of any Socialist candidate in the 1900–1908 era. He received about 9 percent of the vote, trailing the Democratic and Republican candidates. In Globe he polled nearly a quarter of the vote.

Looking forward to the 1908 contest, the editor of the socialistic *Graham County Advocate,* who also happened to be president of the WFM local in Clifton, Arizona, declared that the Republican party was under the thumb of the "master class." At the head of the Democratic party was a particularly evil bunch of reform demagogues who were out to hoodwink the workers.[102] Rule by these parties, the editor concluded, meant rule "by an oligarchy of wealth as cruel and vicious as ever wasted the wealth of the past."[103] The editor predicted better times for the Socialist party.

In 1908, however, the party slumped a bit, receiving but 1,912 votes. Some of this may have reflected the decision of the national and local AFL unions to abandon their long-standing policy of nonpolitical intervention by endorsing the Democratic ticket. While it did little good for the Socialists, the effect of the endorsement in Arizona was to produce a territorial legislature more sympathetic to the demands of a growing labor movement.

Looking at the returns, we find Socialists in 1906 and 1908 doing their best in Gila (where the Socialist percentage was more than twice as high as it was in the rest of the territory), Mohave, Yavapai, and Yuma counties. The party drew more heavily on past Democratic voters than it did Republicans and drew about equally well from most ethnic groups (the exception being a relatively high negative vote from Hispanics). Socialists, like the Populists some twenty years earlier, tended to do best in areas that had been Democratic and especially well where miners were relatively numerous.

Socialist support in Arizona appears comparable to that found in other areas in the West during this period. Robert Hoxie, for example, relying on informed observers in various parts of the country in the early 1900s, noted the existence of a radical form of socialism in western mining areas.[104] Hoxie added that this socialism rested "very largely on the support of men with European blood in their veins."[105] Multivariate analysis, however, suggests that European birth, as such, probably had relatively little to do with Socialist support in Arizona. Rather, the occupation of mining, regardless of the nativity of the worker, provided the strongest link to Socialist support.[106]

The findings here appear more compatible with Hoxie's later observation: "That there is apparently this special type of socialist victory at mining centers in otherwise unaffected territory leads to the thought that there is something in the working environment of these miners which makes them think in different terms from those about them and gives them a different outlook on life and society."[107]

4

THE REFORMERS TAKE OVER

"I am delighted that Cameron has been elected. I shall of course urge separate Statehood for Arizona and New Mexico in my message." Thus wrote Theodore Roosevelt to Edward Kent, Chief Justice of the Supreme Court of Arizona, November 9, 1908.[1] Republican Ralph Henry Cameron defeated Marcus Smith in the 1908 contest for Congress. Cameron's victory was a clear sign to Roosevelt that Arizona was politically ready to join the Union.

Ten days after writing to Kent, Roosevelt instructed Albert Beveridge, who still wanted joint statehood for Arizona and New Mexico: "You will have to take them both in. You cannot take them both in together, and by keeping them out for a short time (which is all you can do) you merely irritate the people there against the Republican party."[2]

Roosevelt urged immediate admission. The go-ahead to frame a state constitution, however, did not come until after William Howard Taft assumed office. On June 19, 1909, Frank Murphy dined with Taft at the White House. He later told reporters that Taft favored statehood.[3] Taft toured the state in October, offering his support for statehood. Taft, however, warned against radicalism.[4] He told a Phoenix audience that the recently adopted Oklahoma constitution was "a zoological garden of cranks" and, thus, a poor model.[5] At Prescott, Taft emphasized the need to elect good (conservative) people to the constitutional convention. Arizonans, he felt, were so anxious for statehood that they were likely to vote for whatever constitution appeared on the ballot.[6]

Authorization to formulate a state constitution came in the summer of 1910. Governor Richard E. Sloan (a Taft appointee) scheduled the election of fifty-two delegates for September 10, 1910. Sloan's action set off a scramble for control of the new state. Hunt Democrats won the struggle. They proceeded to place their imprint on the constitution and, later, a volume of measures passed by the legislature.

The Struggle for Control

While serving in the legislature, George W.P. Hunt, by his own account, became disillusioned over the prospect of arriving at progressive reform. Railroad and mining interests stood in the way of reform. The opportunity to frame a constitution for the state, however, rekindled Hunt's enthusiasm for the reform struggle.[7] Hunt's supporters looked at his image "as the father of the initiative and referendum in Arizona" as putting him in a good position to lead the new state.[8]

During the summer of 1910 Hunt and other progressive Democrats got off to a quick start, lining up delegates to the constitutional convention. In particular, they sought delegates who were "friends of the initiative, referendum and recall."[9]

Meanwhile, more radical groups were also trying to make an impact on the constitution. On July 11, 1910, labor officials from all parts of the territory attended a meeting in Phoenix called by W. E. Stewart, secretary of the Bisbee miners' union. The purpose of the meeting was to draw up a platform of general provisions labor wished to have incorporated in the new state's basic document. Elected chair of the convention was J. C. Provost. Like others in attendance Provost was a member of the Socialist party. At one time he had also been connected with the Denver branch of the Western Federation of Miners.[10]

Among the twenty-seven items recommended for inclusion by the labor group in the constitution were woman suffrage, the initiative, referendum, and recall, the right of the state to engage in industrial pursuits, an anti-injunction law, and an employer liability act. Several of these planks, according to one prominent Socialist in attendance, came from the immediate demands of the Socialist party's national platform.

On the second day of their meeting the delegates decided to form a Labor party that would not only pursue these demands but would try to get its own members elected to the constitutional convention. Delegates reasoned that a new party was far more likely than the Socialist party to secure these objectives. Past elections showed the Socialist party had only a limited following.[11] The delegates left open the question of whether the new party would be necessary following the formulation and adoption of a constitution. Convention leaders announced that they had already raised some $3,200 for the Labor party's campaign. A thousand dollars of this came from the Western Federation of Miners. Leaders also noted that activists were forming party organizations in the various counties.[12]

Selected to head the campaign were several prominent radicals. One of these, A. A. Worsley of Tucson, took responsibility for leading the new party's efforts in central Arizona. Joseph D. Cannon, the Socialist candidate for Congress in 1906, was chosen to lead the campaign in the southern part of the territory. His fellow Socialist, Ernest Liebel, was to take charge of the Labor party's effort in northern Arizona.[13] Liebel did not consider himself to be a wild-eyed revolutionary but someone who accepted "the fundamental principles and ethics upon which the co-operative state" of the future would be founded.[14]

Included in the coalition formed around the new party was the Arizona State Suffrage Association, an affiliate of the National Woman's Suffrage Association. Frances Munds, president of the state organization, offered to support the new party. As a price of this support, the Labor party made "universal and equal man and woman suffrage" a prominent part of its platform. The Laborites felt that they would do well in several parts of the state, for example, Maricopa County, because of the support of the hardworking suffragettes.

The new party had its critics. Samuel Gompers, president of the American Federation of Labor, told reporters the action of the labor element in Arizona displeased him. When told of Gompers's displeasure, delegates to the Arizona convention indicated that they really did not care what the conservative AFL president had to say.[15]

Reporters attending the convention expressed surprise that leading members of the Socialist party (including none other than the 1906 standard-bearer Joseph D. Cannon) would, in the eyes of purists, defect by participating in the formation of another party.[16] Socialist regulars bitterly denounced the turncoats. They later expelled six locals from the Socialist party for their participation in the creation of the Labor party.[17]

The prospect of a new party perhaps most thoroughly frightened progressive Democratic leaders. Many of these, like Hunt, had been depending on the labor vote. The essential task from their point of view was holding the reform elements together. Hunt, as a leader of the progressive forces, received reports on how this problem appeared in various parts of the territory.

As an example, his friend Mulford Winsor (a newspaper editor of the *Yuma Sun*) reported on July 26 from Yuma: "The Labor party is causing me some uneasiness, though we are hopeful that no ticket will be placed in the field in this county. The Socialists, at least, are more inclined to come in with us than they are with the Laborites, and we hope to be able to show the latter that their true interests also lie with the Democratic party."[18]

Eventually, the progressive Democrats were able to withstand the challenge from the left. Led by Hunt, they lessened the third-party threat simply by accepting the Labor platform. This occurred officially in August 1910 when the Democratic party met in convention. In return Labor leaders agreed to support the Democratic ticket.[19] According to Labor party leader Joseph Cannon, the Progressive element in the Democratic party stampeded at the threat of a Labor party:

> So sure did the Labor party seem of electing its candidates to the convention that the candidates of the Democratic party promised that if elected they would grant all the demands of the Labor party, and for three or four days before the election, they promised that they would make the constitution even more radical than the one promised by the Labor party.[20]

The mines, railroads, and conservative press sought to head off the Hunt-Labor element during the contest for delegates. At first, they proposed a nonpartisan election to the convention. Said the *Arizona Republican:* "To republicans and to democrats alike, the time has come for laying aside all considerations of petty partisanship. The man of either party who is so shortsighted as to think of party instead of thinking of all the people of Arizona, is not the man for delegate to the constitutional convention."[21] The Hunt-Laborites, however, had control of the Democratic party. They were confident of their ability to win any territory-wide election and saw no merit in the idea of a nonpartisan convention.

Railroad and mining interests also attempted to form an alliance of Republicans and conservative Democrats against the reform Democrats. Conservative Democrats, hoping to find a role in the new government, refused to bolt the Democratic party even though reformers were in control.

During the contests in the fall of 1910 for seats in the constitutional convention, the choice in most counties was between progressive Democrats and more conservative Republicans. The latter, if not openly hostile to progressive reforms such as the initiative, referendum, and recall, argued that their inclusion in the state's basic document would prompt President Taft to veto the constitution and thus further delay statehood. Republicans put up a slate of candidates to challenge the Democrats in twelve of the thirteen counties. Socialists managed to put together slates in five counties (Cochise, Maricopa, Mohave, Pima, and Yavapai).

The objective of the Labor party evolved during the campaign into one of pressuring the Democratic party into accepting the new party's more radical platform. Although they were able to do this, slates of Labor candidates remained on the ballot in the five counties where the Socialists had entered the field and in Gila and Graham counties.

Some Democratic organizations, such as in Cochise and Graham counties, were relatively hostile to reform-minded candidates. Faced with this situation, "ultraprogressive" Democrats, such as William Cleary of Cochise County, felt compelled to run as Labor candidates. In other

Cochise County, felt compelled to run as Labor candidates. In other counties radical labor appeared willing to go along with Democratic candidates. One example was in Yuma where Mulford Winsor was the Democratic candidate for the county's only delegate position.[22]

The election of September 10, 1910, brought victory for the reform Democrats. Of the fifty-two delegates elected, forty-one were Democrats and all of these but one (E. E. Ellinwood, an attorney for Phelps Dodge) leaned toward the progressive side. The remaining delegates were Republicans. For Democrats and Republicans the chief component in their followings were those who supported the respective parties in the past. For Democrats this included farmers, Mormons, and southerners. Aside from the partisan vote, Republicans did their best (which was not particularly good) in economically mixed cities and towns. The combined Socialist and Labor vote was especially strong where Socialists had done well in the past and, more important, in mining areas. In this respect the Socialist-Labor following resembled that of the Populists years earlier.

Following the delegate election, the *Arizona Republican* lamented: "Arizona yesterday declared unequivocally vocal for the initiative, referendum, and recall. Hope of statehood was pitted against the doctrine in so plain a manner that it can not be misunderstood."[23] The paper attributed the "catastrophe" of the election to "overwhelming popular sentiment in favor of direct legislation."[24] The essential problem from the paper's point of view was "every man who had a grievance of any character thought he saw relief in the initiative, referendum, and recall."[25]

By 1910 the devices of direct democracy had achieved shibboleth status on par with statehood and, in an earlier era, free silver. Indeed, according to one authority, "even conservative Democrats loudly proclaimed the initiative, referendum, and recall knowing that with no other shibboleth could they hope for a place in the new state government."[26] Opponents of these devices found it prudent to avoid attacking them directly. Rather, they warned that the inclusion of direct democracy in the new state constitution was likely to bring about a veto from President Taft and an indefinite delay in statehood. This warning fell on deaf ears.

With the victory in 1910 the friends of direct democracy won control over the statehood process and received a green light to experiment with implementing a broader progressive agenda.

The Progressive Constitution

The state constitution framed in Phoenix in late 1910 was the initial product of the progressive wing of Arizona's Democratic party. A majority of the members had pledged to support inclusion of such reforms as the initiative, referendum, and recall.[27] The convention insured its reform character by electing Hunt president of that body.

As president of the constitutional convention, Hunt was influential in producing a document that was progressive by existing standards. It was not, however, all that the Socialists, Laborites, and other reformers desired. The progressive Democrats at the convention had their own agenda, tempered by their perceptions of political reality. They were unwilling to appease the most radical among them. Many of the statements of policy found in the constitution, moreover, were only symbolic, requiring subsequent action by the legislature before they had the force of law.[28]

The document produced was daring in that, in spite of President Taft's warning, it contained the initiative, referendum, and recall. To Taft's alarm, the Oklahoma constitution and the Oregon constitution provided the models. Bending somewhat to conservatives and President Taft's objections to direct democracy, however, the requirements relating to the number of signatures needed on petitions were among the most difficult in the nation.[29] Opponents of direct democracy focused their attack on making the requirements so strong as to discourage the use of the devices.[30]

To further accountability to the voters, the document did provide for direct primaries and an advisory vote of the people for U.S. senator and instructed the legislature to safeguard the purity of the election system through registration laws and laws providing public disclosure of campaign contributions.

The completed document extended general control over "foreign" corporations such as the railroad and mining enterprises headquartered in the East that had been active in Arizona. One section banned monopolies, trusts, and attempts to restrict trade. Another banned corporate campaign contributions. Several provisions were aimed at various types of corporation-related abuses. One section, for example, prohibited laws making irrevocable grants of privileges, franchises, or immunities such as tax exemptions to particular business enterprises. Another provision forbade those with information regarding corporate bribery or illegal rebating from refusing to give such evidence on the grounds of self-incrimination. No corporation was to be given privileges and immunities not given to other corporations.

Railroads in the new scheme of things were declared "public highways" and "common carriers" subject to control by law. Directly pointed at the railroads was a prohibition on the long complained about practice of giving passes to public officials. Another section prohibited railroads from discriminating among shippers in regard to charges or services. The mines were foremost in the thoughts of the framers when they adopted a provision that exempted from the general right to bear arms the right of "corporations to organize, maintain, or employ an armed body of men" such as those used in territorial years as strike breakers.

The creation of a powerful corporation commission to regulate business, including the rates charged by railroads, demonstrated the progressive character of the constitution. Also progressive, in the anti-corporate mode, were numerous provisions to protect the interests of workers. The constitution authorized the legislature to outlaw blacklisting, prohibited contracts or agreements in which employees released employers from liability for on-the-job injuries, disallowed the use of the fellow servant doctrine as a means by which employers might avoid liability for job injuries, and banned any law limiting the amount that workers could recover in damages for work-related injuries. Also created by constitution was the office of mine inspector to implement safety standards.

One measure that passed in modified form had to do with alien labor. This proposal, supported by a petition signed by five hundred workers from Globe, required employers of five or more people to hire at least 80 percent of their employees from out of the citizen population. The petition deplored the increased employment of illiterate nontaxpaying foreigners in mining camps.[31]

The Immigration Restriction League of Arizona declared in a letter to Hunt: "Every day that goes by sees the American citizen workingman displaced by out and out alien labor, aliens that come from countries whose laws, institutions and ideals of living differ utterly from our own."[32] To the league, the invasion of alien labor had already meant "that some large industrial concerns have denied to American workingmen their God-given privilege to work in their own country under their own flag" and could mean "in a very few years Arizona will be an alien state peopled by an alien race."[33]

Convention delegates supporting the measure also contended that alien workers were causing a massive drain of wealth out of the state. Supporters argued that many of the aliens were Hispanics who sent the bulk of their pay back to Mexico. Similarly, supporters charged, European workers commonly sent money home or hoarded much of their income against the time when they could return to their native land with their savings.[34]

Delegates agreed that the use of foreign labor in private industry carried with it a variety of evils. They concluded, however, that about all they could do was regulate use of such labor in regard to public employment. Thus, the constitution prohibited noncitizens, except for prisoners, from securing employment with any state, county, or municipal agency. A related proposal that would have barred non-English-speaking persons from doing hazardous work did not pass. This measure aimed to drive Hispanics out of the mines.[35]

Although labor did well in the constitutional convention, it did not secure all of its goals. The anti-alien 80 percent proposal passed only in modified form. Labor failed completely not only in regard to the hazardous work proposal but also in getting a ban on the use of court injunctions against strikers (although the recall of judges was a valuable backup remedy) and a clause in the Declaration of Rights that guaranteed the right of working people to boycott and strike against their employers.

On other long-standing issues, the delegates rejected an equal suffrage provision and, after much debate, turned down a petition bearing the signatures of 3,200 women calling for prohibition. When questioned by supporters of equal suffrage for an explanation for his stand against the equal suffrage amendment, Hunt contended that it would have jeopardized President Taft's approval of the document. Frances Munds, head of the Arizona Equal Suffrage Campaign Committee, was, to say the least, unconvinced by this explanation. In a letter to Hunt, Munds pointed out:

> You say you think it is unwise to put a suffrage plank in the constitution and then you go on to say that it should contain the initiative and referendum and recall by all means. Either you think that we women are very dense or else you are not sincere. You know as well as can be that there is nothing that Mr. Taft will so seriously object to as that very thing that you are advocating so strenuously. On the other hand you have no authority whatever for saying that he is opposed to woman suffrage.[36]

Years later, Hunt claimed that the equal suffrage and prohibition proposals came from enemies of the constitution who felt that their inclusion would make the document unpopular with the voters.[37]

The document did not satisfy every reform group or any reform group completely. Most observers, however, considered it highly progressive in character. To those not in favor of the current wave of reform sentiment, the document was downright radical. Conservative Governor Sloan told President Taft that the constitution was about the "worst affair ever turned out, and objectionable to all classes."[38] Sloan attributed some of the push for direct democracy to politicians coming into Arizona from Texas and Oklahoma who hoped to win election to the new state offices.[39] As far as Sloan could see, the constitution as adopted by the Convention was received with such enthusiasm by all those who called themselves progressive, for the sole reason that to them progress meant change, and that not social but political change. To a great many of those the initiative, the referendum, and the recall meant nothing except that they were new and were opposed by the old crowd of conservatives then running things, including the President.[40]

The document expressed many of the aims and aspirations of the Labor party and of organized labor. Labor party officials credited this to their influence on progressive Democrats during the delegate elections. Socialists contended that credit belonged to their party rather than the Labor party.[41] The WFM also claimed its share of the credit for the development of "a constitution more liberal and progressive than the constitution of any other state in the union."[42] Joseph Cannon proudly proclaimed that in Arizona "we have at least one state in the Union in which a Western Federation of Miners constitution is the basic law of the state."[43] In its 1911 annual meeting the WFM resolved to defeat U.S. senators who were opposing acceptance of the Arizona constitution.[44]

Hunt and the others finished their work on December 9, 1910. Shortly after, they formed a statehood league and launched a campaign for voter approval of the new document. As part of this effort, Hunt wrote to Woodrow Wilson, governor of New Jersey, as "one of the great leaders of our party" for his endorsement of the document. Hunt acknowledged that "from the standpoint of some of the older Commonwealths" the new Arizona constitution "may be too advanced." Nonetheless, it represented "the views of the vast majority of the people of Arizona."[45] There is no record of Wilson's response.

The committee sought and received the active support of William Jennings Bryan. Lecturing in Tucson early in February 1911, Bryan spoke glowingly about the document. The most important provisions in the new constitution, Bryan felt, were those providing for the initiative, the referendum, and the recall. These were the most important "because they put the government in the hands of the people, and enable the people to coerce obedience to their will."[46]

Bryan suggested that the recall was far less important than the referendum or initiative. Overuse of the recall, Bryan felt, was unlikely, in part, because the convention had given Arizona lawmakers short (two-year) terms. Nor, volunteered Bryan, was the recall likely to lead to hasty or unjust results. If an error should occur, "the people are much more apt to overlook official wrong-doing that ought to be rebuked than they are to administer an undeserved rebuke."[47]

Bryan found no reason why the recall, which he characterized as "merely a form of impeachment in which the people are the jury," should not apply to judges. Judges, Bryan concluded, "are as much servants of the people as other officials."[48]

While Bryan applauded Arizona for its stand on direct democracy, others opposed these measures. Writing to the president of the Arizona Statehood Committee, U.S. Senator Weldon B. Heyburn, Republican from Idaho, declared: "Your adoption of the recall and a lot of other frauds disgusted me." Arizona, as a new state trying to be a reform leader for the established states, was like "a high school boy who assumes that he had acquired all the wisdom on earth and demands the right to rule men of experience."[49]

During the debate over the proposed constitution, former governor T. T. Geer of Oregon was brought in by opponents of direct democracy. He contended that it was unreasonable to assume that voters could make knowledgeable decisions about the laws passed by legislatures or make proper choices as to what new measures should be adopted.[50] Proponents of direct democracy called upon insurgent Senator Jonathan Bourne of Oregon to refute these contentions. In a letter to Hunt published in territorial newspapers, Bourne pointed out the beneficial effects of direct democracy in his state.[51]

On February 9, 1911, Arizona voters approved the proposed Arizona constitution by an overwhelming vote of 12,187 to 3,303. President Taft held different views than Bryan about the wisdom and propriety of subjecting judges to popular controls. He refused to approve the resolution granting statehood primarily because the new constitution provided for the recall of judges.

Taft was a strong believer in an independent judiciary. Theodore Roosevelt's attacks on the judiciary while campaigning for Republican candidates in the fall of 1910 alarmed Taft. He decided to use the statehood issue to make known his views on courts as the "cornerstone" of individual liberty and on the damage the application of the recall to the judiciary could bring.[52]

Congress on August 19, 1911, adopted a new statehood bill without the recall provision. At an election held on December 12, 1911, the voters, having little choice, eliminated the recall provision. This last remaining obstacle to statehood fell by a vote of 14,963 to 1,980. At the same election, however, the voters chose candidates who pledged to work for the reinsertion of the recall provision after statehood.

In choosing the state's first officials, the voters favored Democrats for all the major positions. The GOP had been weakened during the territorial period by a migration of Democrats from the South into Arizona and by its identification with "carpetbag rule." After 1910 it had the additional negative image as enemy of the popular new constitution. As the platform of the Democratic party of Arizona for 1911 put it: "We denounce the action of the standpat elements which have been and are now in control of the Republican party of Arizona for their continued and determined opposition to the progressive ideas incorporated in the Arizona Constitution."[53]

Viewing the 1911 contest, the *Los Angeles Examiner* declared that the Republican party was trying without much success to convince voters that they now supported progressive principles. Said the paper of the GOP effort: "Its infant progressive history covers a period of just one week."[54]

Radical parties also faced tough times. Leaders of the Labor party met in the miners' union hall in Globe during the middle of September 1910. They vowed to keep up the battle, perfect their party's organization, sweep Gila County, and eventually carry the territory.[55] The Labor party, however, did not survive the 1910 delegate contest. The Socialist party, weakened by the rise of the Laborites and Hunt Democrats, also struggled for survival. It conducted only a feeble campaign in 1911.

Sent to the U.S. Senate in 1911 was the irrepressible Marcus A. Smith, now sounding like a lifelong progressive. This was so much so his conservative friends began to worry about him.[56] Also elected as part of the progressive team that toured the state together was Henry F. Ashurst to the U.S. Senate and Carl Hayden to the single seat given Arizona in the House of Representatives. Hunt also won election as governor, although only after a close struggle.

Commenting on the campaign, Hayden said he sensed "determination to oust standpatism in every audience of voters we addressed." This determination, Hayden noted, was manifest in the "spontaneity with which some particular reference to the standpat party would be applauded, the quick response to appeals to elect the progressive ticket, and the grave interest of our audience." Hayden referred to the "psychological feature" of the campaign and the existence of a "telepathic force" between him, as a speaker, and the audience he was trying to reach.[57]

Hunt's principal challenger in the Democratic primary was Colonel Thomas P. Weedin, publisher of the *Blade-Tribune* at Florence. Weedin was a progressive Democrat and a firm supporter of statehood and the constitution. At the same time, he was acceptable to corporation newspapers as a gubernatorial candidate, especially in comparison to Hunt.[58]

Brady O'Neill (no relation to Buckey), a supporter of Hunt, wrote the candidate on September 8, 1911, and warned him that the progressives in the party had better get together because "the corporation and stand pat element is now at work and will be constantly at work to defeat us and to secure control of the Democratic party."[59] O'Neill viewed Weedin as the candidate of the "corporate bunch" and an ally of intraparty enemy Marcus Smith.[60] Looking at the campaign situation, O'Neill concluded: "The Gazette will be for you and this means . . . an overwhelming vote in Maricopa but there are other counties and lots of work to be done."[61]

Hunt did receive the endorsement of the *Phoenix Gazette* in the primary campaign.[62] Statewide, he disposed of Weedin by a vote of 5,241 to 3,532. Hunt emerged the victor in all but the three smaller counties of Graham, Greenlee, and Pinal. Rumor had it several Socialists entered the Democratic primary to help Hunt.[63]

The Republican primary for governor featured a two-way contest between Edward W. Wells, a conservative judge, and George U. Young, mayor of Phoenix and leader of the progressive wing of that party. Wells agreed to run only after party leaders convinced him that the state could well go socialist unless he carried the Republican banner.[64] The press identified Wells as the Phelps-Dodge candidate. Wells won the primary. In this rather clear-cut choice between standpatter and insurgent, Wells received 61 percent of the vote and carried every county except Maricopa (Young's base) and Yuma.

During the campaign Hunt took considerable pleasure in pointing out that Wells was one of the delegates to the constitutional convention who had refused to sign the document. Hunt, on the other hand, emphasized his leading role in the convention and, through the document produced at that meeting, his role in bringing the "people's rule and progressivism" to Arizona.

Hunt's supporters viewed the 1911 election as a choice "between progress and reaction, between money and morals, between dollars and men," and "between privilege and equal rights."[65] Hunt appeared to his supporters to be on the side of progress, morals, men, and equal rights. His opponents viewed him as an embarrassment, a crude and nearly illiterate man who sided with the wrong class of people and whose radicalism threatened prosperity.

Hunt, to his critics, was the candidate of "the dissatisfied and the incompetent" while Wells was "a man of affairs, backed by the safe and sane sentiment" of the state who would give the state prestige and economic development.[66] Frank Murphy, with Hunt in mind, warned that "the greatest stumbling block that could be put in the road of investors from outside would be a bunch of radicals in the state house."[67] A newspaper editor in a northern county summed it up:

Vote for Judge Wells, and if he is elected Governor, we will have a sane, sound, safe, and sensible administration of state affairs; an administration void of wild-eyed "isms," and other bunco schemes that are used by demagogues solely to catch the sucker vote. Don't allow yourselves to be buncoed into supporting "isms" but keep on the right side by casting your vote for Ed. W. Wells for governor of our new state.[68]

Although some of Hunt's supporters had to defend him against charges of radicalism, others had to counter claims that he was not radical enough. A letter from a Hunt supporter that went to every miners' union in the state, for example, praised Hunt as being as much in step with working men as any Socialist.[69] As the result of such efforts, Hunt and other Democrats received the endorsement of some WFM locals. The more radical locals, however, condemned such action. To them, Hunt or no Hunt, the Democratic party "opposed the demands of the working class and sided with the master class."[70]

Hunt defeated Wells 11,123 to 9,126. Like other Democrats, Hunt retained the party vote evidenced in 1910 and did well among those who favored the constitution. He also drew relatively well in places (including mining areas) where the Socialists had done well in 1908 and the Socialist-Laborites had done well in 1910. The reform Democrats under Hunt, in effect, had put together a governing coalition of loyal party followers, southerners, people attracted to the party because of the constitution or statehood issue, and people in the more radical sector of the electorate.

Hunt and the Progressive Agenda

On inaugural day Hunt, in a show of democratic simplicity, decided to walk the mile or so from his hotel to the state capitol, rather than ride in an automobile. At the capitol he expressed the hope that Arizonans would remember him as the man who "started the state off right" using the foundation established in the "People's Constitution."[71] Hunt asked no higher praise "than to have it said that in some measure I added to the happiness and contentment — and therefore in its most tangible form, the advancement — of the citizenry of the state."[72]

Former territorial governor Richard Sloan, a Republican, later noted that Hunt's walk on inaugural day was the last time the state's first governor made "the same, or any similar journey, on foot."[73] Sloan attended Hunt's inaugural. He was struck by the inaugural prayer that, after lauding the Democratic party, added: "O Lord, we even have it in our hearts this day to ask the divine blessing upon these Republicans. May their eyes be opened so that they may see the truth."[74]

Among the many letters of congratulation Hunt received upon taking office was one from Ernest Liebel, the Laborite, now trying to scratch out a living in New Jersey. Liebel ended his letter with the request that Hunt pursue the unenacted provisions of the Labor party's platform: "These measures must become laws before Arizona is really free from the capitalistic tyranny which has reduced states like Pennsylvania to a condition worse than slavery."[75] Hunt, while not unmindful of corporate abuses, had several matters on his mind. He made known his views on a wide variety of matters while addressing the legislature a few months later.

Speaking to the first state legislature on March 18, 1912, Hunt expressed his relief "that the seemingly endless struggle for recognition as a sovereign commonwealth" had "finally come to a successful, triumphant end."[76] The struggle had been painful but had, in the opinion of the governor, "molded the Arizona character and brought to her name immortal fame."[77]

Immortality came from the Arizona constitution, which gave "the most definite expression ever pronounced by man, of a social and political organization in which every citizen is the equal before the law of every other, and government is truly by consent of the governed."[78] Legislators now had a historic obligation to put provisions of the constitution into life.[79]

Some of the governor's recommendations had to do with legislative abuses he had observed during the territorial years. He sought to end secret or private lobbying by registering those who represented various causes and confining their activities to open public hearings. Hunt also condemned another practice of territorial legislators: wasting time and public funds by taking unnecessary "investigative" junkets around the territory.

More generally, the state's first governor pledged himself to economy, and to the goal of running Arizona like he would a successful business: "I look upon the State's business as I would my own, and I want to see it placed upon an economical, systematic basis, with graft eliminated, the leaks stopped, and every man from the Governor down, like the employees of a great department store, doing their duty."[80]

Hunt, as his remarks on inaugural day suggested, believed that government should make life better for its citizens. Yet like other progressives of the period, he was careful to stress that a positive and powerful government must be accountable to its citizens. It also had an obligation to operate on a sound businesslike basis. Unlike other progressives, however, Hunt did not consider nonpartisanship to be essential to the cause of good government. Hunt was a highly partisan Democrat who believed, moreover, that the Democratic party had a historically important role in Arizona of implementing what he called the "triumph of militant Progressive Democracy."[81]

The term "progressive democracy" meant to the governor "that this country, its institutions, its resources and its rewards for industry belong to the people whose labor makes them possible."[82] To the governor progressive politics was "the faithful application of Thomas Jefferson's equal rights to all and special privileges to none."[83]

The most desirable Democrats, from Hunt's point of view, were progressive ones. He eagerly assumed the task of doing what he could to ensure the nomination of ideologically compatible Democrats. Hunt also, however, professed a willingness to close ranks behind nearly anyone who won a Democratic primary on the theory that it was highly unlikely "matters would be improved by the election of a Republican."[84]

Progressives in California who came to power about the same time as Hunt toyed with antiparty reforms like nonpartisan elections and a cross-filing system for partisan primaries in which a candidate could enter the primary contest of any or all of the parties. The Hunt forces, contrary to their counterparts in California, set out to maintain and enhance their partisan advantage. Although committed to the direct primary, Hunt and his followers insisted that this be of the closed variety that restricted participation to people registered with the appropriate party.

In pushing the closed primary, Hunt complained about what he saw to be a common practice of Republican bosses "loaning" large numbers of voters to the Democratic party. The Republican crossovers sought to bring about the nomination of undesirable or weak candidates.[85] Hunt himself was probably the beneficiary of Socialist crossovers in primaries. In this case he would have been the last to contend that the "raiders" sought to nominate a weak candidate.

Hunt relied extensively on patronage in building what his critics commonly characterized a "political machine." From the earliest days of his administration critics accused the governor of creating a small army to run the state and having to raise taxes to keep his party machine alive.[86] Patronage workers did not get a free ride. They had to work for the party's nominees, Hunt or candidates backed by Hunt, and contribute a percentage of their salaries to the cause.

J. C. Callaghan, the first state auditor and bank controller, who was later to become one of Hunt's most vocal foes, advised the governor early in his administration that an assessment of 5 percent would meet with considerable resistance. A 2 percent assessment "in these days of the rule of the proletariat and the investigation of slush funds" would be safer and combined with individual contributions and popular subscriptions bring in a plentiful amount of campaign funds.[87] Contrary to Callaghan's advice, the assessment on state employees apparently did go as high as 5 percent.[88]

The progressivism of the Hunt Democrats as they came into office continued to show the nativistic biases that had been evident at the convention. Although Hunt was later to take a dramatic stand supportive of striking Hispanic miners, the progressive movement he led up to 1915–1916 contained little of value to Hispanics. Once in power the Hunt forces pushed for job protections against immigrants and measures that would eliminate those not proficient in English from the electorate. The job protection theme appeared in the resurrection of the 80 percent and the hazardous occupations proposals rejected at the convention. The latter could have cost some five thousand Hispanics and recent immigrants from Europe their jobs.[89]

The legislature also produced a law in 1912 that denied the franchise to those unable to "read the Constitution of the United States in the English language in such manner as to show he is neither prompted nor reciting from memory, and to write his name." The law was intended, in part, to eliminate "the ignorant Mexican vote."[90] As indicated by this language, voter registrars had considerable discretion in applying the law.

This discretion was later used against Hispanics in several counties. Because of the decline in Hispanic voters in Cochise and Pima counties, nearly half of the precincts lacked enough voters to justify holding primary elections in 1912.[91] In Apache County Democrats began recall campaigns against two GOP officeholders, in the belief that enough Hispanic voters were purged from the voting rolls to defeat the incumbents.[92]

The attitude of the Hunt forces on woman suffrage continued to be lukewarm at most. Having arrived at a point where they had captured office, the progressive Democrats had little to gain and a great deal to lose by extending the franchise.[93] Yet they did not wish to offend a large group of potential voters. Hunt approached the problem by calling upon the legislature to submit the question of woman suffrage to the male elector-ate. He attached to this recommendation the simple observation that in adopting suffrage "the State's high standard of intelligence will in no wise suffer."[94]

Some five hundred women crowded into the council chambers at the capitol to attend a public hearing on the suffrage question conducted before a joint House and Senate committee. Despite this and other demonstrations of support for suffrage, the legislature refused to act. Suffragists had to take the initiative. They did so in 1912.

Hunt, at least initially, received a favorable response from the first state legislature on policy matters. This resulted, in part, because he had a strong partisan and progressive majority with which to work. In the first state legislature, which met from 1912 to 1915, because the courts decided that state contests were not necessary in 1912, there were fourteen

Democrats and four Republicans in the Senate. Democrats dominated in the House by a thirty-one to four margin.

Among those serving as Democrats were William E. Brooks from Globe in the House and A. A. Worsley of Tucson in the Senate. Brooks's colleague in the House from Gila County, J. Tom Lewis, was later to remark that the influence of the corporations was remarkably low in the first legislature. Constituents, moreover, had definite opinions on labor and regulatory issues. Legislators who differed from their constituents on matters like the 80 percent law, for example, found themselves accused of lining up with the corporations.[95]

The first legislature took a regular and three special sessions called by Hunt to set up the new government and consider various reform proposals. It started on March 18, 1912. It ended its activities on May 17, 1913. The legislature spent what some felt to be an exorbitant amount of money, some $304,000 over the previous fiscal year, to implement the state constitution. It passed ninety-six measures.

One editor, Fred S. Breen, a Republican who also served in the Senate, summarized the flurry of legislative activity and moaned: "There are now laws for nearly everything." A few weeks later he continued the theme by noting: "The one great failing of the recent session of law makers was that of attempting to do all things for all time, forgetting that successive legislatures might want something to do."[96]

Brooks, like other legislators, received scathing condemnations from businessmen. The directors of the Warren District Commercial Club, for example, telegrammed that they were "uniformly indignant at the tendency of the legislature to willfully waste the taxpayers' money." Brooks, in response, said he deeply resented the telegram and the assertion that the businessmen were more concerned about the welfare of the state than he was.[97]

Another legislator, C. W. Roberts from Cochise County, faced the charge of favoring socialism because he liked the idea of free textbooks for school children. Roberts responded by declaring that if people wanted to label him a Socialist, so be it; he was still going to vote for free textbooks.[98]

In response to Hunt's recommendations came laws on workman's compensation, mine inspection, limits on the employment of women and children ("the world," Hunt told the legislators, "has too many over-worked, underfed and scarcely educated children"[99]), an eight-hour day for miners, and a number of regulations regarding railroad rates, safety, and employment practices. In addition, the legislature produced a pension system for teachers who had taught at least twenty-five years in Arizona public schools and, socialistic or not, a law providing free textbooks for students.

Legislative approval of many of these measures constituted a victory for organized labor, which had grouped together early in 1912 under the umbrella of the Arizona Federation of Labor. Holding its first annual convention in Globe, some sixty delegates declared for a wide variety of reforms of interest to labor and for broader social programs such as free school books.[100] The WFM also retained an interest in the course of reform in Arizona and sent lobbyists to the state capitol to work on measures like the eight-hour law.[101]

The principal spokesman in the state senate for the more radical element of the union movement was A. A. Worsley. He chaired the Senate Labor Committee. The *Tucson Citizen,* a Republican paper, called Worsley a blowhard who introduced "an average of one freak bill a day."[102] Among the measures introduced by Worsley early in the session was a proposed constitutional amendment that would allow the state and local governments to engage in industrial pursuits such as light and power plants, irrigation projects, and mining activities. Worsley argued:

> Arizona is what we make it. . . . Why should not Arizona build a saw-mill and convert her vast pine forests into lumber and thus put the lumber trust out of the state? Why should not Arizona build dams and power plants and convert all the dormant power in her great streams into living, active force for the use of her own? Why should not Arizona convert her vast coal fields into electric energy and transmit it all over the country for the people's use and profit?[103]

The industrial pursuit measure passed both houses and appeared on the ballot as a constitutional amendment in 1912. The idea appealed to

Worsley and other legislators as a means of establishing public enterprises to control the development of the state's natural resources.[104] Others, however, looked forward to other types of public enterprises that would compete with private establishments. For example, workers unhappy with the price of meat looked to use the law to create a public meat market owned and operated by the city of Phoenix.[105]

Many of Worsley's more radical proposals died in the legislature. Worsley reacted by encouraging workers to use the initiative to bring about collective ownership of the means of production and other changes.[106] The legislature also failed to implement constitutional provisions in regard to blacklisting. Somewhat ironically, moreover, organized labor, which had supported inclusion of the referendum in the constitution, had no choice but to stand by while the railroads and others used this device to challenge various labor measures passed by the legislature.

Of particular importance in the flow of progressive reform was the creation in 1912 of a three-member state commission tax that, Hunt hoped, would not only bring more uniformity to the tax system but actually raise the assessed valuations of mines and other corporations. The tax commission, although often finding itself locked in combat with local county boards, proceeded to raise the assessment roll some $255 million.[107] Much of the increase came at the expense of the mines and railroads. The assessed value of the mines alone increased from $19 million in 1911 to $45 million in 1912.

In 1914 special legislation increased the value of mines to $146 million. From 1911 to 1914 the percent of total taxes paid by the mines rose from 27 percent to 36 percent. Increased assessment of the railroads meant that by 1916 taxes rose to $627 per mile of line, a figure above the national average of $608.[108] In territorial years the tax per mile was far below the national average. Hunt later argued that the increased tax load, particularly on the mines, had a great deal to do with his subsequent political difficulties.

During his first few years in office, however, considerably more public attention focused on Hunt's attitudes and policies regarding punishment and prison reform than on his policies regarding tax reform. In his address to the first legislature on March 18, 1912, the governor called capital punishment "a relic of barbarism" and asked for its repeal. On the subject of prison reform he called for more humane treatment of prisoners and an end to the "archaic idea that society's ends are best served by the punishment and degradation of those convicted of transgressing the law of the land."[109]

Hunt proposed that prisoners have useful employment such as working for minimal pay in building a badly needed state road system. Hunt became rather well known nationally for articles he had written on penal reform. At home the response was not always positive. Having read one of these articles, Fred S. Breen, the editor of the *Coconino Sun,* declared that it should have been titled: "First Aid to the Wicked."[110]

The governor, nevertheless, wasted little time in making as many changes of this nature as he could. He ordered the elimination of the use of the ball and chain and the silence system within prisons. Next came an honor system that allowed trusted prisoners to work on state highway projects without the supervision of guards.

Hunt's policies in regard to prisoners were to cost him politically. Both labor unions and private contractors opposed the idea of using prisoners to build highways. Residents of Florence, the location of the prison, opposed policies allowing convicts to roam the street dressed like ordinary citizens. Others objected that the new policies had made the prison a pleasure resort. One prominent but very irate Democrat wrote to the chair of the Democratic State Central Committee that under Hunt, "honest, industrious and law-abiding citizens" received harsh treatment "while the convict is a hero, treated as the 'petted, curled darling' of the State."[111]

Also increasingly critical of Hunt on the prison reform issue was State Auditor Callaghan. He used his first official report to complain that discipline in the prison system was challenged "by maudlin sentiment and heroics." Callaghan complained that discipline had suffered because inmates were encouraged to think "they are, in reality, victims of a conspiracy formed by society, and by its legislatures, peace officers, prosecuting attorneys, courts, and juries."[112]

In his message to the state legislature on February 3, 1913, Hunt acknowledged that his policies concerning prison reform had been the storm center about which his critics had raged. The governor contended that, in fact, "nothing sensational or yet very startling has been done or attempted."[113] Rather, he had been simply trying to adapt modern humanitarian reforms already made in other states.[114]

The legislature mildly censured Hunt for a too lax attitude toward prison discipline. It showed considerably more displeasure over how the governor used his powers to grant reprieves and pardons. Hunt opposed capital punishment. He granted reprieves to a dozen murderers who faced this penalty while he sought public and judicial approval of his position.

The legislature struck back in the third special session by creating a board of pardons and reprieves that assumed most of the governor's authority in these matters. Under the legislation the governor could grant a pardon or reprieve only if the board recommended that he do so. The governor, moreover, was to have no control over the appointment of the board members. The acerbic Breen in June 1913 noted progress: "Governor Hunt hasn't pardoned, reprieved, paroled or stood guard on the prison walls so far this week."[115]

Hunt felt that the first session of the legislature was truly responsive to the will of the people in pursuing progressive reforms. When it met in special session a year later, however, the governor found that the legislature had changed its attitude about reform. In the interim, Hunt speculated, legislators fell under the influence of various special interests.[116]

Hunt attributed much of the problem over capital punishment and prison reform to his traditional enemies, the mines and railroads. As the governor saw it, these interests had simply been looking for an issue and had decided to make his program for prison reform the battle ground and the opening wedge in their war to unravel the general reform program. Speaking to his fellow governors at a conference in Colorado in August 1913, the governor outlined the situation:

Prison reform is linked and allied with all other reforms. If it fails and if its enemies are placed in charge of the state government because of its fall, then all other reforms, such as corporation regulation, just taxation, better labor laws, and many that suggest themselves, will also fall. It is doubtful if the opposition to prison reform in Arizona is at all concerned over it, or cares how far it goes. In forcing it as the issue, the interests are after bigger game and seek to use an inefficient legislature to that end.[117]

Some of Hunt's critics within the party declared that the governor had betrayed them and, indeed, most voters in 1911. Whatever Hunt might think, "the voters had not chosen to abandon representative democracy or the sacred principles of Jeffersonian democracy to experiment with the revolutionary theories of socialism."[118]

Other Democrats, such as activist Reese Ling from northern Arizona, whom Hunt considered a reactionary, complained that the governor's actions were in conflict with the goal of economic development. While back East in search of capital, Ling declared he stayed "busy explaining to persons contemplating investments here that we were not anarchists and that we did not believe in confiscation, and that if capital were invested in Arizona it would receive the protection of the law and would not be harassed."[119]

Press criticism prompted Hunt to sponsor a bill that would have required newspapers to publish in a prominent place in every issue the names of their owners, stockholders, and creditors. Hunt felt the copper interests were busy buying up papers for use against him.[120] One did find some normally Democratic papers becoming increasingly critical of the governor. Within the party structure, moreover, the conservative elements began to organize. Several members of the anti-Hunt group won election to the state committee in 1912. One of Hunt's major critics, George A. Olney, became state chair. As the following chapter indicates, however, the bulk of the voters had not yet turned against Hunt or against reform.

George W.P Hunt in 1885. Courtesy of the Arizona Department of Library, Archives and Public Records.

Captain Buckey O'Neill of the "Rough Riders" and mayor of Prescott, Arizona, 1898. Courtesy of the Arizona Department of Library, Archives and Public Records.

100

The inauguration of George W.P. Hunt as governor of Arizona, February 14, 1912. The march to the Capitol. Courtesy of the Arizona Department of Library, Archives and Public Records.

Loading cars during the deportation of suspected Wobblies at Bisbee, Arizona, July 12, 1917. Courtesy of the Arizona Department of Library, Archives and Public Records.

Train filled with deportees leaving for New Mexico, July 12, 1917. Courtesy of the Arizona Department of Library, Archives and Public Records.

Governor George W.P. Hunt knitting, 1918. Courtesy of the Arizona Department of Library, Archives and Public Records.

5

REFORM AND THE MOOD OF
THE ELECTORATE

Conservative newspaper editors looked forward to campaigning against Hunt and the reform Democrats in the 1912 general election. The state Supreme Court, however, put this attack on hold by deciding that Hunt and other state officials elected in 1911 did not have to face the voters until 1914. One anti-reform editor predicted that, at the present rate of governmental spending, the delay meant "the state will be bankrupt when these fellows go out of office."[1]

Arizonans had a choice among several candidates for president and for the state's sole seat in the House of Representatives in the fall election of 1912. The general election also gave the voters an opportunity to express their sentiments on the recall for judges, woman suffrage, and several reforms passed by the first legislature. Two years later, Arizonans voted on reform candidates, including Hunt, and on another batch of measures placed on the ballot by the initiative and referendum procedures.

Progressives, Socialists, and Suffrage

The 1912 presidential contest amounted to "a national decision on the future of progressivism."[2] In Arizona, as in several other states, voters had a choice among major party candidates Woodrow Wilson (Democrat)

and William Howard Taft (Republican) and third-party candidates Theodore Roosevelt (Progressive), Eugene Debs (Socialist), and Eugene W.
Chafin (Prohibition).

Neither Wilson nor Taft campaigned in Arizona in 1912. Both
Roosevelt and Debs, on the other hand, made the trip. Both had visited
the territory on numerous occasions and, thus, were relatively familiar to
Arizonans.[3] Chafin was a resident of Arizona, having moved to Tucson in
1909. He was a Wisconsin native and a former Republican who ran for
the U.S. House from Arizona as the Prohibition party's candidate in 1911.

Wilson, a recent convert to progressivism, offered a somewhat
ambiguous "New Freedom" program that combined moderate reform
largely intended to restore conditions of economic opportunity with
traditional Democrat beliefs in weak government and states rights. Wilson
was an unknown quantity to many Arizonans. Arizona Democrats had
favored Champ Clark in the primary. Yet Wilson stood to benefit from
the strong traditional Democratic vote in Arizona. His endorsement by
the AFL also helped his prospects in the new state.

Taft was the most conservative candidate. For him, the campaign
became a crusade for constitutionalism, that is, for representative democracy as opposed to direct democracy.[4] Taft was particularly unpopular in
Arizona because of his stand on the recall issue, his opposition to the state
constitution, and his reputation as an antilabor "injunction judge" while
on the bench. He did, however, have the endorsement of leaders in the
Mormon Church.[5]

Roosevelt offered voters a long list of social and political reforms.
His program of "New Nationalism" added up to a more democratic
society in which the federal government would play a more prominent
role. Roosevelt reserved his greatest scorn for reactionaries who refused
to see any need for change.[6] During the campaign he told audiences in
Phoenix and Tucson that because Taft had little chance of winning, the
"bosses and representatives of special privilege were rallying to the
support of Wilson."[7]

Local officers of the new Progressive party greeted Roosevelt on his
arrival in the state. Several prominent former Republicans — Joseph A.

Kibbey, Dwight B. Heard, J.L.B. Alexander, and John C. Greenway among them — led the new party in Arizona.

Some of the leading Arizona Progressives had been delegates for Roosevelt at the 1912 Republican convention. The convention chose to recognize a delegation pledged to Taft. Rejected, the Roosevelt delegates came home and called for a new party. They claimed that both major parties were controlled by reactionaries. Roosevelt Clubs soon sprang up throughout Arizona. Heard, a Massachusetts native who came to Arizona in 1895 to regain his health, purchased the *Phoenix Republican* and turned it into an organ for the new party. Through this means and an enthusiastic though underfinanced campaign, the Progressives attempted to woo voters from all sides of the political spectrum.[8]

The National Progressive party of Arizona, in a statement of principles adopted in Phoenix, July 30, 1912, endorsed woman suffrage, direct legislation, and a variety of labor reforms to secure "industrial justice." The platform emphasized the new party's support of the recall, including the recall of judges. "The just and intelligent use of" the initiative, referendum, and recall "will assist more completely in the actual rule of the people."[9] Party leaders also pointed out that voters in Maricopa County owed Roosevelt for his support of federal reclamation projects that made development and prosperity possible.[10]

George Young, the unsuccessful candidate for the Republican primary for governor in 1911, proclaimed during the 1912 contest: "The Progressive party and movement will go on. It is not a creature of one man, but the expression of a whole people against a condition. Theodore Roosevelt would die happy tonight because he knows that the movement will go on."[11] The conservative press in 1912 saw considerable danger in Bull Moose candidates, whose "progressive ideas smack strongly of socialism," canvassing the state.[12]

The Progressive party's platform included a variety of reforms that had long been part of the program of the Socialist party. Roosevelt's adoption of the Socialist planks angered Debs.[13] He feared that Roosevelt and, to a lesser extent, Wilson would siphon off the Socialist votes, particularly those of the more conservative "parlor socialists."[14] Roosevelt, Debs argued, was nothing more than a tool of the capitalists trying to head off fundamental change. Wilson, Debs added, "has as rotten a labor record as any man possibly could have."[15]

The Labor party episode almost destroyed the Socialist party in Arizona. In 1910, shortly before the Labor party emerged, the Arizona Socialist party had close to six hundred dues-paying members scattered around the territory in twenty locals. Defections to the Laborites reduced the Socialist party membership to less than one hundred and the number of locals to three. Yet by early 1912 the party's national committee representative for Arizona was happy to report that most of the comrades who had been "deceived by the self-seeking leaders" of the Labor party had come back into the fold.[16]

By the fall of 1912 Debs's candidacy and a well-organized national party had further rejuvenated the Arizona party.[17] Party workers campaigned enthusiastically on Debs's behalf throughout the state. They also campaigned for A. Charles Smith of Douglas, candidate for Congress, described as a "fluent talker and gentleman" by the conservative press.[18]

As the Socialist campaigners saw it, they were educating the voters rather than saying whatever was necessary to secure votes. They assumed that once the people became informed about the Socialist program their party would not have to worry about votes.[19] Debs, in particular, placed strong emphasis on education and the need for the masses to think for themselves rather than rely on leaders. He pointed out to an assembly in Bisbee: "It would do no good for me to lead you to the promised land — Roosevelt would only come along and lead you out again."[20]

Prohibitionists, likewise, set out to educate the voters, hoping to pave the way for greater electoral success in the future. The liquor traffic, Chafin contended, was not a business but a crime accountable for untold damage. Beyond the liquor issue, the prohibitionists offered a variety of reforms also found in the other third-party platforms. Chafin argued that the Prohibitionists had the "only real progressive platform." Like Debs, he directed the bulk of his attack on the impostor Roosevelt.[21]

The result of the 1912 contest was a decisive victory for Wilson. The percentage of the Arizona vote going to Wilson, 43.6, was just slightly above the 41.8 percent he received nationally. Roosevelt also did slightly better in Arizona than he did on the national level, polling 29.3 percent compared to 27.3 percent. Taft, on the other hand, received only 12.6 percent of the vote in Arizona compared to 23.2 percent nationally. Debs did better than Taft in Arizona, receiving 13.4 percent of the vote. This was way above his national average of about 6 percent. The only states in which Debs did better were Montana (13.5%), Nevada (16.5%), and Oklahoma (16.4%). Chafin received only some two hundred votes.

November 1912 also brought victory to Democrat Carl Hayden as a candidate for the U.S. House of Representatives. He captured 48 percent of the some 23,000 votes distributed among five candidates. Both the Republican and Socialist candidates received 13 percent of the vote while the Bull Moose candidate, riding on Roosevelt's coattails, received 25 percent of the vote.

The popularity of the Progressive party with Roosevelt at the head of the ticket came as no surprise. The relatively strong finish of the Socialist party, however, was unexpected. Not only was Deb's percentage surprisingly high but, as Debs himself pointed out, it was a "true socialist vote" because those interested in mere immediate reform supported Wilson and Roosevelt.[22]

The Socialist party in Arizona after the 1912 election saw itself in the mainstream of reform. Greatly encouraged by Debs's performance, local Socialist party leaders predicted a "rising tide of socialism" in the state.[23] The possibility of this happening did not go unheeded in the general press. The fear of socialism provoked a variety of responses, ranging from efforts at co-optation to, as indicated in the following chapter, violent repression.

Republicans and Democrats both called attention to the rising popularity of socialism. They offered their respective parties as the only safe alternative. The GOP emphasized resistance to socialism or anything that looked like radical reform. The Democrats, as represented by Hunt and his supporters, argued that the only way to meet the socialist challenge was to avoid reactionaries and provide needed changes. As the *Arizona Gazette*, at that time a Democratic paper, put it: "The democratic party is pledged to progressive principles which, if carried out in good faith, will check the growth of socialism."[24]

Among the propositions on the ballot in 1912 were those involving the recall of judges, woman suffrage, and the wisdom of several regulations on railroads. Voters removed the recall from the state constitution as the price of statehood. With statehood they were free to express their true sentiments on the topic. By an overwhelming vote of 16,272 to 3,491, Arizonans decided to put the recall provision back into the constitution. This vote came over objections from Republicans. The GOP platform continued to oppose the proposal. Also largely ignored were newspaper warnings that the recall "undermines the stability of courts and leaves room for dissension, strife, and turmoil."[25]

Theodore Roosevelt, among others, had no doubt about what Arizona voters would do on this issue. Writing in 1911, he noted: "Arizona, of course, will now with practical unanimity reinsert the recall of the judiciary in the Constitution, simply because both its opponents and its advocates felt that it was something for Arizona itself to decide, and bitterly resented the action of the President and the Republican majority in seeking to force them to abandon the proposal."[26]

Hunt remarked shortly after the reinstatement of the recall: "Thus is the State's right to a Constitution of its own making vindicated, its legitimate independence of executive interference asserted, and the consistent belief of the people in their ability to govern themselves established."[27] Earlier, Hunt declared that although the people would seldom use the recall, it was an essential safeguard against those who would misuse power.[28] Ironically, Hunt himself would become the object of the first serious recall effort.

The first state legislature declined to refer the equal suffrage question to the voters. Suffragists reacted by taking advantage of the initiative procedure to put the measure on the ballot. The male voters responded by approving the proposal by a better than two to one majority: 13,442 to 6,202. Suffragettes credited endorsement of the suffrage measure by the Progressive party in 1912 as the key factor in its success because this action prompted the major parties to do likewise.[29] The Progressive party, many felt, would benefit from the addition of women to the electorate.[30]

Nationally, the Socialist party was divided over the suffrage issue. The party endorsed the reform, professing to believe that women, particularly those employed outside the home, were natural allies with male workers in the struggle against capitalism. Some Socialists, however, dissented from this view. They contended that the party was only fooling itself and would find that women, once given the vote, would use it in a conservative manner.[31] In Arizona, Socialists actively worked for the reform. The mainstream press dismissed these efforts as motivated by an attempt for political gain rather than by conviction.[32]

Suffragists' strategy in Arizona centered on making an orderly, conservative, and nonconfrontational case that stressed such themes as the debt owed to pioneer women for building the state.[33] This approach undoubtedly helps explain why the suffrage movement faced little organized opposition. On the positive side suffrage received the backing of groups as diverse as the business-oriented Phoenix Trades Council and labor's Western Federation of Miners.[34] As in the past, it also had the support of groups favoring prohibition. Shortly after the 1912 election the corresponding secretary of the Arizona WCTU reported to her group: "The success of the suffrage movement in Arizona can but mean that the battle for statewide prohibition will soon be waged, and our Union should take fresh strength and courage."[35]

Like the suffragettes and the prohibitionists, organized labor supported the adoption of the devices of direct democracy at the convention in anticipation that it might have to use them to circumvent hostile legislatures. Ironically, in 1912 labor did well in the legislature but later found many of their successful measures challenged by protest referenda filed by railroad interests.

Placed before the voters by the railroads in the November 1912 general elections were legislative measures that called for: (1) the installation of certain types of headlights on locomotives; (2) limits on the number of cars on freight and passenger trains; (3) regulations on the number of crew members employed on trains; (4) more stringent job qualifications for engineers and conductors on trains; (5) maximum rates for the transportation of passengers; and (6) a semimonthly pay day for rail workers (as opposed to the existing monthly pay day system).

These regulations hardly qualified as new or radical. Nor did they impose harsh conditions on the rail industry.[36] The railroads, however, strongly opposed all six measures.[37] The Santa Fe, which led the drive, had already demonstrated its opposition to similar rail regulation in other states. It had often threatened to discontinue service if it did not get its way.[38]

The various railway brotherhoods and the state AFL worked for approval of the measures. They defended the regulations as being in the public interest. Regulation, from this perspective, brought fairer rates and improved safety. Critics charged that many of the measures were simply attempts to protect jobs. Several railroad employees signed the petitions calling for referendum votes. Rail workers were willing to sign the petitions, one paper suggested, because they "felt that the railroads would be forced to make retrenchments in wages paid and in improvements if these measures are put into effect."[39] Supporters of the reforms argued that employers had coerced rail workers into signing the petitions.[40]

Opponents contended that the legislation inhibited the progress of the railroads and thus choked "the arteries through which the commercial and industrial life blood of the state must flow."[41] Spokespersons for the rail industry also took the time to portray the broader danger to economic freedom presented by these measures:

> If laws can be enacted that dictate the manner in which railroads must be operated, when such operation is not at present in conflict with public safety and public policy; if laws can be enacted that compel expenditures for services that are not required, or for equipment that has not yet proven satisfactory, or best; if laws can be enacted that arbitrarily reduce fares and lessen the earning power of the railroads, then indeed, what promise is there that the merchant, the farmer, and the miner will not each suffer similar restrictions in his own business?[42]

During the 1912 campaign, rail interests made many additional arguments against the legislation. Concerning the proposal that locomotive engineers and conductors have three years of railroad experience, for example, railroad spokespersons warned "Mr. and Mrs. Parent" that their boy, whom they had "raised and educated at great personal sacrifice," would lose out when it came to these positions. This would not be because he was unqualified but because "roving railroad men coming from the four corners of the earth" will show up in Arizona with letters, "that may be forged, for all the railroads know," stating that they have the required experience.[43]

In opposition to the semimonthly pay legislation, railroads attempted to win over the antisaloon element by arguing "such a plan would play into the hands of that class of business that makes its living by inducing the workingman to spend his substance, on pay days, in riotous living."[44] Two pay days per month, the railroads warned, would double the amount of riotous living and such activity was not in the interest of the individual, the home, or the state.

Voters approved the labor-supported measures over these protests. They also approved Worsley's industrial pursuits proposal and a tax measure making it easier for the state to assess the property of large corporations. Thus, the voters kept in motion progressive tendencies that had been apparent at the constitutional convention and the first state legislature.

A deeper probe of the election returns suggests that Wilson did particularly well with the party faithful in the state (past Democratic voters) and, over this, people in farming areas. Regionally, he had more appeal to voters from the South and West than he did to voters from the East and Midwest. He had relatively little support in mining areas or in places with large numbers of Europeans. Wilson supporters were comparatively negative about increasing governmental authority (for example, through industrial pursuits), labor-inspired regulations on railroads, and woman suffrage.

Wilson's Arizona constituency, in short, was not highly progressive in nature. Many who supported Wilson may have viewed him as essentially a traditional states rights, limited-government Democrat.[45] Voters appeared to have viewed other mainstream Democrats in a similar manner. Wilson's following in 1912, for example, was comparable to that of Carl Hayden.

Taft and his congressional running mate found regular Republican support fortified by those who were unhappy with the industrial pursuits measure, labor regulation, rate regulation, suffrage, and, most strikingly, the recall. Many of the most determined opponents of the anticorporate reform cause found their candidate in Taft. Like Republicans before him Taft did relatively well in economically diversified cities and relatively poorly in mining areas. Regionally, his vote was nonsouthern. Taft appears to have made a slight inroad in the Mormon vote. Church leaders, however, were not able to produce a massive change in the voting behavior of Mormons. On the other hand, Hispanics appear to have moved away from the Republican party headed by Taft and as represented by the GOP candidate for Congress. Some switched to the Democrats but more appear to have moved to the Progressive party.[46]

Progressives, on the ballot for the first time in 1912, did not draw strongly from any particular party. There is only a slight correlation between the Roosevelt vote in 1912 and the GOP vote in 1910. The new party had little, if any, appeal to the reform-minded who had voted Socialist in previous elections. Both Roosevelt and the Progressive congressional candidate picked up some support from Hispanics and people in mining communities.

More directly related to party support, however, was the appeal it had to those who favored certain reforms, especially as represented by the industrial pursuits measure. Supporters of the Progressive party, on the other hand, did not approve suffrage and other reforms to the extent one might have expected from the campaign. Reporters who witnessed the counting of ballots in some precincts were surprised at the number of progressive tickets marked against woman suffrage.[47]

The Socialist party anchored its support in the party vote evidenced in previous elections. The party vote was relatively strong in mining areas and, in the 1912 presidential election at least, more directly in places where one found large numbers of European-born. The Socialist vote was, as one might expect, also a highly ideological or programmatic vote. It was positively and often strongly correlated with all the anticorporate reforms on the ballot. Compared to other party voters, Socialists were also unusually supportive of suffrage.

Looking at specific issues, one finds different clusters of support. Labor issues involving the railroads did relatively well with people in mining communities and with those who supported third parties. On rail rates more central differences emerged between Socialists and Republicans, and between economically diversified cities and towns and other types of communities (mining and farming). Farmers were a force for rail rate regulation but not for rail regulations in the interest of labor.

Third-party supporters were again a leading source of support on economic reform measures such as centralizing tax assessment (thus making it easier to raise corporate taxes) and Worsley's industrial pursuits proposal. On the recall and woman suffrage partisanship was also an important factor, with third-party voters particularly supportive and major party voters relatively unsupportive. The recall was particularly attractive to Socialist voters and particularly unattractive to Republican voters.

Suffrage did well in Mormon and farming communities. These places, perhaps not incidentally, had comparatively large female populations. Suffrage also did well where Socialists were relatively strong. Further analysis of this vote, done elsewhere, suggests that suffrage enjoyed the support of two otherwise somewhat antagonistic groups.[48] One group for suffrage consisted of native-born westerners and Mormons who wanted both prohibition and suffrage but who did not favor the radical third parties or any of the other reforms on the ballot. The second group consisted of third-party supporters, among whom miners and the European-born were relatively numerous, who favored suffrage and a wide variety of reforms, but not prohibition. Given common assumptions about the policy implications of giving women the vote, those in the first category acted in a rational, instrumental manner. Many of those in the second group, on the other hand, appear to have supported suffrage even though they had severe misgivings about what this would mean in the future.

Hunt, Prohibition, and Labor

Hunt, taking a positive view of the 1912 elections, called Wilson's victory a triumph for progressive democracy. He expressed his delight about how the initiative and referendum had allowed the voters to both defend reforms already made and bring further reform.[49]

Early in 1914 Governor Hunt also spoke with considerable pride about his own accomplishments. These included increased corporate taxation, more spending on education (at a level four times greater than in 1911–1912), stronger regulations on utilities, and several laws "to insure relative justice between men and women who work for a living and those who live without toil or through the skillful display of capital."[50]

Hunt's reforms had angered the corporate elite and conservatives in both parties. Railroads staved off some of the unwanted regulations by successfully challenging them in court. The Arizona Supreme Court in February 1914, for example, agreed with their contention that the three-cent fare law was invalid. The broader and more immediate goal of the anti-reform forces, however, was to remove Hunt and his followers from power.

Shifting political sentiments, increased migration, and the addition of women to the electorate made the 1914 elections difficult to predict. Thanks in large part to the adoption of the suffrage amendment, the voting population increased from some 81,000 in 1912 to about 152,000 in 1914.

Progressive party leaders were encouraged by the performance of their candidates in 1912 and by the addition of female voters to the electorate in time for the 1914 contest. Roosevelt, filled with enthusiasm, urged them to continue the fight in 1914.[51] Feeling secure, Arizona Progressives rebuffed Republican offers of fusion in the belief that the GOP was about to disintegrate.[52]

Just prior to the 1914 primary season, rumors circulated that the Bull Moosers and Hunt Democrats might be able to counter the conservative forces by working out an agreement to control the state. At the heart of this proposed endeavor was a deal whereby the Progressives would help Hunt unseat Marcus Smith for the Senate seat, and the Hunt forces in turn would help Progressive leader Heard become governor.[53] The bargain, if ever a serious possibility, fell through and Hunt turned his full attention to getting re-elected.

Much of the attack on Hunt coming from the conservative press focused on his death penalty and penal reform policies. These issues, strategists assumed, were his greatest negative with the public, especially the new female voters.[54] Editors critical of Hunt took considerable pleasure in describing his release program by conjuring up images of "life-term murderers" at Florence, the site of the state prison, "dancing with innocent girls."[55]

Hunt backed off from his release program. In something of a master stroke, he also abandoned the practice of using convicts to build roads. This ended a controversy he had with organized labor. It also allowed Hunt to give the freed-up jobs on a paying basis to miners who were looking for work. Without Hunt's help many of these miners would probably have left the state. With their new employment the miners remained in the state. Many voted, as they had in the past, for Hunt.[56]

Hunt secured renomination by nearly two to one over a challenger who attacked the governor's stand on capital punishment. Hunt went on to defeat Ralph H. Cameron, the Republican candidate, George U. Young, the Progressive candidate, and J. R. Barnette, the Socialist candidate, in the general election. Republicans and Progressives attacked Hunt for inefficiency, mismanagement, and extravagance; building a political machine; making prison a luxurious boarding school; and driving capital out of the state.[57] Cameron, addressing the Democrats, claimed that Hunt had "in many instances substituted socialistic principles for those of the democratic party."[58] The Progressives denounced Hunt's boss rule and mismanagement of state affairs. On their own behalf they took credit for securing woman suffrage in the state.[59]

Progressives and Republicans spent a good part of the 1914 campaign attacking each other. Republicans argued that a vote for Young would be a wasted vote because Cameron was the only candidate who could defeat Hunt. The Progressives countered in a full-page newspaper ad: "Don't be fooled by exaggerated reports of Republican strength. The Progressive party is on the political map to stay, and offers the only plausible chance to elect a clean, level-headed business-man to replace Governor Hunt."[60]

In the end the GOP and Progressives split the anti-Hunt vote. Hunt, however, would still have had a narrow victory even if a single opponent had combined the GOP and Progressive votes. Without prominent presidential candidates at the top of the ticket, support for the gubernatorial candidates of both the Socialist party and the Progressive party severely declined. Both too may have been hurt by the Hunt candidacy. Together, the third parties received only about 15 percent of the votes cast for governor.

On the negative side for reformers, the 1914 elections cost Hunt some strong supporters in the legislature. A half-dozen of Hunt's more vocal legislative supporters went down to defeat in primary elections. One of these was C. W. Roberts, the legislator accused of being a Socialist because he had supported measures like free textbooks. Other Hunt supporters in the legislature, perhaps seeing the handwriting on the wall, decided not to run again. Much to Hunt's displeasure, his candidate in the primary for the state auditor's office lost out to J. C. Callaghan, a leading critic of the administration's spending and prison reform policies.

In addition to these defeats, the voters expressed their disagreement with Hunt's views on capital punishment by turning down a proposition that would have abolished the death penalty. As a further rebuff to the governor, they agreed to curb his ability to grant pardons and reprieves.

On the plus side came Hunt's re-election and, as noted below, voter approval of several long-sought changes. The Democratic *Arizona Gazette* rejoiced after the 1914 contest that the "people of Arizona are still in the saddle, looking after their political and business interests."[61] "Progressive democracy," the paper continued, had been "placed on trial" but had been able to turn back the reactionary forces, led by former tax dodging corporations, who had worked both inside and outside the party.[62]

In partisan terms 1914 was good for Democrats, radical or otherwise. All Democratic candidates up for statewide election in 1914 were victorious over their Republican and third-party challengers. Marcus Smith had little trouble in defeating candidates of the Republican, Progressive, Socialist, and Prohibition parties for the Senate. Smith received 53 percent of the vote. The Prohibition candidate for the Senate was its 1912 national standard-bearer, Eugene W. Chafin. Added to his general platform was the pledge: "If elected, I'll go to to Washington and stay sober. I'll set an example to the rest of the senate."[63]

Chafin surprised observers by coming in third behind the Republican candidate with about 15 percent of the vote. He, no doubt, benefited from the turnout for the vote on the prohibition measure on the ballot. Coming in behind Chafin with about 7 percent of the vote was Socialist Bert Davis, who was also president of the Arizona State Federation of Labor. The Progressive candidate came in last with about 5 percent of the vote.

Carl Hayden, successful Democratic candidate for the single House seat in Congress, received more votes than any other candidate up for election that year (33,306), easily turning back his Republican and Socialist opponents (the Progressives did not nominate a candidate for this position). Of the 53 seats in the legislature, 52 went to Democrats. One lonely Republican managed to win a Senate seat.

The great issue on the list of propositions voted on in 1914 was prohibition. Acting together under the banner of the Temperance Federation of Arizona, the dry forces developed an initiative measure calling for absolute prohibition. This made it illegal to get liquor even on prescription or for sacramental purposes. Supporters contended that Arizonans should vote for prohibition, in part, as a matter of state pride. Arizona, drys argued, "deserves the best" and prohibition was vital to the "mental, moral and physical integrity of its people."[64] Having the most to gain out of all this, drys argued, were members of the wage-earning class:

With liquor unobtainable the wage-earner's self-efficiency will be increased; his mentality will be clearer; his working conditions improved; his manhood awakened; his ambition fired; his home more nearly ideal; his children better fed, better clothed and better educated; his life longer and more useful. To abolish the liquor traffic is to remove one of the greatest obstructions to the laborer's social and industrial progress.[65]

Wets formed the Arizona Local Self Government League. This organization primarily pushed for local option as an alternative to statewide prohibition. The league was particularly strong in Cochise, Maricopa, and Yavapai counties. It also had support in the Roman Catholic Church and the Arizona AFL.[66] Wets argued that statewide prohibition would be impossible to enforce and costly to the taxpayers. In addition, the loss of tax revenue from the saloons would force the government to look elsewhere for revenues.

Other arguments against the measure, commonly found in newspapers and handouts, were that it interfered with religious freedom, restricted personal liberty (or made people outlaws to exercise that liberty), and could lead to an increase in the number of drug fiends. Wets blamed much of the trouble on "itinerant prohibition agitators" moving from state to state.[67]

Some of those who favored prohibition portrayed unionists, Socialists, and Hunt as allies of the whiskey lobby.[68] In truth, the reform had little support from these sources. All three shared a clientele in mining areas where saloons were an important part of life. In these places saloons were the poor man's social club and an important gathering place for males from various ethnic backgrounds.

Long after the 1914 vote, some labor leaders publicly stated their support of prohibition primarily because it produced better workers and better union members.[69] Union leaders probably had similar good thoughts about prohibition before the 1914 election but, considering the attitude of workers on the subject, were reluctant to express these views. From the WFM came the word that "working people need no guardian to keep them sober and moral" and that the real danger to workers' health was not rum but the conditions of labor created by the monopolies.[70]

Socialist leaders also had mixed emotions about prohibition. They had little good to say about the liquor business, regarding the selling of liquor "as bad as the selling of any other poison," but opposed prohibition because of the enforcement problem and the possibility that the exercise would only substitute a worse poison from the bootlegger for one not so dangerous.[71]

Prohibition carried the Arizona electorate by a margin of 3,144 votes out of some 48,000 cast. Contemporary observers saw the newly created women's vote behind the 1914 approval of the prohibition amendment.[72] Yet while women's organizations worked for prohibition and the women may have tended to vote toward this end, other interests also headed in the same direction. In particular, the experience of communities that had decided to go dry under local option appears to have helped convince business interests that banning alcohol was a worthy course of action. As a historian of the period has noted: "Contractors employing many laborers had learned that, under local option, labor was at least five per cent more efficient in a dry town than in a wet one, so they decided that they would like to try the experiment of a dry state."[73]

Prohibition also appealed to businessmen because they feared developments in the law would make them accountable for drink-induced industrial accidents. Other than economic interests some observers have given considerable emphasis to the support of Mormon and Evangelical churches in rural areas in explaining why prohibition passed.[74]

At the Bisbee convention of the state AFL in 1913, Arizona labor leaders decided to use the initiative route for reforms they had long favored. Unhappy about the prospect of reform in the legislature, they decided to use the 1914 elections to take their case directly to the voters. Labor-sponsored measures placed on the ballot included the long-sought goals of outlawing blacklisting and limiting competition of alien labor through a measure that required employers of five or more people to hire at least 80 percent of their employees from out of the citizen population.

Organized labor in 1913 was on the upswing in Arizona, and various locals were steeped in activity. A dance and cafeteria dinner in Globe hosted by the Globe miners' union on Thanksgiving, for example, netted some $440 for striking miners in Michigan.[75] Other WFM locals in Arizona, however, were less active and, indeed, had problems surviving. John P. Striegel, in the process of resigning as secretary of the WFM in McCabe, noted:

> I was hired twice in the last five months by a corporation, and worked just long enough for them to find out that I was Secretary of this local when I got the axe. Joe Comer had the same trouble when he was Secretary. Since he quit the union he can get work. I am in the same fix he was in. I have a family to support, and am tied down here, so there is but one thing for me to do."[76]

At the time, Striegel's local had seven members in good standing, though none of them had paid their dues recently.

Blacklisting was a serious enough problem in 1913 to prompt labor leader Bert Davis to declare it "the most despicable form of persecution the mind of man can devise. It is founded in hate, born of cowardice and given to gratifying the ignoble passion of revenge."[77] The labor official concluded: "Any company, corporation or individual that deliberately sets out to prevent a man from earning a living for himself or his family is to our mind committing a crime as bad if not worse than murder."[78] Opponents of the measure argued that an antiblacklisting law violated the constitutional right of contract and, more vaguely, "the right of the employer to know something about the man or woman he employs."[79]

Organized labor defended the 80 percent proposal as a necessary protection against aliens. Labor spokespeople used offensive rhetoric in referring to the need to attain "a superior class of citizens for Arizona." They also, however, placed emphasis on the need to protect people of foreign birth from exploitation.[80] Critics contended that the measure would result in the massive unemployment of Hispanics, hurt existing industries, and scare away capital needed for development. AFL sponsorship of the measure widened the gap between it and Hispanic workers.[81]

The nub of the economic problem, from the critics' point of view, was that employers were unlikely to find citizens for section work on the railroads, common labor at the smelters, or low-grade miners who were willing to work for the same wages as the aliens. The problem of having to pay more for labor, opponents argued, would probably be more severe in the mining than in the railroad industry. In the latter the costs could be shifted to consumers, with the approval of the Corporation Commission, in the form of higher rail rates. If the cost of labor went up in mining operations, however, there was no guarantee that the market price for copper, silver, or lead ore would also increase. Thus, some operations especially the low-grade ones, would no longer be worth pursuing and would have to shut down. Opponents of the plan went on to remind the voters: "The best invitation that can be extended to the capital needed in Arizona is to let it be known that the people of this state are not disposed to uselessly nag and harass those who have made investments in Arizona."[82]

In the 1914 general election, however, the voters were in the mood to do some nagging. They approved both the antiblacklisting and 80 percent proposals. Other labor-backed measures submitted for voter approval were an old age and mothers' pension plan that provided for a minimum of $15 a month for destitute mothers, separate grants for their children, and the elimination of alms houses; a proposal permitting the state to engage in industrial pursuits and abolishing the letting of contracts; an Australian Tax Bill that equalized taxes by allowing the state to take over property at an assessed valuation figure determined by owners; and a safety measure regulating electric poles, wires, and cables. All passed except the Australian tax measure. Also passing was a proposal supported by labor prohibiting the governor or legislature from vetoing or altering initiative and referendum measures approved by a majority of the voters.

Looking closer at the voting patterns evidenced in 1914, we find Hunt doing only modestly well among past Democratic voters. Indeed, his vote had a higher correlation with the Socialist vote in 1912 than with the Democratic vote for that year. Hunt did particularly well with Europeans. He retained some support among Mormons. Many Mormons, however, apparently turned away from Hunt because of his stand on issues like capital punishment.[83] Regionally, Hunt, like other

Democrats, did better with people from the West and South than he did with people from the East and Midwest. The most important regional factor was his relatively poor showing with Midwesterners. As expected, Hunt did relatively well with those who favored the elimination of the death penalty.

The death penalty was also an important element, along with traditional partisanship, affecting support of the Republican gubernatorial candidate, Ralph Cameron. In addition, Cameron supporters differed from Hunt supporters in tending to oppose control over rail rates, the blacklisting law, the 80 percent proposal, and the proposal to protect initiative and referendum measures from legislative or gubernatorial tampering.

The Socialist candidate for governor drew heavily on the established party vote and, like Hunt, received considerable support from those opposed to blacklisting and capital punishment. With Hunt on the ticket the Socialist candidate for governor lost much of the following Socialists normally received from Europeans and people in mining areas. Socialist candidates for other offices in 1914, for example, the Corporation Commission, retained that support. Socialists up and down the ticket did not do well with female voters.

Hunt Democrats and Socialists in 1914 appeared, in terms of both program and electoral support, to be part of the economic–political reform tradition dating back to the Populist movement. The Progressives by 1914, however, looked somewhat outside that tradition. Without the heavy vote produced by having Theodore Roosevelt at the top of the ticket, the Arizona Progressives in 1914 became a minor party with some particular appeal to Midwesterners, farmers, and people who supported prohibition but few anticorporate reforms, especially of the labor–oriented variety.

On the issues, data indicate particularly strong support for prohibition among Mormons, farmers, Progressives (those who voted for the Progressive party), and female voters. On issues more central to the anticorporate reform effort, such as blacklisting and rail rate regulation, one finds particularly strong support in mining areas, among Europeans and

Hispanics, and in areas where the Socialist vote was the greatest. On the opposite side, westerners, easterners, Mormons, farmers, Republicans, and females were relatively prominent. Democrats were split between the Hunt forces and the more traditional elements on these issues.

The addition of female voters had a moderate to conservative influence. As Appendix D indicates, Republicans and Progressives gained the most by this expansion of the voting population. As noted above, women in particular rejected the Socialists. Democrats, up and down the ticket, also had little to cheer about in the extension of suffrage.

Influencing these partisan trends to some extent were the activities of the Congressional Union for Woman Suffrage, which took aim at the Democratic party because it was the party in power on the national level and thus responsible for the failure to secure a suffrage amendment. In 1914 the "Defeat the Democrats" effort of the Congressional Union was aimed at all Democratic candidates for national office. In Arizona the group concentrated its efforts on winning over the vote of women in mining communities in the belief that these women were the most inclined toward feminist causes. Democratic candidates in Arizona easily survived the campaign against them, although perhaps because of this they did not do particularly well with women.[84]

As predicted, women in Arizona supported prohibition. On other issues, however, they were negative. Although female reformers such as Frances Munds worked for the penal reform measures, women tended to take the opposite position.[85] Women were even more negative on issues involving rail regulation, blacklisting, and the employment of aliens (the 80 percent law).

Trends and Directions

In both 1912 and 1914 the Arizona electorate appeared supportive of reform candidates and causes. This was shown in the strength of radical-progressive third-party candidates in 1912. Two years later the reform-minded in the Arizona electorate rallied behind the candidacy of George W.P. Hunt. While Hunt and the changes he favored (except for penal reform) appeared to enjoy broad support, signs of a countermovement centered around the goal of economic development. The sanctity of private property rights had begun to develop. Changes also occurred in the composition of the electorate through the adoption of woman suffrage — changes that were not conducive to the anticorporate reform program. Within the electorate, moreover, it was evident that a wide range of reform proposals divided the electorate. These divisions, as the following chapter illustrates, were to widen over the next two years.

6

DISCORD AND DIVISION

A wide assortment of charges had done little in the 1914 general election to damage Hunt's standing with the voters. Yet cracks in public support had appeared. As Hunt entered his second term, moreover, several developments began to make life difficult for him. Reform momentum stalled in the legislature. Increased social and economic tensions divided Arizonans. With the outbreak of war, attention was distracted away from the progressive agenda.

The Shifting Mood

A distinguishing aspect of the second state legislature, meeting for the first time on January 11, 1915, was that two women were members of that body. One of these was Frances Munds, the suffrage leader, who represented Yavapai County in the Senate. The other senators warmly applauded Munds as she rose to preside over the Senate sitting as a committee of the whole. Munds, however, cut the greeting short, declaring: "We are here for business."[1]

As it turned out, the lawmakers actually had very little important business before them, especially when compared to the first legislature. Hunt addressed the lawmakers, all of whom but one were fellow Democrats. Hunt stressed his strong views on labor issues, penal reform, the value of direct democracy, and corporate taxation. After the regular and three special sessions the legislature decided on a closed primary system but neither considered nor passed anything else of consequence.

The second legislature had, on balance, fewer progressives than the first legislature. The lack of activity in the second legislature, however, may have been equally influenced by other factors. Considering the volume of activity in the previous legislature and the number of measures voted on by the voters at the polls, reformers may have simply run out of ideas or wanted to catch their breath. Legislators and others may also have been somewhat disillusioned with reform. Critics inside and outside the legislative chambers complained that direct primaries and elections on initiatives and referendum matters were expensive, confusing to the voters, and divisive.

Critics also pointed out that use of direct democracy had frequently resulted in policies that could not stand up in court.[2] In 1913–1915 state courts invalidated measures on rate regulation, headlights on trains, car train limitations, and the old age and mothers' pension plan. The 80 percent law met a similar fate in the U.S. Supreme Court in a decision announced by Justice Charles Evans Hughes — a decision that later haunted him when he became a presidential candidate — who declared the law unconstitutionally denied to aliens the right to make a living.[3]

Some reformers faulted the courts for siding with the railroads and employers. Legislators, however, tended to fault the voters for approving the measures even though the legislature itself had also approved several of these measures. Out of this concern emerged a proposal by the legislature that appeared on the ballot in 1916. The proposed law stipulated that, to be successful, initiative and referendum measures must have a majority of the votes cast at the election, rather than simply a majority on the particular question. Because there was usually a fall-off in voting on proposition measures, the proposed law would likely reduce the number of successful measures. Opponents argued that had this law been in effect in previous elections the railroad bills and prohibition would have failed.[4]

Labor leaders saw the weakening of the initiative and referendum as a plot by the corporate interests "to gain control of the industries, the commerce, the government, and even to a degree the lives and property of the workers."[5] On a more theoretical level the Arizona Federation of Labor complained:

> It is absurd to claim that the people as a whole are not as intelligent or as able as the members of a legislature. It is ridiculous to assert, as the advocates of this measure do, that the initiative leads to more ill-advised legislation than the representative system. . . . Truly it is a rash commentary on Arizonans to say that the Legislature is wise, but the People are foolish.[6]

The change in attitude found in the legislature reflected, in part, the growing conservatism of the Arizona people. Some of this was due to migration. From 1910 to 1920 relatively affluent and conservative middle-class families from the Midwest were particularly prominent among those migrating to the state.[7] Many of the newcomers gravitated to the cities. Phoenix more than doubled in population between 1910 and 1920. Farm areas in the Salt River area, never hot beds for radical reform, also grew during the second decade of the twentieth century because of large federally financed irrigation projects. Meanwhile, older mining centers like Globe changed little or even lost population. Over the decade power was shifting from the mining areas, which constituted the base of support for Hunt and other reformers, to the farms and growing cities.

With population growth, Anglos, if anything, became more outspokenly hostile and exclusionary in their attitudes toward minorities.[8] Much of the attention of the Anglo population focused on Hispanics, who evidenced signs of growing discontent. One cause of this was increased pride built around the popularity of the Mexican revolutionary Pancho Villa. Another cause was the socio-economic situation in which Hispanics found themselves.[9] In Phoenix, Hispanics and blacks were living in the south-central part of the city in an area characterized by poor, substandard housing.[10] Booker T. Washington, after a trip to Phoenix in 1911, noted: "As a rule, people do not speak very respectfully of the Mexicans. As a class, they are regarded as unprogressive, unsteady and unthrifty."[11] Hispanics in mining towns, although often not in abject poverty, did far less well than Anglos in regard to housing, pay, and working conditions.

From 1913 to 1918, throughout the state there were rumors of attempted violence by small bands of Mexican revolutionaries aimed at mining operations, lumber mills, and other industries.[12] The fear of an armed revolt by Hispanics increased after disclosure of the famous Zimmerman note written by the German foreign secretary to the Mexican government. The German official proposed that Mexico form a military alliance with Germany out of which Mexico would regain Arizona, New Mexico, and Texas at the conclusion of the war.

The drift toward the involvement of the United States in World War I generated discontent among workers in the copper mines. Among the population at large, however, the war created strong feelings of patriotism. This led to intolerance for those who opposed the involvement of the United States in the effort. In Arizona, as in much of the West, the most widely detested symbol of dissent was the Industrial Workers of the World (IWW). The Wobblies, to their critics, engaged in treasonable collusion with Germany.

Arizona in 1915–1917 still had numerous labor leaders committed to reform, if not radical action. The movement, however, was divided. Conflicts between Socialists and anti-Socialists, wets and drys, the large miners' union and other unions that resisted the miners' attempts at domination of the state federation, and those who believed in craft unions and those who sought some other plan of organization mitigated against unity.[13]

Conflict took place in mining areas between the Western Federation of Miners (which changed its name to the International Mine, Mill, and Smelters Union), affiliated with the American Federation of Labor, and the IWW over the organization of workers. Tension in mining areas also reflected increased opposition of older highly skilled hardrock miners, generally native and foreign-born Anglos, to the massive influx of unskilled labor, largely non-English speaking Hispanics, Slavs, and Italians. The latter group captured mining union locals at Globe and other places and formed the core of a militant faction that captured the state federation.[14]

During Hunt's second term, difficulties in mining areas gave the governor's opponents their first real opportunity to topple his administration. The beginning of a war in Europe in 1914 initially had a depressing effect on the mining industry in Arizona as elsewhere in the nation. By 1915, however, the price of copper had soared. With this, mining wages went up, although not nearly as dramatically as the price of copper. Miners enjoyed greater job security because the stream of immigration to the state slowed to a trickle with the outbreak of hostilities. If the times were good for labor, they were also good, labor leaders reasoned, for making demands on management for benefits truly commensurate with the rise in the price of copper and for greater worker control over the conditions of their employment.

The most serious disruption growing out of increased labor demands took place in the Clifton-Morenci and Metcalf copper-producing districts in the fall of 1915. These districts had long been nonunion territories. WFM agents entered the area early in 1915. At that time prices for copper were low and owners had recently cut back on wages. Guy Miller, an organizer for the WFM, reported to President Charles H. Moyer in July that the "Mexicans are alive and enthused throughout Arizona, if the sentiment can be crystallized into organization it will mean much."[15] Later, Miller reported he had met with considerable success although, given the scarcity of property not owned by the mining companies, the only meeting places he could find for organizing were in the red light district.[16]

Salaries in the Clifton-Morenci district were the lowest of any mining camp in Arizona. To compound the problem for Hispanic miners, they received considerably less than others for the same work.[17] Mine owners defended these practices and fiercely resisted the attempt of the Western

Federation of Miners to organize and represent the workers. Finally, on September 15, some five thousand miners and workers, 80 percent of whom were Hispanic, went on strike to secure higher wages and union (WFM) representation.

According to the conservative press, a reign of terror took place as authorities stood by while WFM members dragged strike breakers out of their beds. "Threats of lynching, abuse and curses heaped upon men and their families at every turn caused many to leave."[18] The owners responded to the strike by closing down their mines. Managers of the involved companies and nonunion workers fled the mining camps where the strikes occurred. Eventually, the AFL local in Phoenix stepped in to represent the miners, because the mine operators refused to deal with the WFM, and reached a settlement with the owners.

Hunt, by his words and actions concerning the strike, won the applause of organized labor and, at the same time, helped solidify those opposed to him. Hunt made it clear that he was sympathetic to the workers and their demands. More important, he ordered the national guard into the area to protect those who were on strike and to prevent strike breakers from entering the camps. In other states during this period it was more common to find that mine owners had the ear of the governor and, thus, were able to use the state militia to protect the strike breakers. Use of the militia in this manner led to bloody confrontations in Colorado and other states. In Arizona, thanks to Hunt and to local law enforcement officers who protected the mine owners' property during their absence, a peaceful settlement was possible.

National as well as local labor leaders praised Hunt for his actions in Clifton-Morenci. One AFL official placed Hunt on the same level as the "immortal Altgeld" as one of the greatest governors of all time.[19] Praise also was forthcoming from legendary labor organizer Mother Jones, who had been in the state assisting in the organization of the miners.[20] On the negative side Hunt enthusiasts were quick to point out that he had also "earned the undying hatred of a great many of the employers of labor."[21] As Mother Jones later noted, "the financial interests set out to 'get' Governor Hunt."[22]

Careful scholarship suggests that the copper companies did, indeed, respond with alarm to the demonstration of labor's strength during the fall strikes. They decided to band together in opposition to both labor and Hunt.[23] Mining companies gained control over an increasing number of newspapers (including the *Arizona Gazette,* once favorable to Hunt) and used them to lambast Hunt for siding with the radicals and, in the context of the war, unpatriotic worker demands.[24] The fact that most of the striking miners were Hispanic made Hunt, in the eyes of some of his critics, a traitor to his own people. One paper complained: "The speech made by Governor Hunt in Clifton recently was wholly inflammatory in its effect. He caused the strikers to spit in the face of good citizens by telling them that they were as good as anyone."[25]

By October 1915 Hunt's activities in regard to the striking miners, combined with older grievances involving his penal reform program and liberal spending amounting to "wanton and reckless extravagance," became part of an open effort to recall him from office. Referring to the situation in the Clifton-Morenci-Metcalf districts, the recall petition declared that Hunt "has deliberately attempted to foment and encourage class hatreds and divisions" and, "by a program of unconcealed and deliberate catering to the most radical elements," had "created a condition approaching anarchy in certain sections of the state."[26] Behind the movement for a recall were the publisher of the Arizona Gazette in Phoenix and some prominent citizens from Mesa, including O. S. Stapley, a state senator.

Hunt's initial response to the petition was to dismiss it as the work of a few people trying to discredit his efforts to have a federal investigation of the situation in Clifton.[27] Hunt, however, worried about the recall effort. Writing to Mulford Winsor on December 9, 1915, he noted that most of the recall activity was taking place in the rapidly growing Salt River Valley area, including Phoenix, which he characterized as the "center of the standpat, reactionary, furies." Hunt went on to note "the howling dervishes hereabout seem to be continually concocting some wild and startling story, which, as you may readily conjecture, keeps me on the jump, as is undoubtedly their intention." The governor concluded:

The sad part of all this business is to think that the people of Salt River Valley, especially the farmers, can be so gullible as to allow themselves to be used by the agents of the big interests to pull the chestnuts out of the fire. They don't realize that if the big interests control the situation, it is only their own taxes that will be reduced and those of the rest of the people will be higher than ever. And now it looks as if some of the very people for whom I have fought to get a square deal were turning against me; it is heart-rending, not only to realize their ingratitude, but their inability to see what they are doing to themselves as well.[28]

Toward the end of the year, Winsor wrote back to Hunt and communicated his wish that 1916 would give the governor "added strength to resist the attacks of all reactionaries, and particularly the traitorous attacks of renegades and turncoats."[29] By this time the recall campaign was beginning to peter out. Hunt, however, continued to be the target of criticism, often from people within his own party. Those who favored prohibition looked at Hunt as being in league with the whiskey ring. Others objected to his labor policies and his connection with radicals like Mother Jones.

In June 1916 Mother Jones wrote Hunt to thank him for his kindly treatment on a visit she had made to the capitol. The visit, she wrote, "was so foreign to the treatment I get as a rule from Governors of States where I enter to educate the workers to their own class interests. Generally speaking, the bayonets are sent to receive me."[30] Jones also offered her help in the 1916 election "because the miners are more than anxious to have you returned to the executive chair."[31] Later, in the middle of the summer of 1916, Jones came to the state to campaign for Hunt, a fact duly noted by Hunt's enemies as further proof that the governor was a socialist who had ridden the Democratic party into power.[32]

Prospects were not encouraging for Hunt in the upcoming 1916 election.

The 1916 Election

As the 1916 election grew nearer, there were signs of considerable division within the Democratic party. Some observers contended that the Arizona delegation in Congress, Senators Smith and Ashurst and

Representative Hayden, lined up solidly against Hunt and in favor of George Olney for governor. Olney had entered the Democratic gubernatorial primary with the support of copper mine owners. As a sign of the conspiracy, newspapers pointed out that many postmasters and other federal officers in Arizona appointed by the congressional delegation were working for Olney. Rumor had it that prominent labor attorney William B. Cleary informed President Wilson that he would run as an independent candidate against Ashurst unless the administration used its influence to line up the federal officeholders behind Hunt.[33]

Carl Hayden, who had appointed many of the postmasters in question, was, according to some of Hunt's supporters, behind the conspiracy. There was little love lost between Hunt and Hayden, although their differences appear to have had as much to do with personality as with policy or philosophy.[34] Hayden, however, denied any involvement in the "alleged political activity of the Arizona postmasters." He considered himself a friend of both Georges and stated, as a general policy, that he strove to avoid involvement in matters of state politics.[35]

Despite these denials, Hunt made peace with former socialist activist and state senator A. A. Worsley of Tucson, who was opposing Hayden in the primary. Worsley, in turn, endorsed Hunt for renomination. Worsley, like Hunt, had considerable appeal to the socialist and radical labor vote. Hayden received conflicting advice about how to regard Worsley. One Hayden supporter warned that Worsley was an effective orator, "the most forcible and forceful speaker in Arizona, especially when appealing to class prejudice."[36] Others contended that Worsley's candidacy was "not viewed with alarm by anyone."[37] Hayden decided to take the contest seriously. He wrote one supporter:

> The way I size up the situation, Mr. Worsley will get practically all of the votes of the Socialists who have registered as Democrats. I have had letters from my friends in all parts of the state and every one says that his strength is limited to that element. If such is the case I should defeat him without difficulty. Nevertheless, I am going to keep on writing letters.[38]

During the primary contest, Worsley's campaign received very little press coverage. This may have reflected the success of an effort organized by publisher W. B. Kelly, a Hayden supporter. In August 1916 Kelly wrote Hayden: "I am writing my newspaper friends in the state to keep Worsley's name out of the papers and let him get his own publicity."[39] Although several Socialists may have registered Democratic, this had little effect as Hayden easily defeated Worsley, 19,600 to 7,780.

Hunt had more trouble disposing of Olney, winning 18,122 to 12,261. Many Republicans, reportedly, had registered as Democrats to vote for Olney.[40] Throughout the primary campaign Hunt was the object of attack from nearly every daily newspaper in Arizona. The *Coconino Sun,* under the editorship of Fred Breen, set the pace in June by charging: "Governor Hunt has not interposed or objected to any fad, fancy or new stunt in the way of freak legislation proposed by the most violent of agitators." As a consequence, "our state has been the laughing stock of all the states of the union, and, to their disgust, the people have had to pay for it dearly."[41]

The *Arizona Gazette* attacked Hunt just days before the primary election. The paper contended that Hunt was undemocratic in seeking a third term and ignored the fact that this was against the "American practice." The paper also charged that his administration had been extravagant and wasteful, that he had built a political machine, and that he had put himself above the law in regard to penal reform.[42]

Hunt, in return, contended that the corporate interests were behind the attacks on him and were using the

> hue and cry concerning taxation, prison reform, capital punishment, socialism, and the third term bugaboos — anything to divert the public's attention from the real issue — the troublesome insect in the corporate ointment — the fact, in brief, that the big alien corporation and the absentee capitalist, for the first time in the history of Arizona, are paying their just share of the public's taxes along with the stockman, the farmer, the proprietor of a small business and the home-owning wage earner.[43]

Commenting upon Hunt's successful primary, one paper noted his solid support among labor and acknowledged that he "is a better friend to the miners, building trades, and the day laborers generally than they have ever before known." Sounding what was to become a familiar theme, the paper went on to conclude, however, "the trouble is, Governor Hunt is not equally a friend to the farmer, the real estate dealer, the small grocer, the mining company and the salaried man."[44]

The Progressive party had disappeared by the time of the 1916 primary election. Two years earlier the party finished far below expectations. Leaders saw little chance for improvement. J.L.B. Alexander, as provisional state chair of the Progressive party of Arizona, in an open letter to all Progressives dated August 25, 1916, declared that the Progressive party was dead and urged his fellow former Progressives to work with the Republican party as the party of "nationalism and progress."[45]

The Socialists, more ideologically centered and accustomed to a small vote, continued to nominate candidates. In 1916 the party had but a few hundred members organized in twenty or so locals around the state. Included among the Socialist organizations were Hispanic locals in Clifton and Metcalf, a Finnish local in Miami, and a Slavic local in Globe.[46] Yet although small in membership, Socialist party leaders saw their program to be in the mainstream of popularly supported reform. As one Socialist official put it during the 1916 campaign: "We must recognize that the dominant political thought in Arizona is not reactionary, that it is in fact progressive and even radical."[47]

The problem from the Socialist point of view was that since 1910 the party had been at least partially co-opted by the Democratic party. Some Socialist activists had become Democrats. Socialist papers noted switches of this nature in a somewhat caustic fashion. The *Arizona Socialist Bulletin* of October 11, 1916, for example, noted:

Our former Comrade, Lester B. Doane, who ran for nomination for state senator on the Democratic ticket, was turned down so hard that the fall was almost audible. He received fewer votes by several hundred than his nearest competitor, which can be taken as proof that the Democratic voters want in addition to good men, good democrats, as well. Mr. Doane's faux pas does not seem to discourage others, however, as Mr. L. W. Wyman, has just been elected Secretary-Treasurer of the Gila County Democratic something or other and is trying to do his former political friends as much damage as possible.[48]

The number of Socialists who registered in the Democratic primary to support candidates like Worsley and Hunt is difficult to determine. It is clear, however, that the possibility that many party members (and countless others who might otherwise have favored Socialist candidates) would, out of error, vote for Hunt greatly concerned party officials. A Socialist editor openly acknowledged "many working men and others with Socialist convictions will vote for Gov. Hunt chiefly because they consider him a 'friend of the workingman.' " Yet the editor declared:

We Socialists challenge his right to such a title in all that the name implies so long as he is part and parcel of a capitalist political machine. Possibly, in a Pickwickian sense, a capitalist candidate or politician can really be a "friend of labor." We demand something more. We demand of our representatives that they be proven heart and soul of and for labor, first last and all the time — not only on occasion when it will bring them political advantage, granting the best of motives.[49]

The 1916 general election found Hunt face to face with Thomas E. Campbell, a popular Republican who, two years earlier, had won election to the State Tax Commission. Campbell had an organization of relatively young workers. Their average age was thirty-seven. Some had registered as Democrats because they saw little life in the Republican party. With Campbell, however, they saw a chance to reconstruct their party. To raise funds, the group put together the "hundred club," open to people who would contribute $100 or more to defeat Hunt. Campbell toured the state with slogans: "Good Government versus Huntism, Industrial Peace Versus Wobblyism," and "Tax Payers versus Tax Eaters."[50] Campbell felt that Hunt and the IWW — he tended to link the two — were traitors. Campbell condemned Hunt for arraying labor against capital and inciting class conflict.

Campbell also spoke against the pleadings of organized labor for privileges denied to individual or unaffiliated workers. He spoke with special vigor against class-conscious agitators, declaring "class prejudice is more injurious and destructive to industrial and social welfare than sectional, racial or religious animosity."[51] Hunt called for "a square deal for labor" in attacking the corporations. Other than this, Hunt's campaign consisted largely of a defense of his administration, although he also took time to champion an amendment abolishing capital punishment that was on the ballot in the 1916 election.

The gubernatorial contest was the featured election in 1916. It drew more voters than any other contest, including the presidential one. At first count 58,293 voters, or about 36 percent of the voting population, turned out to choose a governor. This compares with 48,007 (32 %) in 1914.

On the first count Campbell won 27,976 to 27,946. The victory led a Republican paper to gloat: "George Hunt today stands a man without a party, discredited and with only a shred of his former pomp and vanity clinging to him in the shape of former appointees and a part of the Western Federation of Miners."[52] Later, as a recount ate into Campbell's thin margin, the editor noted: "There is nothing cheap about the people of Arizona. They have evidently elected two governors when one would do as well and probably better."[53] The final decision by the Arizona Supreme Court, coming a year after Campbell had taken office, gave the election to Hunt. Hunt was the victor by forty-three votes.

Hunt's friends argued that the Socialists, by putting up a gubernatorial candidate, cost Hunt some 2,000 votes in 1916. Although the state had only an estimated 700 "red card" Socialists in 1916, they allegedly were able to convince some 1,400 American Federationists into supporting Peter T. Robertson, the Socialist candidate.[54] Hunt needed all the votes he could get. In fact, however, as noted below, Hunt had less reason to complain about the lack of Socialist support than any other Democratic candidate. More detrimental to Hunt were his losses among members of his own party.

Woodrow Wilson and the remainder of the Democratic ticket had relatively little difficulty turning back the Republicans in Arizona. Wilson won easily with 57 percent of the vote, although the Republican national committee reportedly poured large amounts of money into the state on Hughes's behalf.[55] Wilson ran on a slogan, "He kept us out of War." This seemed to be a popular position in Arizona and in much of the West in 1916.[56] Later, after the United States entered the war, the state became extremely hawkish.

Democrats depicted Hughes as a foe of labor because of his voting record as justice of the Supreme Court. Among his anti-labor decisions was deciding against Arizona's 80 percent law. The GOP attempted without any apparent success to cultivate discontent over Wilson's policies in regard to Mexico — there had been some concerns over the safety of Arizonans as a result of the Mexican revolution and the marauding of Villa.

Wilson picked up some support with the Mormons. His gains with this group in Arizona, however, were not as dramatic as in other Mountain States because Arizona Mormons had long tended to vote Democratic. Increased Mormon support for Wilson in Arizona and elsewhere appears to reflect a more neutral stand by church leaders. To some extent it also reflects the efforts of the Wilson administration to cultivate the Mormons through patronage appointments.[57]

Wilson did not do noticeably well with those who had voted for third-party candidates in 1912. With Debs declining to head the ticket, the total vote for the Socialist candidate fell off considerably. While some of those who supported Debs may have switched to Wilson, the Socialist candidate, Alan Benson, received a strong regular "party vote."

The 1912 supporters of the Progressive party tended, as suggested by their leaders, to return to the GOP. Elsewhere in the West, they tended to shift to the Democratic party, apparently because the Democrats were the more liberal of the two parties and, therefore, were more ideologically compatible with the Bull Moose Republicans.[58] Democrats in Arizona, especially at the state party level, were more liberal or progressive than the Republicans. The Bull Moosers in Arizona, however, appeared not all that liberal, especially when it came to the type of labor issues championed by the Democrats, and, thus, would not have felt comfortable in the Democratic party.[59]

A few months before the 1916 election Phoenix lawyer Leon Jacobs wrote Carl Hayden that "progressive" had become "a worn out word in Arizona." People, Jacobs suggested, were tired of "progressive" as a rallying point and of reform in general.[60] The election of 1916 in Arizona did not constitute a total rejection of progressivism but it did show diminished voter support for reform.

The voters, in re-electing Wilson, apparently found little to quarrel with in Wilson's record in regard to such matters as the income tax, the federal reserve system, and labor reform. The proposal to make passage of initiative and referendum measures more difficult failed, although by a margin of only 605 votes. The weakening of the initiative and referendum was opposed by groups within the electorate as diverse as Europeans and Mormons.

More surprising, the proposal abolishing the death penalty passed, although by an even smaller margin of 152 votes. Republicans, Mormons, and females were prominent among those against abolishing the death penalty. Socialists were prominent among the supporters of this action.

Antiprogressive sentiment prevailed on several issues. Labor lost all the measures it sponsored. These included proposals to abolish the state senate in favor of a unicameral system, to create an office of state architect, and to create a department of labor. Also a sign of conservatism was the failure of a tax exemption for widows measure referred to voters by the legislature in 1916 and supported by labor.[61]

Hunt and labor leaders favored abolishing the state senate and instituting a single-house system. They were frustrated with the "high-browed Senate" that in the second legislature was found to be "nearly 100 percent copper." The move was also defended on the grounds that the two-house arrangement prevented the effectuation of the people's will by providing more opportunities for the corporations to exert influence.[62] Opponents argued that "the spirit of American politics that calls for two houses, one to act as a check upon the other, and there seems no good reason for making a change."[63] Farmers, Mormons, Republicans, and females stood out among those against experimenting with unicameralism. Socialists, especially, tended to support this reform. From 1912 the national Socialist party had been on record in favor of abolishing the U.S. Senate.

The department of labor issue brought strong disagreement between farmers and miners and, on a partisan basis, Democrats and Socialists versus Republicans. Controversy over the state architect position, proposed to implement the industrial pursuits measure, was largely along economic lines. Conservative critics contended that both new departments were unnecessary and expensive. A new department of labor was also considered dangerous in that the commissioner of labor "would be entitled to enter every home and every business office in the state at his own pleasure and there make such investigations as he might see fit to undertake."[64]

On one remaining issue, prohibition, a proposition tightening the existing law passed while one favoring local option went down to defeat. Farmers and Mormons particularly favored the measure to strengthen prohibition and opposed local option. The last of these, opponents argued, was "the entering wedge for the restoration of the liquor traffic."[65]

The gubernatorial contest between Hunt and Campbell found the electorate polarized on the basis of issues. Labor issues (the department of labor) and criminal justice issues (the death penalty) particularly divided the supporters of the gubernatorial candidates and played important roles in the contest (see regression analysis in Appendix D). Also important were partisan differences in the electorate and differences in regard to regional backgrounds. Of particular significance in 1916 was the appeal Campbell had to the growing number of people from the Midwest.

On the issues, Hunt supporters tended to oppose the effort to make initiative and referendum votes more difficult. They tended to favor local option on prohibition, a unicameral system, abolishing the death penalty, giving a tax exemption to widows, the creation of a department of labor, and the establishment of the office of state architect. Campbell supporters lined up on the opposite side on all of these measures.

Hunt, overall, did best in districts with relatively large percentages of foreign-born, males, miners, and people bent on liberal-labor reform but not prohibition. Hunt did well in districts with large numbers of Hispanic voters. This was due in part, no doubt, to his stand on labor strikes. Hunt drew unusually well in precincts where Socialists as well as Democrats had done relatively well in previous elections. Evidence suggests, however, that registered Democrats were at the core of Hunt's support and far more likely than registered Socialists to vote for him.

Campbell's best districts were those where Republicans, Mormons, farmers, and females were particularly numerous and where there was opposition to nearly all changes but prohibition. Campbell also did well among those in the electorate who had supported Bull Moose candidates in the previous election (this included a number of midwesterners).

The Socialist candidate for governor, Peter T. Robertson, was somewhat separated from his natural constituency with Hunt on the ballot. His appeal was limited mainly to party loyalists. Robertson received a total of 1,975 votes, far below those cast for other Socialist candidates in statewide contests. Vote totals for other Socialist candidates ranged from 2,827 to 4,467 or from 852 to 2,492 above those going to Robertson.

Sizable segments of the voting population had clearly split their ticket in voting for candidates in the gubernatorial and presidential elections. Looking at the presidential contest for comparative purposes, we find Wilson attracting a far more traditional Democratic vote (including Mormon support) and GOP strength resting, as it had in the past, on the party faithful and people in economically diverse cities and towns. The Socialist vote, likewise, had a traditional radical base in mining communities and among the European-born. Hunt tapped this support in the gubernatorial election. Differences between Wilson and Hughes supporters on the issues on the ballot were in the same direction as between Hunt and Campbell supporters. The differences, however, were less extreme or important in the presidential contest.

By 1916 the electoral base of the Democratic party in general had become more liberal or progressive than it was just two years earlier (see Appendix D). When we compare those who registered Democratic in 1916 with those who had voted for Democratic candidates in 1914, we find those in the first group were more likely to favor extending a tax exemption to widows, establishing a department of labor, creating the office of state architect, and making a unicameral legislature. People from mining areas were far more prominent in the Democratic coalition in 1916 than they were in 1914.

By the same measurements, Republicans in 1916 were stronger in their opposition to political reforms like unicameralism and measures to benefit labor such as the department of labor than they were in 1914. Republicans in 1916 were far stronger with midwesterners than they were two years earlier.

Contrary to those who supported the major parties, the Socialists in the electorate in 1916 appear to have become less issue-oriented, especially on labor issues. This is due in large part to the continued evolution of the Democratic party, under Hunt, as the party of organized labor. Demographically, and in association with the decline of the labor orientation, the Socialist partisan in 1916 was less likely to be a European or a miner.

Women in 1916, as two years earlier, tended to be negative on Socialist candidates. Campbell did well in precincts with relatively large numbers of women, while Hunt did poorly in such districts. Wilson did better than Hunt in this regard. Some scholars have suggested that the peace issue may have worked in Wilson's favor with female voters. In this case it may have helped him do better with women than did other Democrats or, looking at registration figures, the Democratic party in general in 1916. On the other hand, other factors that may have cut into Wilson's support among women in Arizona were his stand on suffrage, the efforts of the Women's party to defeat him, and the reaction of women to his remarriage so soon after the death of his first wife.[66]

On the issues gender gaps occurred on the unicameral, the death penalty, department of labor, state architect, and other measures with women on the conservative side.

The End of an Era

On February 8, 1917, George Powell wrote fellow labor official Henry S. McCluskey: "While I was in Phoenix, I met a fellow by the name of Perry, he is from New York, and came to Phoenix to establish IWW headquarters there. He says that they have $35,000 to organize this state, now they may not be able to organize Arizona, but they can raise an awful lot of h —— with that amount of money."[67] Powell was referring to IWW activist Grover H. Perry.

The first major strike attributed to IWW conspirators occurred in May 1917 in Jerome where, reportedly, less than one hundred Wobblies were able to convince some six thousand miners that strike activity was warranted.[68] Following the Jerome strike came strikes in Globe, Miami, Clifton, Morenci, Metcalf, and Bisbee. Discontent was particularly high in Hispanic mining camps. Workers in these camps told *New York Evening Post* investigative reporter Robert W. Bruere that they were striking for "an American standard of living" and greater control over working conditions in the mines.[69]

Mine managers saw a number of factors involved in strike activity. Among these were the general unrest of Hispanics, greater job security growing out of the scarcity of labor, and the relatively high income miners already enjoyed, which gave them the ability to afford a lay off if it came to that. Mine owners also attributed some of the problem to prohibition. With the saloons gone, owners contended, workers had too much time to think of their problems and, thus, fell into the hands of agitators.[70]

While strike activity reflected a number of problems, most Arizona newspapers and many prominent government officials saw the striking miners to be in league with a pro-German conspiracy. Mining company officials refused to meet with union organizers for the IUMMSW. The acknowledged leader of the copper group, Walter Douglas of the Phelps Dodge Corporation, declared: "We will not compromise with rattle-snakes; this goes for the International of— the A.F. of L. organization — as well as for the I.W.W."[71]

Hunt, temporarily out of office in 1917, accepted an appointment from President Wilson as a commissioner of conciliation in the mining areas. Several labor leaders applauded the appointment. Some conservatives also saw it as having some value. Eugene Ives, prominent conservative Democrat and lawyer from Tucson, wrote Wilson that Hunt "unquestionably has more influence with the miners than any man in Arizona." Hunt, Ives argued, would be willing to use his influence to induce miners, for patriotic reasons, to withdraw or modify their demands.[72]

Marcus Smith and mining officials opposed the appointment. They charged that Hunt favored strikers and, thus, was unacceptable to the operators.[73] E. E. Ellinwood, attorney for the Phelps Dodge company at Bisbee, argued: "It is preposterous to appoint as conciliator the very man who is primarily responsible for the labor unrest in Arizona and who was defeated because of that fact."[74]

On June 26, 1917, while Hunt was attempting to mediate labor disputes in the Globe-Miami district, copper workers in the Warren district south of Bisbee called for a strike for the next day. Not long after the strike occurred, Cochise County Sheriff Harry S. Wheeler formed a vigilante group of some two thousand men, called the Citizen's Protection League, to protect mining properties. The group, on July 12, 1917, proceeded to round up some twelve hundred persons they felt were Wobblies or professional labor agitators, loaded them into railway cattle cars, and deported them to Columbus, New Mexico.

Authorities in Columbus refused to allow those in charge of the deportation to leave the men there. Vigilantes put the deportees off the train in the nearby desert town of Hermanas, New Mexico, and left them to fend for themselves. The War Department, on July 14, 1917, sent troops to escort the deportees back to Columbus. They remained there under federal protection until the middle of September.

Mine managers helped plan and execute this clearly unlawful act. Indeed, they were proud of their involvement. They defended their action on the need to head off violent acts planned by the strikers. Campbell, governor at the time, attributed the problem "to the presence of large numbers of members" of the IWW "coming from outside the state and agitating their propaganda." Campbell noted in his request to

President Wilson for the assistance of federal troops: "It is generally believed that strong pro-German influence is back of this movement, as the IWW appear well financed and are daily getting into their ranks many aliens, particularly Austrians."[75]

Wilson, on July 12, 1917, wired back to Campbell that the situation was under investigation. He added: "Meantime may I not respectfully urge the great danger of citizens taking the law in their own hands as you report their having done. I look upon such action with grave apprehension. A very serious responsibility is assumed when such precedents are set."[76] Labor spokespersons in Arizona and elsewhere wired the White House demanding that federal troops escort those deported from Bisbee back to their homes. Arizona labor officials, irritated by the lack of federal action, asked the president: "Are we to assume that Phelps Dodge interests are superior to the principles of democracy?"[77] Wilson found the tone and intimation in the telegram to be harsh.[78]

In September 1917 Hunt visited the deportees in Columbus. He found between nine hundred and one thousand of them. "I spent five days in camp, talking to the refugees, singly and in groups, receiving their confidences and learning their views, judiciously questioning them when necessary to ascertain their real frame of mind," Hunt later reported to President Wilson.[79]

Hunt found that about half of the deportees were Wobblies. Some had joined the IWW since the deportation and largely because of that event. At the same time, Hunt concluded that the deportees as a whole were not pro-German or unpatriotic. Rather, "they are just ordinary human beings, struggling in their own ways and according to their own lights for a betterment of the conditions which they expect will be their lot through life." They were people, Hunt continued, who took a "rather personal outlook upon affairs" rather than acting out of concern for humankind in general. "The situation to them seems very simple and practical, and they are wholly unable to comprehend why their strike should be associated with the war, or held by anyone to be an act of unfaithfulness to the government in its emergency." Those who went on strike simply wanted a share of the additional profits enjoyed by the

147

copper companies because of the war. "They cannot understand why the war should be so one-sided in its effect upon capital and labor, as to justify extraordinary gain to the former while denying to the latter the right of organized action to secure a living wage."[80]

As to the cause of the deportation, Hunt concluded:

> I am possessed of the firm conviction — a conviction supported by the scarcely veiled utterances of the mining companies' chief spokesmen — that these incidents are manifestations of a determination entered into by the great copper mine operators of Arizona to crush organized labor in this State, and that, while employing the "camouflage" of patriotic protestations they are in reality using the nation's extremity to serve their selfish ends, and they are going about their enterprise in a manner that would shame the Prussian autocracy.[81]

A presidential commission looked into the matter and roundly condemned the deportation as an action "wholly illegal and without authority in law either State or Federal."[82] Writing to Felix Frankfurter, counsel for the presidential commission, Theodore Roosevelt took exception to the report. He noted that John Greenway, a personal friend and one-time Bull Moose spokesperson in Arizona, was one of the prominent leaders in the deportation. Based on what he learned from Greenway and others, the federal report was "thoroughly misleading." To Roosevelt: "No human being in his senses doubts that the men deported from Bisbee were bent on destruction and murder." Local citizens had the right to protect themselves and had acted properly.[83]

In December 1917, about a month after the commission report, Hunt returned to the governorship. Anti-Wobbly hysteria, however, did not die down. Writing to Hunt in 1918, Frances Munds declared "it is getting so that every working man who dares to say his life is his own is called and denounced as an IWW."[84] Similarly, Bruere concluded that "all labor leaders, all strikers and all persons who sympathize or are suspected of sympathizing with strikers are lumped under the general designation of 'I.W.W.' or 'WOBBLY.' "[85] Continuing on the hysteria of the times, Bruere noted:

This fantastic enlargement of the meaning of WOBBLY we found to be universal. Very few people had any accurate knowledge of the tenets or tactics of the IWW. The three letters had come to stand in the popular mind as symbol of something bordering on black magic; they were repeated over and over again by the press like the tappings of an Oriental drum, and were always accompanied with suggestions of impending violence. It was in this way that it became possible to use them to work ordinarily rational communities into hysterical mobs resorting to violence.[86]

Hunt, upon regaining the governor's chair, was increasingly the target of attacks questioning his affiliation with the IWW and his loyalty to the nation. Several papers published a picture of Hunt between two indicted leaders of the IWW, Charles McKinnon and Grover H. Perry. The *Bisbee Daily Review* of June 7, 1918, ran the picture along with statements declaring its indignation that the state's chief executive had been "hobnobbing with traitors and enemies of society." Hostile papers also declared Hunt had made statements indicating that he opposed the war.

Hunt decided not to run again in 1918. He was a political realist who saw Campbell would probably win and that a defeat might do his political career permanent damage. Drawing upon his status as a long-standing leader of the Democratic party, Hunt was able to secure an appointment from President Wilson as ambassador to Siam (Thailand). In his farewell address, Hunt concluded that he could

take courage and satisfaction from the fact that I know that our institutions will never return to the medieval condition they were in when we passed from territorial to state government, and I know that the burden of taxation will never again fall on the individual and entirely miss the corporate interests as it did in the old days.[87]

Stepping into the spotlight as the Democratic nominee in Hunt's absence was Fred T. Colter, commonly viewed as a progressive in the Hunt tradition. He lost by a small margin (25,927 to 25,588) to Republican Campbell in the general election. In all probability, Campbell benefited from the sympathy felt for him when he left the governor's office after having served for a year without compensation.[88] Campbell won another term in part because of Harding's landslide victory in 1920. In 1920 the Republican tide was so strong in Arizona that the GOP captured the state senate and came within a single member of matching the Democrats in the state house. During the competitive 1920s, the state voted Republican in presidential elections in 1920, 1924, and 1928.

Frances Munds, writing to Hunt in September 1917, predicted "we will have the time of our lives to keep our state in the progressive line" after the war was over.[89] The radical or progressive element in the Arizona electorate did not altogether disappear in the 1920s. Once again, however, this sentiment was most noticeable in third-party movements. For example, some 23 percent of those Arizonans who voted in the 1924 presidential contest favored Progressive party presidential candidate Robert LaFollette.

The major parties who vied for control of state politics in the 1920s, on the other hand, shunned experimentation. As Senator Ashurst noted in his diary, following the 1920 election, Arizona and the rest of the nation appeared "tired of ideals, altruism, and high endeavors."[90] Coming full circle, Arizona once again became increasingly concerned with the politics of development, an ambition that underlay the effort to build highways and to protect the state's water resources.[91]

7

THE ANATOMY OF A REFORM EFFORT

"If people get accustomed to regarding progressivism as merely aimless going ahead anywhere and to any degree, a reaction is sure to come, and I want to avoid government by oscillation, so to speak." Thus wrote Theodore Roosevelt in December 1911.[1]

At the time Arizona was in the midst of its Progressive period. A number of reform efforts dating back to the 1880s had culminated or were about to culminate, and within a few years, a reaction began to set in. The term "progressive" to many Arizonans may have come to mean nothing much more than aimless change simply for the sake of change.

The Progressive era in Arizona politics was, as previous pages indicate, characterized by a number of movements heading in various directions. Among the major reform efforts taking place was the one aimed at large corporate enterprises. The anticorporate reform effort began in response to the rapid economic development of the state and found expression in programs offered by organized labor, third-party candidates, and the reform wing of the Democratic party that came to power from 1910 to 1916.

Anticorporate reformers over this period reacted to similar stimuli, shared broad programmatic themes, and enjoyed a common thread of electoral support emanating from mining communities. At times support from mining areas was about all the support forthcoming. At other times the reform vote from mining areas was part of a broader consensus.[2]

In this chapter we review the previous discussion and focus more directly on the nature and career of the anticorporate reform effort. We are concerned with its goals and relations to other movements, the conditions for reform, the roles played by third parties in bringing change, and the rise and fall of those who brought about reform.

The Nature of the Effort

The anticorporate reform effort represented, in a broad perspective, an attack on the political and economic influence of organized wealth. One might well argue that the attack on large corporations or "monopolies" was the distinguishing characteristic of the Progressive period in general and at the heart of the reform activity.[3] The nature and success of the reform effort were, however, affected by its relations with other movements.

Anticorporate reformers in Arizona, as elsewhere, called for changes in the political process to offset corporate influence, tax reform that would shift a greater portion of the burden to large business concerns, governmental assumption of certain economic activities, and the adoption of regulations to protect or advance the interests of the producing class. In the producing class category were industrial workers, farmers, owners of small businesses, and others who, as Hunt put it, worked for a living rather than lived off the skillful display of capital.

Anticorporate reformers in Arizona placed considerable emphasis on making government more responsive to the will of the majority. They were divided, however, over the proper size and composition of the electorate. To some reformers, implementing the will of the majority required expanding the number of potential voters by extending suffrage to women. This position was generally taken by third-party leaders. Some anticorporate leaders of third parties argued that women would support the cause of anticorporate reform. Others essentially ignored the possible effects of expansion on the reform program because they thought the change was merited and/or could work to their benefit at the polls. From our previous discussion, Socialists appeared likely to see merit in the idea but to worry about its effects.

The reform Democrats had a more limited electorate in mind. Many were fearful of the "ignorant Mexican vote" as well as of enlarging the electorate through woman suffrage. While this stand reflects the biases of Anglo males, it also reflects fear that enlargement of the electorate would have adverse effects on the anticorporate reform effort. In a real practical sense, moreover, reformers who captured the Democratic party felt they already had the votes necessary to gain and maintain power and saw no need to risk tampering with the size of the electorate.

Although anticorporate reformers divided over the proper size and composition of the electorate, they agreed on increasing the number of opportunities for those qualified to vote to make their influence felt. The end goal was to reduce corporate control. Making as many governmental positions as possible elective was an important step in this direction. Reformers argued, however, that more was needed. The major threat to public accountability, Worsley and others contended, occurred after a legislator or other official took office. It was then that the corporations exerted their greatest influence. Direct democracy was the cure for this evil. Through the initiative, referendum, and recall, the majority could combat or circumvent corporate influence over those in office.

Reformers also valued unicameralism to avoid problems such as deals fashioned in conference committees that made it difficult to implement the will of the participating majority. Another barrier to this will, an independent judiciary, likewise incurred the wrath of reformers. The recall was the remedy of choice for this problem.

To George Hunt the goal of corporate control required not only electoral and structural changes, but the establishment of a strong Democratic party. Progressives elsewhere thought nonpartisanship was a viable way of attacking corporate abuses. Hunt, in effect, attempted to build an anticorporate political machine. He acted on the assumption that a strong Democratic party, based on patronage and other machinelike attributes, could exist apart from and in opposition to the corrupting force of large corporate interests.

Although the ultimate goals of the various anticorporate reformers differed somewhat, there was considerable consistency in the immediate demands of the Populists, Socialists, and progressive reformers like Hunt. Populists focused on devising solutions to current problems such as iniquities in taxation, excessive railroad rates, and corruption in government. While critical of the effects of growth, they favored "the fostering of every legitimate industry" that was not oppressive to labor. Even the Socialists, whose revolutionary message was strongest, put considerable emphasis on immediate reform. Less radical corporate critics, like Hunt, targeted particular abuses or specific capitalists rather than industrialism or economic development as such. They wanted economic growth and were willing to accept large corporations as essential to the growth process but were insistent on the need for safeguards against corporate abuse.[4]

Despite occasional revolutionary rhetoric, the general thrust of the movement as it evolved from the Populists to the Socialists to Hunt was toward improving the industrial system. As elsewhere, reformers in Arizona helped channel whatever anti-industrial or anticorporate sentiment existed in the population into a quest for ameliorative reform.[5]

The immediate reform message was not revolutionary. It was, however, met with alarm. Similarly, though one might dismiss the reforms made as token, they did not come easily. Corporate defenders marshaled a counter attack. They warned against departing too quickly from the past with untried and possibly dangerous ideas. Countering Worsley's claim, "Arizona is what we make it," were cries of alarm over the danger of attempting to construct a new society out of whole cloth. Critics warned against rationally constructed schemes or "isms." They also cautioned against reliance on legislation or so-called scientific governmental managerial techniques to solve social and economic problems. Lack of respect for traditional ways, conservatives contended, also invited disruption of social relationships. With reform, Anglos could face the challenge of groups no longer content with their place in society.

Political reforms in the name of the "people" or "majority," such as direct democracy, were countered with warnings against instability caused by mob rule and violations of the constitutional system. Critics of the reformers emphasized the sanctity of private property rights. Unlike the reformers, they saw no distinction between the rights and obligations of large corporations and those of small businesses and family farmers. Voters were told, while it might seem appropriate to regulated large corporations today, small enterprises and farmers might be the victims tomorrow. "It could happen to you" arguments were prominent in debates on initiative and referendum measures regarding the regulation of railroads.

Economic arguments against corporate taxation and regulation commonly centered on the detrimental effects they would have on investment and economic growth. Labor reform, to critics, could possibly have even more disastrous effects. Reformers, especially those who championed the cause of radical labor, threatened the stability of the new industrial order. Appeals to class consciousness and conflict, from the conservatives' perspective, could do nothing but create havoc. To capitalists in Arizona, as elsewhere, because everyone in the industrial system had a vital function to perform, no matter how lowly some of the jobs might appear, class divisions interfered with the harmony needed for overall productivity and prosperity.[6] Unabated, industrial class conflict would bring down the system. For these reasons, it was far better, as Campbell argued in his 1916 gubernatorial bid, that Arizonans divide up along ethnic and racial lines than along class lines. Indeed, from the employers' view, ethnic and racial divisions were helpful in that they weakened worker solidarity.

The reform effort was controversial because it challenged established interests and, thanks in part to the countercampaign, appeared to conflict with widely shared values. The course of reform was further complicated because it was influenced by a number of other reform efforts.

Over the course of its career the anticorporate reform effort both benefited and suffered because of other movements. The drive toward statehood was a plus in that skillful reformers, with the unwitting assistance of William Howard Taft and others, were able to make some of the desired changes matters of civic pride. The silver movement also was helpful in so far as it gave the anticorporate Populists a forum.

On the other hand, many anticorporate reformers did not welcome female suffrage or prohibition. Some, as indicated above, were uncomfortable over how suffrage extension would affect voter support for economic and political change. Some anticorporate reformers saw value in prohibition. Union leaders, for example, felt it would help them in organizing workers. Anticorporate reformers, however, could not publicly favor prohibition even if they found the reform desirable. Prohibition prescribed a life-style that was unacceptable to many in the electorate (such as people from mining communities) who otherwise supported anticorporate reform. Both suffrage and prohibition had their major support in an element of the population — rural, agricultural, pietistic — quite distinct from that which supported most of the anticorporate reforms and reformers. The ultimate effect of the suffrage movement was largely detrimental to anticorporate reformers, especially the most radical component of the movement.

Penal reform was probably far more central to the cause of working people than commonly recognized in that members of this class were far more likely than others to be victims of an injustice. Especially likely to be caught up in the system were foreign-born workers.[7] Penal reform, however, while popular with some elements of the anticorporate coalition, especially Socialists, divided the general public. Opponents of anticorporate reform used the issue as an opening wedge to attack Hunt and his supporters.

Also damaging to the cause of reform was a nativistic movement directed in particular against Hispanics and "new" Europeans. Nativism usually refers to the hostility of established residents to new immigrant groups. For many Hispanics, the process initially worked in the reverse direction in Arizona. Hispanics dominated the Arizona territory when it came into existence. By treaty, Hispanics living in the territory became citizens of the United States. They became the victims of discrimination as newcomers entered Arizona. The Mexican-born who came to Arizona in the early 1900s thereafter suffered in the same way. Whether an old or new resident, Hispanics continually faced exclusionary economic, social, and political practices.[8] Anti-Catholicism played a role in the discrimination.

Many anticorporate reformers were part of the Anglo-Saxon, Protestant community and shared the cultural views of that community.[9] Reformers in Arizona were not out of line with reformers elsewhere in these respects. Exclusionary sentiments also characterized Bryan's view of democracy and the broad patterns of southern progressivism.[10] Strengthening the nativistic aspect of the reform effort in Arizona was the resentment of organized labor over the use of Hispanics and European immigrants as sources of cheap labor. Also encouraging exclusionary policies was the resentment of Democratic leaders like Hunt over the historic tendency of some of the non-Anglos, especially the Hispanics, to vote Republican.

Nativism did not initially diminish the popular appeal of the anticorporate reform effort in Arizona. It did, however, interfere with worker solidarity, especially as Hispanics and southern Europeans increased their share of the mining work force. The changing ethnic character of the work force, moreover, made life increasingly difficult for prolabor politicians like Hunt.

The Conditions for Reform

Scholars who focus on the initiation of political reform movements differ over the use of structural strain or resource mobilization explanations. For those who place emphasis on strain, movements come as temporary and somewhat irrational responses to abnormal conditions growing out of rapid social change. Much of this literature takes a dim view of people caught up in such change. Pluralist theorists, in particular, argue that widespread protest activity lacks rationality, sophistication, and appreciation of the need for orderly conflict resolution.[11]

Mobilization theorists, on the other hand, contend that movements can emerge in a rational fashion without the aid of rapid social change. From this perspective, discontent is a constant. Activists may organize this discontent into a movement at any given time. As one scholar has noted:

"While the structural strain theorist may be puzzled by the occurrence of mass protest movements, the mobilization theorist is curious why they do not happen more often."[12]

This study has drawn upon both of the above approaches. Obviously, the anticorporate reform effort could not have existed without the emergence of large corporate enterprises as the focal point of reform. Changing economic conditions were necessary in the emergence of the reform effort. Continuing economic problems and abuses from large corporate enterprises helped keep the movement alive. Yet while economic conditions were necessary in the emergence and perpetuation of this particular reform effort, they do not explain the existence of the reform effort. The reform effort was not the inevitable result of economic conditions. In explaining both its origin and persistence, we must credit factors such as the emergence of effective agitators and the failure of private and public institutions to respond in a timely fashion to demands for change. The existence of this particular reform effort, in short, reflected a combination of determinants.[13]

Both strain and mobilization theories help explain the decidedly anticorporate sentiments of people in mining communities. In these places one finds objective and psychological factors often associated with reform activity. These include rapid socio-economic change, a discovery that society has unjustly treated a collective (relative deprivation), and rising expectations that things will improve. It is also possible to argue that the behavior of people in these communities was a rational response to the conditions or situations in which they found themselves.

Scholars, in probing the question of radicalism or reform-mindedness in mining communities, have often emphasized changes in mining conditions.[14] Some have suggested that, initially at least, one can trace much of the discontent in mining communities to the job alienation felt by former placer miners. As placer miners, they needed little money and little training to engage in mining activity. Miners also acted individually and independently as their own bosses. Whatever wealth they came upon belonged to them.

With deep shaft mining, however, miners became industrial employees of large corporations, often in menial jobs because of their lack of training, dependent on whatever wages the owners were willing to pay them. If anyone was going to strike it rich, it would be the owners of the mining companies rather than the workers. These changes challenged the "myth of success," that is, the notion that poverty need be only a temporary condition because everyone had a good chance of becoming wealthy. This myth had functioned as a psychological safety valve against unrest.

In the commonly advanced scenario, once workers accepted their new position as permanent, they turned to union activity to improve their situation. When this did not provide the needed security, workers turned to political activity, for example, to secure the eight-hour day. When conventional political activity failed, some workers became economic or political radicals or both.

From our examination of the Arizona experience, the above explanation for dissent and the progression from economic to conventional political activity and on to radical political activity places too much emphasis on the placer–miner background and too little emphasis on the ability of labor leaders, radical political organizers, and reform politicians to cultivate and channel discontent.[15]

Arizona mining communities had a mixture of people with different cultural and occupational backgrounds who had a variety of politically relevant grievances. Those doing well had anxieties over maintaining high wages, avoiding job competition from newcomers, and losing their jobs because of technological innovations. Those doing less well had grievances over discrimination and exploitation. This was particularly true of Hispanic mine workers.

Rapid change and the complexity of conditions in mining communities help account for the almost continuous discontent found in these places throughout the period under review. Reform was not simply a matter of doing what could be done while waiting for workers to adjust to the new conditions of employment. Rather, both the conditions of employment, as dictated by the price of copper and technological innovations, and the nature of the work force were constantly changing and, thus, causing dislocations, conflicts, and demands for economic security.

Technology reduced skilled workers to unskilled workers and brought a steady stream of newcomers into the mines who, from the reformers' point of view, needed economic and political education. Discontent was virtually inescapable. It resulted from increases in copper prices because workers sought their share of the new profits and employers tried to hold the line on wages. Workers, in Hunt's words, were apt to take "a personal outlook upon affairs" and saw no reason why they should not share increased profits. Discontent also resulted when prices fell, as miners sought to retain gains already won from employers. At any given time, miners in Arizona, as elsewhere, sought safe as well as steady employment and were apt to object to their working conditions on these grounds.[16]

Going beyond the question of why some miners were unhappy is why some miners supported reform parties and candidates. One logical step, in the days before the ascendancy of the Hunt Democrats, was the conclusion that little or no help would come from the major parties. Those who voted for the Populist or the Socialist parties, on the other hand, presumably not only rejected the other parties but had additional reasons for going to the polls and picking out the third-party alternatives. They could have simply rejected the major parties and stayed home on election day. For those in mining communities, what likely distinguished the Populist and Socialist parties from the other parties, including the Bull Moose Progressives, was that they clearly and unhesitatingly championed the goals of labor reformers and class-conscious workers.

We must credit not only the direct positive appeal of the third-party programs but also the efforts of the third-party reformers and their allies in the labor movement to reach out and cultivate the working-class discontent. Those who experience deprivation and oppression do so in a specific setting and are likely to react against specific targets. As Frances Piven and Richard Cloward have noted: "Workers experience the factory, the speeding rhythm of the assembly line, the foreman, the spies and the guards, the owner and the paycheck. They do not experience monopoly capitalism."[17] Developing worker consciousness of a broader systemic problem requires a strong educational effort. In this case study, WFM, Populist, and Socialist organizers and politicians like Worsley and Hunt performed this function.

One also has to give considerable credit (or blame) to the mine owners and mine managers in Arizona for ignoring the demands of their employees. Opposition to unions in Arizona, as elsewhere, encouraged radicalism.[18] Conflict did not characterize the relations between all western mine owners and their employees.[19] For reasons requiring further study, Arizona mine owners were unusually intransigent.

Third Parties and the Reform Agenda

One popular model in political science has third parties representing the aspirations of wild-eyed reformers, cranks, or discredited leaders of the major parties. Under normal conditions it is not rational for anyone to vote for the candidates of such parties because they have little chance of winning. Hence, one looks for unusual conditions to explain the emergence of third parties that for a short time, at least, secure a sizable number of supporters.[20]

In explaining the appeal of third parties, one finds two basic schools of thought or viewpoints. Some scholars theorize that third parties "are expressions of discontent with major parties and their candidates."[21] Others contend that third parties emerge because "they appeal on fundamental issues to an alienated minority."[22] The first explanation suggests a rather passive role for third parties as simply or largely the temporary by-products of the process of major party readjustment or realignment. They evolve naturally to fill a void. Eventually, however, major parties adjust their programs, siphoning off third-party support, and the third party disappears. The second explanation places more emphasis on the positive appeal of third parties and suggests a more active role for them in bringing about change, although, indeed, the net effect of their aggressiveness may be that they disappear. The second perspective is more compatible with resource mobilization theory. The third parties examined in this study are generally best understood from this perspective.

Some scholars have argued that third parties were easier to organize in western states like Arizona in the last decades of the nineteenth century because voters in these locations had relatively weak attachments to the major parties.[23] Weak partisan attachments, some argue, are a natural consequence of frontier conditions. As one writer notes: "In any frontier society the emphasis is upon the man, rather than upon the organization or party with which he is affiliated."[24] As noted earlier, Governor Hughes in 1893 attributed the independence of the Arizona voter to such factors.

Yet for years up to the time Hughes spoke, voting on the basis of affiliation with one of the two major parties was a regular feature of Arizona politics. The switch of many partisans to the new Populist party, thus, is better interpreted as having had less to do with the natural independence of the voters than with the inability or unwillingness of the major parties to respond to new issues and to the ability of the new party to fill this void.

With economic growth in mind, government officials concentrated on devising various incentives for investors and distributing public facilities around the territory. They found it difficult to face, let alone resolve, conflicts caused by economic dislocations. A political system based on logrolling and horse-trading, such as that which characterized the territory during the 1880s, is, as Michael Paul Rogin once noted, "viable only where individuals are satisfied with small favors."[25] It occurs where there is agreement on basic values. In the 1890s disagreement over values came to the surface and a third party, the Populist party, emerged.

The emergence of the Populist party followed a loss of confidence in the two major parties and their failure to address new and pressing issues caused by growth and economic change. In the process, the Populists took the lead in calling attention to adverse consequences of development, offering an interpretation for the dislocations that occurred and suggesting solutions to these problems. Among the solutions were innovations like the initiative and referendum.

The party attempted to build a broad and diverse following in the electorate. It fell considerably short of this goal. It was most effective at capturing the attention of a class of voters, with a variety of cultural and occupational backgrounds, who were doing neither very well nor very poorly, but who were uncomfortable in an industrial situation new to them and which was beyond their control. The Populists, in particular, offered hope to the new breed of industrial miner.

Socialists and Laborites sent a similar message. Although they did considerably less well with the electorate than did the Populists, they provided linkage in both a programmatic and electoral sense from the Populists to the group of reformers who came to power under the Democratic banner in the period 1910–1916.

Socialists, working through the labor movement and their own party, carried the torch for reform in the early 1900s. Their appeal paralleled that of the Populists. As political scientists Steven Rosenstone, Roy Behr, and Edward Lazarus have noted, the Socialist party, like the Populist party, was a by-product "of an economic transition that embedded in many Americans the feeling that they had been left behind."[26]

Like the Populists, the Socialists undoubtedly benefited from negative events, especially labor disturbances, and the inability of the major parties to cope with these problems. The Socialist party functioned in part as a vehicle of discontent for people with a wide variety of grievances. Indeed, some scholars have argued that the party's prosperity during the Progressive period mostly represented a protest against conditions rather than an acceptance of socialism.[27] As indicated above, however, in explaining Socialist success in Arizona one must place considerably more emphasis on the party's aggressive recruiting and the strength of its ideological appeal, particularly, but not exclusively, among miners. The Socialist party in Arizona, as elsewhere, was "an educational as well as political force."[28]

Socialists in Arizona did unusually well among miners and, unlike the Populists, the European-born. Research published elsewhere suggests that while both cultural (European) and occupational (mining) factors influenced Socialist support in Arizona, the influence of culture was largely indirect. Thus, while the European-born living in Arizona in 1912–1916 were unusually inclined toward radical politics, their decision to vote that way had more to do with the occupational conditions in which they found themselves. The European-born who were miners were unusually supportive of the Socialists. Europeans in other, presumably less stressful occupations were less inclined to vote for radical candidates.[29]

Speaking to a WFM convention in 1907, a prominent Arizona Socialist declared: "The capitalistic class don't fear the Socialist party, as a party, but it fears the great socialist sentiment that is being built up in the United States."[30] The Socialist party in Arizona was never a serious electoral threat. Yet many on the right saw themselves locked in combat with a socialist movement far broader and pervasive than suggested by the amount of electoral support given to the Socialist party. Old guard, standpat Arizona Republicans outright rejected anything that looked like socialism. From 1910 to 1916 they were surrounded by people who were quite willing to experiment with ideas long associated with the Socialists. Reform Democrats, like Hunt, were more concerned with how the electoral support of the Socialist party might affect their ability to gain office. They moved to co-opt the Socialist program or at least the most popular parts thereof. As the Democratic party moved to the left to co-opt the radicals, business interests became even more frightened, conservative, and Republican.[31]

The question of why the United States, unlike most European countries, did not develop and maintain an active Socialist party has been of considerable interest to scholars.[32] In Arizona, at least, the principal problems before World War I were internal disputes and co-optation by the Hunt Democrats. By 1917 the Socialists in Arizona also suffered because of their opposition to the war. "They are a disgrace to the United States, and they are a disgrace to my son that is in the army," said one miner of the Socialist leaders in the mining unions.[33] This may have been a widely shared view. Socialists soon faced the wrath of the right, evidenced in extreme form in the Bisbee deportation, and fell to squabbling among

164

themselves while the public appeared to tire of change. As late as 1918, However, George Hunt was still encouraging Socialists to register as Democrats and line up solidly with the progressive wing of that party.[34]

In 1912 and 1914 the Progressive party challenged the Socialists and Hunt Democrats for leadership of the reform effort. The Progressives offered a platform comparable to the other anticorporate reformers. Yet, particularly after 1912 when Roosevelt no longer headed the ticket, the Progressives had little appeal to the traditional Populist electorate or to those in the electorate supportive of the Socialists, Laborites, Hunt Democrats, or specific anticorporate reforms on the ballot. Rather, the Progressives did best among midwesterners in rather conservative farming areas and in places where interest in reform meant little more than prohibition.

The striking gap between the reform program of the Bull Moosers and the reform sentiments of those who supported the candidates of this party is rather puzzling. It may be that the personality of Theodore Roosevelt rather than the program of the Progressive party attracted or turned away voters. Reportedly, Roosevelt's personality had much to do with the Progressive vote in states like Nevada and Nebraska.[35]

More generally, one study suggests that the Progressive party in Arizona may have been perceived on the basis of its leadership to be not much different from the local Republican party out of which it grew.[36] Somewhat along this line, one scholar, in exploring a similar phenomenon in Colorado, concluded that the failure of the Roosevelt progressives to do well with more radical voters was because the message that got through was, in some subtle ways, different in emphasis than that of the Populists (and presumably the Socialists).[37] Radical voters may have heeded Debs's warning that the Progressives were more interested in preventing change than in bringing it about.

In Arizona the Progressive party's failure to appeal to the anticorporate electorate was influenced more directly by the party's endorsement of prohibition — a reform extremely unpopular in mining areas — the WFM's condemnation of Roosevelt's labor policies, and by the prior claims that the Socialists and Hunt Democrats had on that electorate.

While the impact of the Progressive party in Arizona is a bit difficult to pinpoint, the other third parties — beginning with the Populists and extending to the Socialists and Laborites — clearly played active and important roles in expressing economic and social discontent, agitating for reform, educating the public, building support for innovation, and compelling the major parties to change their positions.[38]

These parties built support for anticorporate reform directly by taking the case for reform to the voters. Perhaps equally, if not more important, was the indirect influence of the third parties in moving the Democratic party to the left and in helping it secure public approval for change. Democrats moved to the left in part to co-opt issues at the heart of the anticorporate reform program that the third parties had helped make salient. Populists, Socialists, and Laborites also helped push the Democrats to the left by infiltrating the party and, sometimes, by assuming leadership positions. For the Laborites the leftward influence came as a matter of exchanging support for platform adjustments.

Also in a strategic vein, third parties were useful to Democrats because of their threat value. Democrats used the threat of radicalism as represented by third parties, particularly the Socialists, to engender support for what they called ameliorative reforms. Although these reforms were very much in the anticorporate reform tradition, Democrats depicted them as moves that would sap the strength of the radicals. Identified in this manner, the reforms gained in their general acceptance.

Overall, this study indicates that third parties during this particular historical era were highly active and visible proponents of change rather than merely reactors to the failure of the major parties to address particular grievances. They were not simply passive by-products in the process of major party realignment.

One should note, however, that the study also indicates that neither economic stress nor the most strenuous efforts to cultivate a following are apt to do third parties much good without highly visible leadership, be it nationally known leaders like Roosevelt or local celebrities like O'Neill. Third parties, moreover, run the risk that major parties may co-opt their program and following in the electorate through ameliorative reform or, perhaps, just the appearance of reform.

The Bringing of Reform

A broad area of disagreement among scholars has to do with the nature of the political conflict in the Populist-Progressive period and the resolution of this conflict. Some scholars, particularly an earlier generation of progressive historians, contend that public officials, faced with public outrage or a mass movement prompted by the abuses of an economic elite, had no choice but to make fundamental reforms. Others argue that the reforms made were neither fundamental nor driven by public demands. Rather, public officials responded to the demands of the economic elite and made changes that were, at best, only symbolic window dressing to pacify the masses.[39] A third approach has been to ignore elite-mass relations altogether and attribute reform to the influence of specific groups, for example, the coalition of farmers and owners of small businesses who shared an interest in rail regulation.[40]

The anticorporate reformers in Arizona depicted themselves as agents of the people fighting the special interests. Reformers in the Hunt era spoke in practical terms of building a coalition among farmers, owners of small businesses, and workers in opposition to the large corporate interests. Their view of the political struggle, however, was not that of a multi-sided group struggle, but of a two-sided contest between the economic elite and the people or between the special interests and the public interest. The Democratic party in Arizona, in their eyes, was the sworn enemy of the special interests.

This reform perspective, some scholars have argued, characterized Democrats throughout the country in the Progressive era. It is, thus, not surprising that the task of making reform in much of the country fell into the hands of Democrats.[41] In Arizona it is more precise to say, however, that the task of making reform fell to the progressive wing of the Democratic party, which slowly emerged from an underdog status in the 1880s, 1890s, and early 1900s to become the dominant element in the party and the state. The victory of the progressive element came only after the co-optation of reform-minded third parties and their followings and after the merger of anticorporate reform with other popular causes, especially statehood. The reign of the reform element in Arizona, as elsewhere, was but for a relatively short period (1910–1916).[42] With changes in popular sentiment, Democratic leaders turned away from reform.

Depicting the anticorporate reform effort as a "mass movement of the people" poses certain difficulties. Certainly, up to 1915–1916 "the people" it represented were Anglos only. On the electoral level only around 27 percent of the eligible voting population participated in the elections that brought the reformers to power, and by no means did all these people vote for reform.

From a more practical perspective it makes considerable sense to look upon the anticorporate reform effort not so much as a mass movement, but as an attempt by certain formal associations (labor groups and political party organizations) to gain general approval of specific programs and objectives calling for what they perceived to be collective benefits. The reformers became involved with the mass of people, particularly the general electorate, because they needed voter support to bring about change. More exactly, their success depended upon securing the approval of a majority of the eligible voters who turned out on election day.

Leaders of the anticorporate reform effort had to move from what was a minority position reflected in the third-party vote to a majority position. In the process they had to move from a core of true believers in the electorate (the highly issued-oriented Populist and Socialist supporters) to attracting those who marginally favored the reform package, who favored a particular type of reform in the package such as direct democracy, or who associated reform with something positive such as statehood or a candidate they liked.

One might partially attribute the success of the Hunt Democrats to their ability to cultivate resentment against the corporations and to present a plausible reform program.[43] More directly, the Hunt Democrats came to power in 1910 by riding a wave of rather widely diffused support for reform in which the initiative, referendum, and recall formed the centerpiece. By 1910 the devices of direct democracy achieved shibboleth status on par with statehood and, in an earlier era, free silver. The battle over direct democracy, which intensified as Arizona entered the second decade of the twentieth century, was central to the conflict between the economic interests and the reformers.

The two sides debated abstract principles concerning democracy and representation. The underlying tension was over who would govern the new state. Direct democracy threatened the ability of railroad and mining corporations to control the legislature, something they had been largely able to do during the territorial period. From their point of view, statehood without direct democracy would be relatively safe and, indeed, even desirable for economic reasons. For the reformer, on the other hand, statehood would be meaningless, perhaps a disaster, without protections against corporate influence offered by the initiative, referendum, and recall.

A broad spectrum of the voting public, including the traditional core of Democratic supporters — farmers, Mormons, and southerners — in 1910 likewise sought both the objectives of statehood and direct democracy. Arizonans, compared to people in other western states, were unusual in their commitment to what some branded as radical reforms. They stayed committed even at the risk of endangering the adoption of their constitution and bringing an indefinite delay in statehood.[44]

Reform Democrats who came to power in Arizona could reasonably claim a broad permissive consensus to experiment with change.[45] Voter support came in approval of the progressive constitution and progressive Democratic candidates in 1911. Later, approval appeared in the large percentage of the vote that went for reform-minded presidential candidates in 1912, in Hunt's re-election in 1914, and in the actions of the electorate on the propositions brought before them in 1912 and 1914. Not surprisingly, in this context conservative Democrats and even some Republicans who were anxious to have a say in the new government suddenly became "lifelong" progressives and former Socialists felt comfortable participating as Democrats.

The progressive wing of the Democratic party under Hunt dominated Arizona politics during the period of accomplishment. Critics within and outside of his own party accused Hunt of being a Socialist who had ridden the Democratic party to power. On the other hand, although Socialists sometimes praised Hunt, they did not claim him as one of their own.[46] Other critics charged that Hunt was secretly receptive to the corporate interests — more than willing to meet with the railroad and mining executives behind closed doors.[47] This type of criticism, however, did not come from the left, but from the right. It came during a period when public enthusiasm for anticorporate reform was high, in the hope it would tarnish Hunt's public image. Looking at the 1910–1916 period as whole, one has little reason to believe that the policies articulated by Hunt in regard to the corporate interests differed from his actual policies. Nor is there any reason to believe that the opposition of the corporations to the reforms he pursued was less than vigorous.

The reforms made in the Hunt years may not have been fundamental. Indeed, the initial goals, funneled through the Hunt Democrats, were not all that radical in the first place. What is remarkable is the extent to which the economic interests resisted change. What is even more remarkable, from a power perspective, is that the system worked, at least in the short run, by producing reforms over the objections of the affected economic interests.

The corporate interests, in fact, lost many battles in the convention, in the legislature, and at the polls from 1910 to 1916, although they recovered somewhat by resorting to the courts. Corporate leaders in Arizona, as in California during an earlier era, had to live with the fact that politicians and a sizable segment of the public resisted their plans, circumvented their authority, and sought, with frequent success, to control their activities.[48] Hunt, a molder of reform sentiment, did not need evidence of public support for change in order to spur him on. Other policymakers felt the pressure. Research suggests that constituency pressure on issues like rail regulation was strong enough in the first state legislature to cause even those who might have had doubts about reform to line up behind such measures.[49]

The Decline of Popular Support

The level of apparent electoral support for corporate reform in Arizona built up over the period 1890 to 1910, peaked between 1910 and 1914, and declined thereafter. What accounts for this decline? One explanation is that reform sentiment died out in part because reformers had accomplished most of their original objectives. The Hunt years produced direct democracy, increased corporate regulation and taxation, and provided more labor protection. The reform effort had, in a relatively brief period, brought an array of legislation and agencies and, as a result, had lost its reason for being. It produced, in a sense, a "policy fad" that was soon followed by preoccupation with another set of issues.[50] The distracting issues had to do with World War I and, involved with this, an escalation of labor problems.

Probing a bit deeper, one might also argue that, to some extent, support for reform among many people in the broader electorate was initially only a temporary product of the statehood struggle. Making Arizona the center of "progressive democracy" partially reflected emerging feelings of state pride and a general desire to demonstrate the political independence long suppressed by decades of territorial rule.[51] Frustration over the failure to achieve statehood may have strengthened the popular resolve to be different, especially in regard to direct democracy. In later years, as the enthusiasm engendered over statehood died out, enthusiasm for progressive reform also diminished.

Some evidence also suggests that enthusiasm for reform also abated as the limitations and costs of reform became apparent. The benefits of direct democracy, in particular, could probably never have lived up to expectations. Their limitations and the effects taxation and regulatory reform had on the climate for investment became matters of concern and public debate. Also alarming was the apparent radicalization of the labor movement, as symbolized by the IWW. Labor continued to have reform goals but by 1916 the public had tired of giving its approval to labor-backed measures.

In explaining the decline in support for reform, one also has to focus more directly on the political consequences of what the reformers did after they took power. Hunt himself and historians like James Byrkit have pointed to the efforts of the mining companies to drive the reformers from power because of taxation and labor relations policies. In his well-documented analysis of the period, Byrkit concludes: "Between 1915 and 1918 the companies, led by Walter Douglas, completely reversed the direction of Arizona politics and destroyed the liberal influence in the state. By 1921 they had secured a closed society."[52] There is no doubt that the corporations did all they could, for example, through the newspapers subject to their control, to reverse the political tide. Hunt, in writing to his friend Upton Sinclair, placed particular emphasis on copper company control of the press in turning sentiment against reform.[53]

Whatever the underlying causes, shifting popular attitudes toward reform brought the rise of Republicans, a growing aversion of Democrats to the progressive label, and a decline in support for radical third parties. On the electoral level the campaign against Hunt brought a shift in the perception of the nature and intent of his agenda.

The reform Democrats took over government by putting themselves on the side of the people versus the special interests. A more refined version of this two-sided conflict, as described by a Hunt associate, was "between the forces of Absentee Capitalism on the one hand, exercising their power through the corporations, and on the other side the citizens of Arizona, the merchants, farmers, professional men, stock growers and the workers."[54]

By 1916 the corporate press was busy advancing the thesis that Hunt was a radical, overly sympathetic to the interests of a special segment of society, Hispanics and foreign-born industrial miners, whose loyalty to the country was questionable. Hunt, the papers charged, had abandoned farmers, owners of small businesses, and others for this special labor interest. The major turning point came in the Clifton-Morenci labor crisis in 1915. When push came to shove, Hunt was prolabor, regardless of the nativity of the workers. Because of the ethnic groups involved, however, his actions could appear as a betrayal of both his own and the dominant social class.

The election returns in 1916 show that Hunt and, indeed, the Democratic party as a whole, had moved from a broad base to an highly issue-oriented one centered among the working class in mining areas. Hunt, in sum, suffered the same fate as Hiram Johnson in California in that by his actions in office, as filtered to the public through a hostile press, he alienated many of those who had voted for him and thus wound up with a much narrower core of support in the industrial working class.[55]

A fuller explanation of the shift in electoral support requires an examination of the behavior of specific groups of voters and of the impact of additions to the electorate. As the statistical analysis in Appendix E suggests, from 1912 to 1916 reform Democrats picked up support among Europeans, Hispanics, and miners. They lost support among the native-born (except southerners), Mormons, and, most dramatically, midwesterners and farmers.

Looking at voting patterns on anticorporate reform propositions from 1912 to 1916, we find the most demonstrable about-face on issues in farming communities. People in these places, while not enthusiastic about labor protection measures, were at least mildly supportive of other anticorporate reforms in 1912. In 1914 and 1916 they were among the strongest opponents of such reforms. Mormons also showed some tendency to become more conservative on the issues over the same period.

During the 1911–1916 period some voters changed their party or policy preferences. Others were new to the electorate, that is, recent migrants or long-term residents who voted for the first time. One must give considerable weight to the importance of new voters in accounting for more negative attitudes about reform. Some of this came from migrant midwesterners, most pronounced in farming areas, who brought with them their Republican politics.

Working in the same direction was woman suffrage. Female voters demonstrated a conservative leaning, being far more likely than men to oppose radical candidates and anticorporate measures on the ballot. That western women were essentially conservative finds some support in the literature and, indeed, a gender gap similar to the one found in this study was found in an empirical study of voter behavior in Oregon in the same period.[56] The voting behavior of women in this study is partly although not completely explained by·cultural and economic variables, that is, the tendency of women to be Mormons, midwesterners, and members of farming communities.

The increased conservatism one finds in farming and Mormon communities, however, is only partially explained by the addition of voters. To some extent, males in farming and Mormon communities who voted for Hunt and reform in 1911 and 1912 became more conservative in 1914 and 1916. For some, this change had to do with a change of heart from liberal to conservative. A more plausible explanation, however, is that the support of reform candidates and issues in farming and, to a lesser extent, Mormon communities in 1911–1912 was an aberration.

Farmers and Mormons before 1911–1912 were far from strong and dependable supporters of the type or degree of change favored by Hunt and others in the Populist tradition. Their support of Hunt in 1911 most likely had more to do with their status as loyal Democrats than with issues. Their disenchantment with Hunt came somewhat naturally as Hunt's stand on issues, including penal reform as well as anticorporate reform, became clear. Thus, on the issues their support for anticorporate propositions in 1912 represents nothing much more than a temporary flirtation engendered by the statehood movement.

Farmers in other Mountain States during the same period also shied away from radical parties and took conservative positions on reform issues with the exception of prohibition.[57] Mormons, as farmers, shared these views. Mormons also had their own reasons for opposing the anticorporate reform effort. This opposition in so far as it related to labor issues reflected earlier struggles in Utah.

Farmers, Mormons, females, and newcomers from the Midwest were at the core of a movement away from experimentation and change. Another and relatively more constant source of opposition to reform was in the economically diverse cities and towns. A plausible explanation for this is the unusual commitment of people in these types of settlements to the notion of economic growth.[58] Throughout the period under review, charges that corporate regulation and taxation would destroy the business climate and scare off out-of-state investors appear to have been particularly effective in these areas.

The finding that a class of industrial workers, the miners, were at the core of reform activity is compatible with the literature.[59] These workers were largely native-born Anglos at the beginning of the reform era. Toward the end of the era, they were new Europeans and Hispanics. Anglos could turn to the Populist party and the new Europeans had the Socialist party. Hispanic miners, however, were, for a considerable period, a group of industrial workers with an anticorporate bent who lacked a protest party. Hispanics did not gravitate toward either the Populist or Socialist party. This was due in large part to the nativism of these groups and the unions with which they associated.

By the first decade in the twentieth century, Hispanics were an important element in the reform effort, especially on the industrial field. While the significance of the Hispanic vote on several reform matters disappears when one controls for mining, Hispanics were an independent source of support for measures like rail regulation and centralizing tax authority to better tap the wealth of corporations. The tendency of Hispanics to vote Republican began to reverse in the early 1900s. They tended slightly toward the Progressive party in 1912, but it was not until 1916 and the Hunt candidacy that Hispanics had a candidate in whom they had confidence. The switch to Hunt and the Democrats represented a new stage in the long struggle of Hispanics for their political and economic rights. This shift, however, accompanied and perhaps helped produce a movement away from the Democratic party by other groups in the electorate.

CONCLUDING NOTE

POPULISTS, PROGRESSIVES, AND THE ELECTORAL DIMENSIONS OF REFORM

Instability due to reliance on a "one crop" (mining) economy, intense labor-management conflicts, high rates of migration into the state, frustrations growing out of a long statehood battle, tensions between Mormons and non-Mormons, conflict between Anglo and non-Anglo (especially Hispanic) communities, and rivalry among economic groups distinguished Arizona politics in the period under review. This combination of factors makes the unfolding of reform in Arizona a somewhat unique story.

Many of the same forces, however, also influenced politics in other states, particularly those in the Mountain West.[1] To some extent or another, other states in this region also experienced an anticorporate reform effort in which miners and mining communities played prominent roles.[2] Anticorporatism was not the whole of reform politics in states like Arizona, Colorado, Montana, and Nevada. It was, however, an important element and one that linked the Populists, Socialists, and early twentieth century non-Socialist progressives.

In undertaking this study the author was mindful that scholars, traditionally, have disregarded the significance of the Populist-Progressive era in the Mountain West. Some have dismissed populism in this part of the country on the grounds that it largely reflected an obsession with the silver issue.[3] Others have faulted this interpretation for taking a far more restricted view of the motives of both Populist leaders and supporters in the electorate than is justified.[4] Critics of the silver-only view contend that Mountain State Populists sought many reforms, some of which had to do with particular developments within their boundaries.

This study lends support to the broader view of the Populist program in the Mountain West. It is also compatible with the notion found in previous studies that if there was a common denominator among Populist activists in Mountain States, it was an obsession with large corporations or monopolies, be they of the land, money, transportation, or another variety, and with the need to protect the interests of working people.[5]

Nationally, it is reasonable to think of two main types of populism, both genuine, but with one having a greater orientation toward labor and another in which farmers and farm issues played a more dominant role. Both types sought political and economic reform. Both types also had a genuine interest in free silver. In the labor-oriented type, increased silver production was a means of increasing employment. In the farm-oriented type, free silver was a means of easing debt problems. Populism in the Mountain States like Arizona had as natural a relationship to the emergence of an industrial labor movement, especially in mining areas, as populism in the South and Midwest had to the emergence of a farm movement.

Historians have traditionally looked upon progressivism as a broadening of the protest of the agrarian populists. If one takes the broader view of the Populist movement, that is, as one that offered a broad reform program centered around anticorporate themes and that included the industrial labor component as well as the agrarian one, the distinction between the two movements in the Mountain West becomes difficult to draw. Programmatically there were differences between the Populist and Progressive movements in places like Arizona, but they shared a common anticorporate focus and a common following in the electorate. In this sense we are talking about one movement rather than two.

Some scholars, in separating the Populist and Progressive periods in the Mountain West, have also depicted the Progressive period in these states as largely imitative of a more genuine movement elsewhere. Western historian Gerald Nash, for example, has concluded that being derivative rather than original, "westerners followed the progressive reform programs of their eastern cousins."[6] Making a similar point, historian Loren Chan has contended: "Nevada's progressive tone in government and politics was merely a manifestation of the states' ability to follow regional and national trends, rather than to set them."[7]

One has to acknowledge the importance of regional and national influences on Mountain State progressivism. Much of the intellectual leadership and inspiration came from the Far West. Mountain State reformers took an interest in the "Oregon System" and several Mountain State governors saw themselves as local versions of Hiram Johnson. Reforms undertaken in Oregon, Oklahoma, and other states interested and encouraged Arizona progressives.

Reformers in Arizona, and presumably elsewhere in the Mountain West, however, were not simply gathering in ideas that became nationally salient in the 1910–1916 period. Populists and Socialists in Arizona had advanced most of the so-called progressive ideas decades earlier. Nor were the progressive reformers simply attempting to be fashionable. The need for reform grew out of events in the state's past and in reaction to serious existing problems. Reform did not reflect a sudden impulse to implement ideas developed elsewhere. It evolved over the years in response to real problems facing Arizonans.

What motivated reform activity? In focusing on the history of the anticorporate movement, one has to give considerable weight to the importance of economic (occupational and class) divisions. Partisan voting in Arizona prior to the rise of the corporations and the Populists largely reflected ethnocultural rather than economic divisions within the electorate. Democrats were, in essence, southerners and Mormons while Republicans were Yankees, non-Mormons, and Hispanics. The emergence of the Populists both reflected and fueled economic differences in the electorate. In 1894 and 1896 differences based on economic factors (mining, farming, mixed or commercial activities) began to have as much or more to do with electoral divisions as did the ethnocultural factors in explaining the divergent followings of the parties and the vote for particular candidates.

The anticorporate effort, of course, was but one of several crusades in the reform period. Its base in Arizona was quite different from the drive for suffrage or the effort to make penal reform. Reform efforts emerged in reaction to different stimuli (or as the result of the efforts of agitators to channel long-smoldering discontent of various types), had a particular group of activist supporters, and enjoyed a particular following in the broader population. They reflected ethnocultural differences, economic differences, or a mixture of each type.

The preceding discussion has also shown that at any particular time during the reform period, the vote for a candidate, party, or cause usually consisted of a combination of different types of factors. Short-term issues or evaluations of particular candidates often affected the vote. This study suggests that the personal appeal of leaders such as O'Neill, Debs, or Theodore Roosevelt can greatly enhance the vote for a reform party. Among long-term factors, this study indicates that values and prejudices prevalent in places where people were born and reared and attitudes associated with membership in various social and occupational groups are often significant indicators of voting behavior.

Also of considerable importance among the long-term factors affecting voting during this period was partisanship. Attachment to a political party, be it one of the major parties or a relatively new third party, was often of importance even when issues were unusually salient. To some extent, party voting, especially for the long-established parties, was habitual voting reflecting psychological attachments.

More fundamentally, however, partisanship reflected issue, economic, and ethnocultural divisions within the electorate.[8] For much of the early twentieth century, Republicans and Socialists in the electorate represented the opposite extremes on reform issues. One, as expected, generally found voters for third parties highly issue-oriented. Voting for the party that dominated most of the period, the Democrats, became far more issue-based in 1914–1916. Throughout the reform era the coalitional nature of parties changed as reform and radical elements of the electorate moved between third parties and the Democratic party and opponents of most reforms of an anticorporate nature gravitated toward the Republican party.

The most fundamental lesson of the Arizona experience is that the functioning of the election and party systems were key elements in understanding reform. Reformers, by cultivating citizen grievances and demands, combining these with other widely shared goals or causes, and co-opting third parties, were able to capture a major political party, assume power, and make changes opposed by a targeted elite. While interest group activity and elite manipulation no doubt also influenced changes made in Arizona and elsewhere during the Populist-Progressive period, this study suggests the central importance of forces emanating through the electoral system.

APPENDIX A

VOTING BEHAVIOR:
THEORY, DATA, AND METHODS

What types of factors condition or determine voter behavior? Political scientists, in answer, have placed considerable emphasis on partisanship. Some theorists look at party identification as a strong psychological bond formed largely through a socialization process in which the family is the primary agent. Other theorists argue that people attach themselves to particular parties because experience leads them to believe that the candidates of a particular party are closer to their values than are the candidates of other parties. Party, thus, becomes a convenient shorthand cue for separating candidates.[1]

Whatever its roots, party identification takes on a life of its own and has an independent impact on voting behavior. Compared to issues or candidate-specific factors, party identification also has a long-term influence on voting behavior. Theoretically, in any given election people will vote for the candidate of their party unless short-term factors, for example, issues or something about the candidates involved, cause them to do otherwise.

Much of the work of party identification in this country concerns identification with the Democratic and Republican parties. Third parties, in the conventional framework, exist as temporary products of new issues or other factors that cause either a short-term disruption in the pattern of two-party voting or, in an unusual case, a realignment of the coalitional nature of the major parties.[2] In either case, they rise with issues that disrupt voting behavior and disappear once the issues fade in importance or are co-opted by one of the major parties. Third parties that continue to capture a small vote year after year are dismissed as little more than ideological clubs or interest groups that happen to nominate candidates.

Identification with the Democratic and Republican parties was, by all indicators, an important factor affecting voter behavior during the Populist-Progressive era in U.S. politics. Yet scholars are divided over what types of factors provide the best explanation for party identification, voting choice, third-party support, and party realignment in this period.[3] Historians disagree over whether reform divided people along economic or ethnocultural lines and over the precise nature of the economic or ethnocultural factors involved.[4] Students of social or protest movements have likewise differed over whether mass behavior, including voting behavior, during this period reflected class or life-style concerns.

This study examines voter behavior by looking at the effects of partisanship, issue orientation, occupation, ethnocultural factors, and, for the elections in 1914 and 1916, gender. Theoretically, occupational and ethnocultural factors are background variables that not only directly affect voting but indirectly affect voting through their influence on issues and partisanship. Issues also have an indirect effect on voting through their effect on partisanship.[5] Logically, gender is a prior variable that may influence issues and partisanship as well as voting behavior.

Election returns and voter registration lists provided materials to estimate partisanship variables. Contests where short-term factors were relatively less important, that is, below the presidential or gubernatorial levels, were chosen to indicate the party vote. Votes on measures put on the ballot through initiative and referendum procedures provided material to gauge voter opinion on important issues and to explore how issues affected the choice of particular parties or candidates. The opinion expressed in such elections presumably is that of those most active in the electorate and those most likely guided by ideological orientations.[6] Election data were collected on a precinct level. Voting variables are the percentage of the total vote in each precinct in support of a particular candidate, party, or proposition.[7]

Information on the background characteristics of people in each precinct comes from a random sample of individual responses of household heads to the 1900 and 1910 national censuses.[8] Background variables gathered from census materials are percentages of the total number of household heads sampled in each precinct. While we do not know all we should know about these people, census material provides what the literature indicates are potentially valuable ethnocultural and economic variables.

By looking at places of birth we are able to estimate the number of household heads from various regions of the United States, Mexico, Europe, and those who belonged to the Mormon Church. The regional variables reflect the percent of household heads in each precinct who were born in the official census designations of eastern, western, mid-western, and southern states.[9] Regional census categories have demonstrated considerable explanatory power in previous studies, although the precise reasons for their importance is not altogether clear.[10] Some research links regional variations with cultural variations identified by political scientist Daniel Elazar.[11]

Historians have long noted the political significance of the migration of southerners and midwesterners to the western part of the United States and the links between these regional backgrounds and partisan activity. Political scientists, of late, have concluded that place of residence is a far more important independent source of political opinion (partisanship and ideology) than previously thought.[12]

Scholars probably have failed to give enough attention to the significance of the foreign-born migrant in western politics. Western historians, in the Turnerian tradition, have focused on cultural traits they choose to characterize as distinctly American.[13] Yet as one western historian has argued: "Had Frederick Jackson Turner projected a different set of statistics, he might have propounded a thesis suggesting that the West was unique because it had been settled by three times as many foreigners per capita as then occupied the remainder of the United States."[14]

The Mormon component of the electorate represents a political culture, based on religious doctrine and the experiences of a people, which champions the Puritan ethic of sobriety, piety, industry, and thrift. To some extent, Mormons also represent a moralistic political culture. This culture emphasizes political participation and the attainment of broad collective objectives.[15] Mormons began moving into Arizona from Utah during the last decades of the nineteenth century as the result of an organized effort on the part of the Mormon Church to colonize other parts of the Southwest. Used to estimate the Mormon population is the percent of household heads in each precinct who were born in Utah.[16]

Economic or occupational variables examined were the percentage of household heads engaged in mining, farming, and mixed economic activities. These variables provide an index of social class or socioeconomic status (SES), commonly employed in behavioral studies. To some extent, they also provide an index of regional divisions among mining communities, farming communities, and cities and small towns based on a mix of economic activity. Included in the last of these categories are towns found by some historians to epitomize attachment to the economic development ethic.[17]

Another set of data, 1916 voter registration statistics, allowed the author to measure the percentage of Democrats, Republicans, Socialists, and eligible female voters in each precinct. This last bit of information also made it possible to examine the impact of expanding suffrage to women. Variables are the percent of registered Democrats, Republicans, Socialists, and women in each precinct.

Technically, the data relate only to the voting patterns of election units.[18] Yet, although one must be cautious, reliance on precinct data that is relatively homogeneous with respect to the variables examined (nativity and occupation) along with contextual information allows us to make reasonable estimates of individual behavior.[19]

The discussion of various elections in the text is often only descriptive in nature. In describing elections, I refer to correlation coefficients to note the association between the vote for a candidate, party, or proposition and particular variables. Appendix D shows these relationships. Appendixes D and E contain regression findings for the various elections. These provide a measure of the relative influence of particular types of variables in any given election. They also show how much the variables in the equations explain election outcomes. Problems of multicollinearity prevented the entry of all variables in each equation. The regression tables also omit those variables that were not found to be significant at the .05 level.

APPENDIX B

MAPS OF ARIZONA (1891, 1895, 1909)

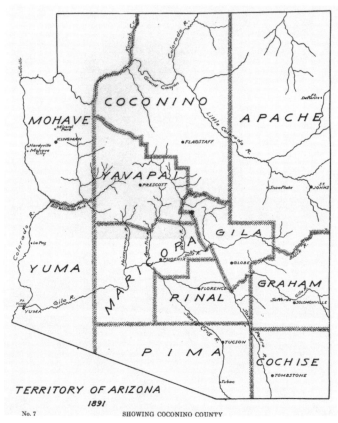

George H. Kelly, ed. *Legislative History of Arizona, 1864–1912.* Phoenix, Ariz.: Manufacturing Stationers, Inc., 1926.

188

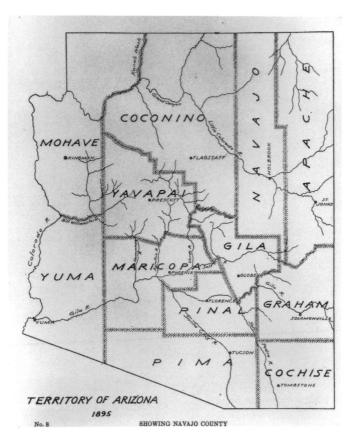

George H. Kelly, ed. *Legislative History of Arizona,* 1864–1912. Phoenix, Ariz.: Manufacturing Stationers, Inc., 1926.

Appendix B

No. 10   SHOWING GREENLEE COUNTY

George H. Kelly, ed. *Legislative History of Arizona, 1864–1912*. Phoenix, Ariz.: Manufacturing Stationers, Inc., 1926.

190

APPENDIX C

VOTING RETURNS BY COUNTY*

	1880 Congress			1882 Congress		
	TV	D%	R%	TV	D%	R%
Apache	599	52	48	1061	42	58
Coch.				2724	55	45
Gila				718	55	44
Graham				563	67	33
Mar.	1012	64	36	891	51	49
Mohave	269	49	51	455	65	35
Pima	3484	49	51	1804	51	49
Pinal	795	68	32	674	72	28
Yav.	1513	46	54	2171	51	49
Yuma	282	57	43	311	47	53
Total	7954	53	48	11364	54	46

	1884 Congress		
	TV	D%	R%
Apache	1255	59	41
Coch.	2349	48	52
Gila	452	42	58
Graham	1013	36	64
Mar.	1446	50	50
Mohave	534	40	60
Pima	1704	42	58
Pinal	748	48	52
Yav.	2578	41	59
Yuma	263	37	63
Total	12342	45	55

Voters in some counties could choose more than one delegate.

Appendix C

VOTING RETURNS (cont.)

	1886 Congress			1888 Congress			1890 Congress			1891 Const.	
	TV	D%	R%	TV	D%	R%	TV	D%	R%	TV	% Yes
Apache	910	64	36	835	66	34	897	62	39	481	83
Coch.	1721	70	30	1673	64	36	1404	57	43	921	75
Coco.										279	38
Gila	514	58	42	433	75	25	713	60	40	436	52
Graham	844	69	31	899	83	17	908	62	38	848	83
Mar.	1539	56	44	1990	75	25	1915	60	40	1727	79
Mohave	516	43	57	470	53	47	497	52	48	277	79
Pima	1564	54	47	1524	59	42	1422	49	51	988	80
Pinal	789	52	48	865	79	21	632	54	46	338	52
Yav.	2132	56	44	2546	56	44	2382	51	50	1172	53
Yuma	298	54	46	403	59	41	308	47	53	271	57
Total	10827	59	41	11538	67	33	11078	55	45	7738	70

VOTING RETURNS (*cont.*)

	1892 Congress			1894 Congress				1894 Council			
	TV	D%	R%	TV	D%	R%	P%	TV	D%	R%	P%
Apache	855	50	50	973	44	48	07	947	44	52	05
Coch.	1255	63	37	1150	30	42	29	1119	36	47	17
Coco.	874	37	63	961	37	46	17	913	43	50	07
Gila	688	60	40	545	30	22	49	512	43	27	30
Graham	915	70	29	1212	47	38	16	1169	52	40	09
Mar.	2298	60	40	3182	35	42	23	3106	41	41	18
Mohave	487	50	50	499	22	22	56	475	32	34	33
Pinna	1329	52	48	1436	39	46	15	1392	43	49	08
Pinal	541	52	48	504	31	50	19	589	36	55	09
Yav.	2043	53	47	2439	33	45	21	2295	40	50	11
Yuma	350	56	44	427	30	39	31	411	42	42	16
Total	11641	54	46	13427	36	42	22	12923	41	45	14

Appendix C

VOTING RETURNS (*cont.*)

	1896 Congress				1898 Congress			1900 Congress		
	TV	D%	R%	P%	TV	D%	R%	TV	D%	R%
Apache	475	48	48	04	485	46	54	522	41	59
Coch.	1140	46	23	31	1359	52	48	1469	55	45
Coco.	998	36	42	23	814	43	57	938	46	54
Gila	822	37	17	46	1017	62	38	1036	63	38
Graham	1266	63	21	17	1392	63	37	1534	59	41
Mar.	3215	44	33	23	3414	49	51	3397	50	50
Mohave	545	34	08	58	642	74	26	557	76	24
Navajo	521	45	47	08	625	46	54	573	53	47
Pima	1306	47	32	21	1591	48	52	1576	56	45
Pinal	523	52	28	20	532	49	51	580	66	34
Yav.	2751	34	28	39	3123	55	45	2883	42	58
Yuma	458	48	22	30	602	43	57	755	62	38
Total	14050	43	29	28	15595	53	47	16330	53	47

Appendix C

VOTING RETURNS (*cont.*)

	1902 Congress			1904 Congress				1906 Congress			
	TV	D%	R%	TV	D%	R%	S%	TV	D%	R%	S%
Apache	568	37	63	510	41	59	00	463	44	54	02
Coch.	2661	57	44	3518	57	39	04	4376	54	34	12
Coco.	1031	44	57	1074	47	53	01	995	57	42	02
Gila	847	52	48	1274	58	30	12	1855	49	30	21
Graham	2098	64	36	2117	53	38	10	2268	51	38	11
Mar.	3361	52	48	3812	45	52	03	3563	52	43	04
Mohave	601	51	49	639	54	33	13	553	66	19	15
Navajo	470	50	50	628	46	53	01	609	60	37	03
Pima	1752	48	52	1977	45	52	03	2208	34	62	04
Pinal	519	51	49	597	62	35	04	528	51	46	03
S.C.				552	43	56	01	580	61	37	02
Yav.	3623	46	54	3514	43	46	12	3113	50	38	12
Yuma	798	56	44	988	47	46	12	976	39	49	13
Total	18955	51	49	21220	49	45	06	22088	50	40	09

Appendix C

VOTING RETURNS (cont.)

	1906 Statehood		1908 Congress				1910 Constitutional Delegation					
	TV	% Yes	TV	D%	R%	S%	TV	Del	D%	R%	S%	L%
Apache	127	37	558	35	65	00	632	1	51	50	00	00
Coch.	3954	13	5115	44	49	07	35992	10	48	39	03	09
Coco.	841	15	1115	45	51	04	1210	2	36	64	00	00
Gila	1660	06	2325	42	41	17	9922	5	37	35	00	28
Graham	1827	22	2738	52	42	06	10290	5	58	30	00	12
Mar.	3421	12	4398	45	51	04	3833	9	54	43	02	02
Mohave	509	18	609	59	32	09	639	1	60	00	00	37
Navajo	438	32	737	41	54	05	1273	2	54	46	00	00
Pima	1634	28	2672	47	49	04	10647	5	35	52	02	11
Pinal	439	08	734	48	49	04	1460	2	61	39	00	00
S.C.	517	23	677	51	46	04	332	1	45	55	00	00
Yav.	2709	11	3190	42	48	10	12801	6	47	41	05	07
Yuma	257	29	1305	43	44	12	3238	3	63	37	00	00
Total	19406	16	26074	45	48	07	126769	52	50	40	02	08

Appendix C

1911 ELECTIONS

	U.S. Representative				Governor			
	TV	D%	R%	S%	TV	D%	R%	S%
Apache	625	43	56	01	633	42	57	01
Coch.	3728	51	42	06	3738	54	39	07
Coco.	680	46	51	03	704	40	57	02
Gila	1793	57	31	12	1843	58	30	12
Graham	1150	58	33	09	1159	56	35	10
Green.	1108	54	41	05	1124	53	41	05
Mar.	4448	58	38	03	4422	51	45	03
Mohave	608	60	20	19	633	57	24	19
Navajo	701	53	46	01	724	46	53	01
Pima	1810	48	50	02	1824	48	50	02
Pinal	743	57	37	05	758	48	47	05
S.C.	568	51	45	03	567	54	42	04
Yav.	2363	52	40	08	2426	45	48	06
Yuma	1056	60	33	07	1070	60	33	07
Total	21381	54	40	06	21615	51	42	06

1912 GENERAL ELECTION

	President					U.S. Representative				
	TV	D%	R%	P%	S%	TV	D%	R%	P%	S%
Apache	255	42	22	31	04	253	53	21	22	03
Coch.	4603	43	09	30	18	4533	47	08	28	17
Coco.	860	39	28	21	11	851	44	27	18	10
Gila	2036	38	10	27	25	1979	44	10	22	24
Graham	1051	51	09	23	16	1048	54	09	20	16
Green.	1173	56	09	24	10	1257	53	09	21	16
Mar.	5672	46	11	32	08	5655	53	11	26	08
Mohave	807	40	09	28	23	805	45	09	23	23
Navajo	733	39	23	32	05	713	46	22	27	05
Pima	1792	39	19	34	06	1776	43	19	32	05
Pinal	802	44	10	39	08	785	52	09	31	07
S.C.	469	53	12	26	08	466	58	13	21	07
Yav.	2364	42	19	23	15	2375	42	28	16	14
Yuma	1070	40	09	34	18	1047	49	09	27	15
Total	23687	44	11	29	13	23545	48	13	25	13

Appendix C

1912 PROPOSITIONS

	Recall		Industrial Pursuits		Suffrage		Railroad Length		Railroad Rates	
	TV	%	TV	%	TV	%	TV	%	TV	%
Apache	195	75	177	69	217	72	173	50	183	72
Coch.	4005	85	3817	85	3941	73	3877	71	3939	86
Coco.	703	80	645	77	712	68	690	66	734	83
Gila	1735	86	1670	84	1737	70	1737	61	1764	79
Graham	1009	63	705	73	878	81	760	31	862	79
Green.	1075	85	1029	87	1071	55	1029	63	1062	83
Mar.	4578	81	4243	79	4539	66	4309	44	4498	70
Mohave	659	89	615	88	525	70	614	71	635	88
Navajo	585	79	543	80	612	66	563	60	696	59
Pima	1357	75	1305	75	1318	65	1377	49	1364	58
Pinal	675	83	630	74	678	65	619	54	644	75
S.C.	419	78	397	84	431	65	396	55	421	79
Yav.	2007	78	1832	75	1991	69	1846	53	1900	68
Yuma	991	88	872	83	994	66	946	62	956	73
Total	19977	81	18530	81	19644	68	18937	57	19658	75

Appendix C

1914 GENERAL ELECTION

	Governor					Corporation Commission				
	TV	D%	R%	P%	S%	TV	D%	R%	P%	S%
Apache	875	63	29	07	02	805	69	18	09	03
Coch.	8376	56	28	10	06	8112	58	16	15	10
Coco.	2032	48	44	06	02	1702	61	29	04	06
Gila	4515	48	34	02	15	4094	60	14	03	23
Graham	2131	51	35	05	09	2016	69	16	03	11
Green.	2204	52	38	04	06	1970	63	21	05	12
Mar.	13952	45	32	19	05	15569	57	21	16	06
Mohave	1485	64	24	02	10	1381	64	21	01	14
Navajo	1746	51	43	03	03	1709	59	28	06	06
Pima	4031	39	47	11	02	3662	52	31	11	05
Pinal	1845	46	38	13	03	1742	65	12	15	07
S.C.	1102	55	40	02	03	1028	60	28	06	06
Yav.	4604	46	41	07	06	4220	58	23	08	11
Yuma	2109	63	23	08	12	2054	68	12	08	12
Total	51007	49	35	10	06	50064	59	20	11	09

1914 PROPOSITIONS

	Prohibition		Railroad Rates		Capital Punishment		Blacklisting		80% Law		Initiative & Referendum	
	TV	%	TV	%	TV	%	TV	%	TV	%	TV	%
Apache	830	67	614	35	593	35	550	23	609	30	563	18
Coch.	7999	48	5649	79	6188	49	6319	69	7085	81	5680	65
Coco.	1907	45	1161	68	1297	53	1235	54	1479	72	1114	44
Gila	4320	47	2968	70	3413	46	3330	64	3581	77	2960	56
Graham	2105	74	1638	54	1638	54	1741	38	1851	62	1663	58
Green.	2049	50	1468	47	1580	35	1440	66	1850	65	1332	59
Mar.	13643	64	9020	52	10755	48	9704	36	10420	49	9363	39
Mohave	1383	41	937	80	1026	51	1018	67	1095	77	927	62
Navajo	1689	64	1122	50	1245	43	1181	45	1261	60	1092	43
Pima	3929	43	2585	52	2837	51	2747	43	2990	56	2577	45
Pinal	1684	48	1196	66	1403	39	1929	48	1456	60	1127	43
S.C.	1016	47	760	78	858	47	773	63	850	72	686	55
Yav.	4007	41	2742	62	3108	48	2898	52	3329	65	2629	52
Yuma	2069	51	1318	80	1485	55	1385	61	1494	66	1338	59
Total	48630	53	33178	63	37510	48	35651	51	39340	64	33051	50

1916 GENERAL ELECTION

	President					U.S. Representative				
	TV	D%	R%	S%	PR%	TV	D%	R%	S%	PR%
Apache	980	66	32	02	01	1047	54	45	01	00
Coch.	10131	60	32	07	01	10099	52	44	04	00
Coco.	2072	57	39	04	01	2200	47	50	02	00
Gila	5733	64	26	09	01	5871	63	33	05	00
Graham	2255	71	22	05	02	2318	44	52	04	00
Green.	2334	64	29	07	01	2376	58	41	01	00
Mar.	14140	54	37	04	05	14460	35	59	03	02
Mohave	2226	60	29	11	00	2253	61	32	07	00
Navajo	1881	66	31	02	02	1865	47	51	01	01
Pima	4922	42	53	03	02	4877	46	53	02	00
Pinal	2179	57	39	03	01	2228	48	50	02	01
S.C.	1442	50	46	03	01	1450	49	49	02	00
Yav.	4983	58	34	07	01	4984	48	49	03	00
Yuma	2240	59	32	08	01	2265	56	37	07	00
Total	58017	57	35	05	02	58293	48	48	03	01

1916 PROPOSITIONS

	Senate		Capital Punishment		Dept. of Labor		State Architect		Initiative & Referendum	
	TV	%	TV	%	TV	%	TV	%	TV	%
Apache	533	08	605	37	536	16	529	10	523	36
Coch.	6119	37	6363	48	6288	43	6393	29	6647	49
Coco.	1200	33	1255	45	1159	38	1160	26	1192	60
Gila	3426	55	3701	59	3456	69	3433	62	3783	38
Graham	1196	18	1309	33	1224	16	1296	11	1403	56
Green.	1407	53	1532	56	1445	56	1463	46	1491	41
Mar.	8892	22	10262	51	9334	22	9764	13	9927	52
Mohave	1291	55	1409	61	1275	69	1255	59	1135	51
Navajo	1017	30	1172	42	1135	32	1153	24	1241	39
Pima	2963	28	3306	52	3176	36	3203	22	3294	57
Pinal	1249	33	1576	47	1337	42	1378	27	1459	55
S.C.	625	38	841	45	723	41	766	28	784	55
Yav.	2826	42	3106	50	2960	46	2945	31	3132	49
Yuma	1173	36	1343	55	1242	43	1232	28	1306	39
Total	33917	34	37720	50	35290	39	35970	28	37317	49

Notes: TV — total votes; D — Democrat; R — Republican; P — Populist; S — Socialist; L — Labor; PR — Prohibition.

Creation of counties: Cochise formed from part of Pima in 1881; Gila formed from parts of Maricopa and Pinal in 1881; Graham formed from parts of Apache and Pima in 1881; Coconino formed from part of Yavapai in 1891; Navajo formed from part of Apache in 1895; Santa Cruz formed from part of Pima County in 1899; Greenlee formed from part of Graham in 1910.

APPENDIX D

ANALYSIS OF MAJOR ELECTIONS
(Precinct–Level Data)

1890s ELECTIONS
SIMPLE CORRELATIONS

Variable	Congressional Delegate 1894			Territorial Council 1894		
	Rep.	Dem.	Pop.	Rep.	Dem.	Pop.
Rep. '92	.47★★	-.30★	-.20	.53★★	-.44★★	-.19
Dem. '92	-.47★★	.30★	.20	-.53★★	.44★★	.19
East	.01	-.25★	.16	.09	-.23	.10
West	-.19	.40★★	-.10	-.23	.36★	-.06
Midwest	-.22	-.05	.22	-.26★	.04	.24★
South	-.31★★	.22	.11	-.23	.32★★	-.04
Europe	.08	-.15	.03	.08	-.19	.08
Hispanic	.48★★	-.20	-.27★	.44★★	-.28★★	-.22
Mormon	-.26★	.46★★	-.08	-.33★★	.45★★	-.04
Mining	-.16	-.54★	.49★★	-.05	-.46★★	.45★★
Farming	-.40★★	.46★★	.04	-.33★★	.49★★	-.06
Mixed	.50★★	-.12	-.35★★	.37★★	-.21	-.22

1890s ELECTIONS SIMPLE CORRELATIONS (cont.)

Congressional Delegate 1896 (N=117)				Congressional Delegate 1898 (N=131)		
Variable	Rep.	Dem.	Pop.	Variable	Rep.	Dem.
Rep. '94	.63**	-.14	-.39**	Rep. '96	.52**	-.50*
Dem. '94	.05	.56**	-.50**	Dem. '96	-.15	.15
Pop. '94	-.59**	-.28*	.70**	Pop. '96	-.30**	.28**
East	-.14	-.27*	.34**	East	-.12	.12
West	.19	.20	-.32**	West	.10	-.10
Midwest	-.07	-.11	.15	Midwest	-.15	.14
South	-.19	.06	.10	South	-.33**	.30**
Europe	-.01	-.13	.11	Europe	-.06	.06
Hispanic	.14	.12	-.21	Hispanic	.30*	-.28*
Mormon	-.08	.39**	-.26*	Mormon	-.12	.12
Mining	-.38**	-.28*	.54**	Mining	-.19	.12
Farming	-.08	.24*	-.14	Farming	-.07	.07
Mixed	.32**	-.06	-.20	Mixed	.20	-.16

Note: 1-tailed significant: * -.01; ** -.001.

REGRESSIONS

(All Variables Significant at .05 Level or Beyond in a Two-Tailed Test)

1894 Delegate Election

Democrat				Republican		
Variable	r	B	Beta	Variable	r	B	Beta
Mining	-.54	-.32	-.47	Rep. '92	.47	.47	.38
Mormon	.46	.38	.42	Hispanic	.48	.32	.37
South	.22	.28	.26	Mixed	.50	.13	.25
	R^2=.51				R^2=.48		

Populist

Variable	r	B	Beta
Mining	.49	.51	.50
Hispanic	-.27	-.26	-.26
Dem. '92	.20	.31	.21
	R^2=.36		

REGRESSIONS (*cont.*)

1894 Council Election

Democrat				Republican			
Variable	r	B	Beta	Variable	r	B	Beta
Mining	-.46	-.25	-.38	Rep. '92	.53	.59	.52
Dem. '92	.44	.23	.24	Hispanic	.44	.33	.42
Mormon	.45	.31	.36				
South	.32	.28	.27				
		$R^2=.53$				$R^2=.46$	

Populist

Variable	r	B	Beta
Mining	.45	.37	.48
Midwest	.24	.31	.27
Dem. '92	.19	.23	.21
		$R^2=.32$	

1896 Delegate Election

Democrat				Republican			
Variable	r	B	Beta	Variable	r	B	Beta
Dem. '94	.56	.61	.51	Rep. '94	.63	.60	.65
Hispanic	.12	.22	.24	Mining	-.38	-.21	-.27
Mormon	.39	.20	.18	West	.19	.21	.25
				Midwest	-.07	.18	.15
		$R^2=.38$				$R^2=.55$	

Populist

Variable	r	B	Beta
Pop. '94	.70	.57	.58
Mining	.54	.22	.23
East	.34	.41	.16
Mormon	-.26	-.18	-.13
		$R^2=.36$	

Appendix D

REGRESSIONS (*cont.*)

1898 Delegate Election

	Democrat				Republican		
Variable	r	B	Beta	Variable	r	B	Beta
South	.30	.21	.17	Rep. '96	.52	.39	.47
Pop. '96	.28	.37	.54	South	-.33	-.24	-.20
Dem. '96	.15	.45	.51	Hispanic	.30	.13	.18
Hispanic	-.28	-.14	-.18				
		R2=.33				R^2=.36	

1906–1911 ELECTIONS
SIMPLE CORRELATIONS

Congressional Delegation 1906 (N=109)

Variable	Rep.	Dem.	Soc.
Rep. '00	.34**	-.23*	-.24*
Dem. '00	-.34**	.23*	.24*
East	.03	-.06	.05
West	-.00	.14	-.23*
Midwest	-.03	-.06	.15
South	-.42**	.42**	.05
Europe	-.20	-.04	.43**
Hispanic	.31**	-.24*	-.15
Mormon	-.25*	.32**	-.09
Mining	-.16	-.12	.48**
Farming	-.28*	.47**	-.28*
Mixed	.41**	-.36**	-.13

Congressional Delegation 1908 (N=129)

Variable	Rep.	Dem.	Soc.
Rep. '06	.59**	-.51**	-.20
Dem. '06	-.45**	.59**	-.22*
Soc. '06	-.26*	-.10	.69**
East	.07	-.12	.09
West	.00	.11	-.18
Midwest	.14	-.17	.11
South	-.40**	.40**	.02
Europe	.05	-.16	.15
Hispanic	.04	-.03	-.04
Mormon	-.17	.24*	-.11
Mining	-.08	-.08	.22*
Farming	-.22*	.34**	-.11
Mixed	.31**	-.30**	-.08

1906–1911 ELECTIONS SIMPLE CORRELATIONS (cont.)

Variable	Congressional Delegation 1910 (N=137)			Vote on Constitution 1911 (N=124)	
	Rep.	Dem.	Soc.-Lab.	Variable	% Yes
Rep. '08	.62**	-.40**	-.13	Rep. '10	-.20
Dem. '08	-.55**	.55**	-.10	Dem. '10	-.05
Soc. '08	-.17	-.20*	.37**	Soc.-Lab. '10	.30**
East	.08	-.10	-.11	East	.10
West	.06	.15	-.25*	West	-.32**
Midwest	-.04	.09	-.11	Midwest	.04
South	-.45**	.23*	.15	South	.19
Europe	.04	-.35*	.39**	Europe	.17
Hispanic	.12	-.09	.07	Hispanic	.06
Mormon	-.14	.23*	-.13	Mormon	-.34**
Mining	-.06	-.34**	.53**	Mining	.20
Farming	-.24*	.40**	-.26*	Farming	-.17
Mixed	.34**	-.15	-.19	Mixed	-.20

Note: 1-tailed significant: * -.01; ** -.001.

VOTE FOR DEMOCRATIC CANDIDATES 1911

Variable	Senate	House	Governor	Secretary of State
Rep. '10	-.65**	-.71**	-.65**	-.59**
Dem. '10	.49**	.59**	.41**	.34**
Soc. '10	.07	-.00	.17	.21
Soc. '08	.16	.08	.23*	.25*
Const.	.28**	.22*	.29**	.21
East	.05	.12	-.03	-.09
West	-.01	.05	-.04	.02
Midwest	-.12	-.00	-.15	-.27*
South	.37**	.37**	.40**	.33**
Europe	-.19	-.27	-.10	-.01
Hispanic	.02	-.12	.02	.03
Mormon	.03	.10	.04	.08
Mining	-.04	-.19	.06	.16
Farming	.23*	.27*	.20	.14
Mixed	-.20	-.14	-.26*	-.03

Note: 1-tailed significant: * -.01; ** -.001

210

REGRESSIONS
(All Variables Significant at .05 Level or Beyond in a Two-Tailed Test)

1906 Delegate Election

	Democrat				Republican		
Variable	r	B	Beta	Variable	r	B	Beta
Farming	.47	.27	.52	South	-.42	-.63	-.42
South	.42	.33	.23	Mixed	.41	.14	.25
Europe	-.04	.25	.20	Rep. '00	.34	.23	.22
Mormon	.32	.49	.49	Europe	-.20	-.46	-.34
West	.14	-.30	-.43	Mormon	-.25	-.36	-.34
				East	.03	-.51	-.21
	$R^2=.43$				$R^2=.50$		

Socialist

Variable	r	B	Beta
Mining	.48	.18	.50
Hispanic	-.15	-.10	-.20
		$R^2=.27$	

1908 Delegate Election

	Democrat				Republican		
Variable	r	B	Beta	Variable	r	B	Beta
Dem. '06	.59	.44	.48	Rep. '06	.59	.44	.48
South	.40	.32	.25	South	-.40	-.33	-.24
Mixed	-.30	-.08	-.17	Mixed	.31	.08	.16
	$R^2=.44$				$R^2=.43$		

Socialist

Variable	r	B	Beta
Soc. '06	.69	.61	.70
Midwest	.11	.10	.17
		$R^2=.50$	

REGRESSIONS (cont.)

1910 Congressional Delegate Election

Democrat				Republican			
Variable	r	B	Beta	Variable	r	B	Beta
Dem. '08	.55	.69	.55	Rep. '08	.62	.52	.49
Midwest	.09	.27	.22	South	-.45	-.31	-.22
Europe	-.35	-.34	-.25	Mixed	.34	.09	.18
				Midwest	.04	-.15	-.13
	$R^2=.41$				$R^2=.47$		

Socialist-Labor

Variable	r	B	Beta
Mining	.53	.26	.48
Soc. '08	.37	.41	.23
South	.15	.23	.17
		$R^2=.37$	

1911 Elections

Dem. Governor				Dem. U.S. House			
Variable	r	B	Beta	Variable	r	B	Beta
Dem. '10	.41	.36	.46	Dem. '10	.59	.43	.57
South	.40	.48	.36	South	.37	.33	.25
Mining	.06	.15	.30	Cong. Yes	.29	.12	.24
Cong. Yes	.29	.12	.24				
Mormon	.04	.13	.17				
	$R^2=.43$				$R^2=.48$		

Dem. U.S. Senate				Dem. Sec. of State			
Variable	r	B	Beta	Variable	r	B	Beta
Dem. '10	.49	.40	.53	Dem. '10	.34	.37	.45
Cong. Yes	.28	.11	.22	Mining	.16	.21	.39
South	.37	.36	.28	South	.33	.47	.33
Mining	-.04	.08	.17				
	$R^2=.42$				$R^2=.32$		

REGRESSIONS (*cont.*)

1911 Constitution Yes

Variable	r	B	Beta
Mormon	-.34	-.47	-.31
Soc. '10	.30	.38	.19
Rep. '10	-.20	-.31	-.17
		R^2=.20	

1912 GENERAL ELECTIONS (CORRELATIONS)
(N=133)

Variable	Presidential				Congressional			
	Dem.	Rep.	Pro.	Soc.	Dem.	Rep.	Pro.	Soc.
Rep. '10	-.24*	.42	.06	-.12	-.27**	.37**	-.01	-.15
Dem. '10	.41**	-.19	.02	-.32**	.55**	-.24*	.07	-.31**
Soc. '10	-.32**	-.28**	-.12	.68**	-.49**	-.13	-.10	.71**
Recall	-.09	-.62**	.14	.42**	-.03	-.54**	.22*	.39**
Ind. Pur.	-.19	-.55**	.23*	.39**	-.18	-.48**	.31*	.42**
Suff.	-.26*	-.19	.11	.29**	-.12	-.13	.01	.26*
R. Lth.	-.27**	-.21*	.05	.45**	-.33**	-.19	.20	.42**
R. Rates	-.11	-.38**	.08	.35**	-.12	-.38**	.18	.39**
Taxes	-.09	-.50**	.22*	.27**	-.09	-.47**	.29**	.32**
East	-.05	.30**	-.15	.28**	-.05	.32**	-.18	-.07
West	.08	.27**	-.05	-.21*	.17	.19	-.11	-.21*
Midwest	-.24*	.13	.09	.01	-.13	.07	-.05	.03
South	.23*	-.28**	-.12	.07	.17	-.24*	-.00	.18
Europe	-.30**	-.09	-.09	.50**	-.40**	-.01	-.06	.46**
Hispanic	.18	-.22	.12	-.13	.11	-.20	.22*	-.17
Mormon	.12	.11	.02	-.20*	.18	.05	-.04	-.19
Mining	-.21*	-.30**	.10	.40**	-.33**	-.20*	.16	.37*
Farming	.18	-.09	.06	-.22*	.33**	-.17	.06	-.13
Mixed	-.06	.34**	.08	-.14	-.09	.32*	.14	-.20

1912 GENERAL ELECTIONS (*cont.*)

Propositions

Variable	Recall	Ind. Pur.	Suff.	R. Lth.	R. Rates	Taxes
Dem. Cong.	-.03	-.18	-.12	-.33**	-.12	-.09
Rep. Cong.	-.54**	-.48**	-.13	-.19	-.38**	-.47**
Pro. Cong.	.22*	.31**	.01	.20	.18	.29**
Soc. Cong.	.39**	.42**	.26*	.42**	.39**	.32**
East	-.21*	-.10	-.09	-.10*	-.30**	-.23*
West	-.15	-.39**	.37**	-.39**	-.12	-.20
Midwest	.03	.04	-.04	-.08	-.18	-.03
South	.23*	.22*	.10	-.02*	.11	.17
Hispanic	.13	.15	.05	.38**	.22*	.06
Mexican	-.02	.21*	-.34**	.25*	.17	.20
Mormon	-.11	-.21*	.40**	-.38**	-.03	-.10
Mining	-.19	.28**	-.14	.52**	.42**	.18
Farming	.22*	.06	.41**	-.35**	.05	.13
Mixed	-.44**	-.37**	-.30**	-.15	-.38*	-.30**

Note: 1–tailed significant: * -.01; ** -.001.

1912 ELECTIONS (REGRESSIONS)
(All Variables Significant at .05 Level or Beyond in a Two-Tailed Test)

Presidential Election

	Democrat				Republican		
Variable	r	B	Beta	Variable	r	B	Beta
Suff.	-.26	-.29	-.35	Recall	-.62	-.48	-.55
Midwest	-.24	-.26	-.34	Hispanic	-.22	-.11	-.25
Dem. '10	.41	.20	.31	Rep. '10	.42	.09	.17
Farming	.18	.06	.20	South	-.28	-.16	-.20
R. Lth.	-.27	-.09	-.17	Mining	-.30	-.08	-.25
				R. Lth.	-.21	.09	.20
		$R^2=.39$				$R^2=.56$	

	Progressive				Socialist		
Variable	r	B	Beta	Variable	r	B	Beta
Ind. Pur.	.23	.25	.26	Soc. '10	.68	.57	.58
Europe	-.09	-.29	-.36	Hispanic	-.13	-.10	-.20
South	-.12	-.22	-.23	Recall	.42	.21	.20
Mining	.10	.10	.24	R. Lth.	.45	.10	.19
				Europe	.50	.27	.34
				Mining	.40	-.13	-.33
		$R^2=.14$				$R^2=.60$	

Congressional Election

	Democrat				Republican		
Variable	r	B	Beta	Variable	r	B	Beta
Dem. '10	.55	.35	.51	Recall	-.54	-.47	-.43
Ind. Pur.	-.18	-.33	-.31	Rep. '10	.37	.15	.21
Hispanic	.11	.19	.31	Hispanic	-.20	-.10	-.17
Farming	.33	.08	.23	East	.32	.24	.15
		$R^2-.45$				$R^2=.40$	

1912 ELECTIONS (*cont.*)

Progressive				Socialist			
Variable	r	B	Beta	Variable	r	B	Beta
Ind. Pur.	.31	.39	.38	Soc. '10	.46	.64	.61
Soc. '10	-.10	-.26	-.25	Hispanic	-.17	-.17	-.30
East	-.18	-.27	-.16	Ind. Pur.	.42	.19	.19
				R. Lth.	.42	.08	.15
	R^2=.26				R^2=.62		

Proposition Voting

Recall				Industrial Pursuits			
Variable	r	B	Beta	Variable	r	B	Beta
Rep. Cong.	-.54	-.37	-.40	Rep. Cong.	-.48	-.45	-.44
Soc. Cong.	.39	.22	.25	Dem. Cong.	-.18	-.28	-.29
Mixed	-.44	-.09	-.25	West	-.39	-.14	-.26
				Mixed	-.36	-.10	-.24
	R^2=.43				R^2=.45		

Railroad Rates				Suffrage			
Variable	r	B	Beta	Variable	r	B	Beta
Mining	.42	.25	.45	Farming	.41	.16	.41
Farming	.05	.17	.41	Mormon	.40	.31	.36
Soc. Cong.	.39	.41	.31	Soc. Cong.	.26	.34	.29
Hispanic	.17	.16	.22	Europe	.05	.18	.18
	R^2=.37				R^2=.40		

Railroad Length				Taxes			
Variable	r	B	Beta	Variable	r	B	Beta
Farming	-.35	-.34	-.60	Rep. Cong.	-.47	-.30	-.46
Mining	.52	.24	.32	Dem. Cong.	-.09	-.16	-.26
Soc. Cong.	.42	.51	.29	Mixed	-.30	-.05	-.19
Pro. Cong.	.20	.34	.19	Hispanic	.20	.05	.15
Mormon	-.38	-.30	-.24				
	R^2=.42				R^2=.33		

Note: The measure restricting the length of railroads is highly correlated with other regulations sought by labor on the railroads in regard to headlights on locomotives, qualifications for engineers, number of crew members, and pay periods.

1914 GENERAL ELECTIONS (CORRELATIONS)
(N=137)

Variable	Gubernatorial				Corporation Commission			
	Dem.	Rep.	Pro.	Soc.	Dem.	Rep.	Pro.	Soc.
Dem. '12	.01	-.08	.19	-.13	.37**	-.21*	.03	-.30**
Rep. '12	-.13	.46	-.28**	-.28**	-.06	.58**	-.31**	-.24*
Pro. '12	-.04	-.06	.27**	-.22**	-.10	-.10	.38**	-.19
Soc. '12	.15	-.24*	-.23*	.58***	-.19	-.28**	-.10	.70**
Female	-.11	.14	.13	-.26**	-.11	.22*	.15	-.27**
Prohib.	-.10	-.18	.40**	-.01	-.09	-.04	.30**	-.18
R. Rates	.27**	-.25*	-.20*	.28**	-.07	-.23*	-.02	.41**
Cap. Pun.	.23*	-.43**	.13	.23**	-.18	-.19	.17	.29*
Blacklist	.26**	-.23*	-.28**	.39**	-.06	-.25	-.13	.54**
80% Law	.30**	-.25*	-.32**	.40**	.02	-.29**	-.16	.51**
I&R	.33**	-.36**	-.15	.32**	-.06	-.32**	-.01	.47**
East	-.28**	.19	.14	-.04	-.34**	.17	.25*	-.02
West	.01	.13	-.08	-.15	.16	.19	-.19	-.22*
Midwest	-.21*	-.05	.36**	-.01	-.36*	.04	.42**	-.03
South	.06	-.16	.12	.29**	.07	-.37**	.08	.23*
Europe	.36**	-.10	-.35**	-.00	.05	-.05	-.22*	.23*
Hispanic	.01	.04	-.08	.02	.09	.01	-.10	-.02
Mormon	.08	.03	-.07	-.14	.16	.13	-.16	-.20*
Mining	.24*	-.08	-.27**	.08	.08	-.15	-.16	.25*
Farming	-.14	-.12	.37**	-.01	-.12	-.10	.37**	-.15
Mixed	-.04	.24*	-.11	-.27*	.07	.32**	-.18	-.25*

Appendix D

1914 GENERAL ELECTIONS *(cont.)*

			Propositions			
Variable	Prohib.	R. Rates	Cap. Pun.	Blacklist	80% Law	I&R
Dem. Corp. Comm.	-.09	-.07	-.18	-.05	.02	-.06
Rep. Corp. Comm.	-.04	-.23*	-.19	-.24*	-.29**	-.32**
Pro. Corp. Comm.	.30**	-.02	.17	-.13	-.16	-.01
Soc. Corp. Comm.	-.18	.41**	.28**	.53**	.51**	.47**
Female	.35**	-.34**	-.15	-.39**	-.33**	-.23
East	-.18	-.15	.07	-.18	-.10	-.20*
West	.51**	-.52**	-.46**	-.53**	-.41**	-.52*
Midwest	.08	-.07	.34	-.11	-.10	-.07
South	.11	.06	.08	.11	.15	.13
Europe	-.40**	.38**	.19	.41**	.42**	.48**
Hispanic	-.24*	.30**	-.02	.30**	.15	.22*
Mormon	.58**	-.49**	-.47**	-.46**	-.33**	-.35**
Mining	-.45**	.55**	.03	.57**	.49**	.55**
Farming	.66**	-.33**	-.10	-.45**	-.40**	-.33**
Mixed	-.34**	-.13	-.01	-.10	-.07	-.21*

Note: 1-tailed significant: * -.01; ** -.001.

1914 ELECTIONS (REGRESSIONS)
(All Variables Significant at .05 Level or Beyond in a Two-Tailed Test)

Gubernatorial Election

Democrat				Republican			
Variable	r	B	Beta	Variable	r	B	Beta
Cap. Pun.	.23	.36	.38	Cap. Pun.	-.43	-.44	-.46
Europe	.36	.34	.32	Rep. Cong. '12	.46	.49	.38
Mormon	.08	.23	.25	Mormon	.03	-.19	-.20
Midwest	-.21	-.24	-.25				
	$R^2=.28$				$R^2=.37$		

Progressive				Socialist			
Variable	r	B	Beta	Variable	r	B	Beta
Prohib.	.40	.24	.43	Soc. Cong. '12	.39	.69	.81
Mormon	-.07	-.19	-.28	Europe	-.00	-.18	-.36
Midwest	.36	.17	.24	Female	-.26	-.16	-.23
Europe	-.35	-.16	-.21	Mixed	-.27	-.11	-.47
Pro. Cong. '12	.27	.18	.20	Farming	-.01	-.11	-.60
				Prohib.	-.01	.07	.20
	$R^2=.40$				$R^2=.57$		

Corporation Commission Election

Democrat				Republican			
Variable	r	B	Beta	Variable	r	B	Beta
Dem. Cong. '12	.37	.50	.51	Rep. Cong. '12	.58	.59	.63
Prohib.	-.09	-.27	-.42	South	-.37	-.20	-.23
East	-.34	-.70	-.39	Pro. Cong. '12	-.10	.18	.20
Hispanic	.09	-.21	-.35				
Midwest	-.36	-.19	-.23				
	$R^2=.41$				$R^2=.43$		

Progressive				Socialist			
Variable	r	B	Beta	Variable	r	B	Beta
Pro. Cong. '12	.38	.29	.33	Rep. Cong. '12	.70	.49	.66
West	-.19	-.13	-.27	Female	-.27	-.20	-.22
Prohib.	.30	.13	.25	South	.23	.09	.12
Farming	.37	.07	.24				
East	.25	.29	.19				
Midwest	.42	.13	.19				
	$R^2=.47$				$R^2=.55$		

1914 ELECTIONS (*cont.*)

Proposition Voting

Prohibition				Railroad Rates		
Variable	r	B	Beta	Variable	r	B	Beta
Farming	.66	.24	.42	Mormon	-.49	-.60	-.42
Mormon	.58	.48	.39	Mining	.55	.29	.34
Pro. Corp. Comm '12	.30	.40	.21	Soc. Corp. Comm. '12	.41	.61	.24
Female	.35	.31	.16	East	-.15	-.66	-.20
East	-.18	-.33	-.12				
		$R^2=.64$				$R^2=.52$	

Capital Punishment				Blacklisting		
Variable	r	B	Beta	Variable	r	B	Beta
Mormon	-.46	-.38	-.40	Soc. Corp. Comm. '14	.53	.96	.34
Midwest	.34	.33	.33	West	-.53	-.40	-.33
Soc. Corp. Comm. '14	.28	.37	.21	East	-.18	-.77	-.22
East	.07	-.42	-.20	Mining	.55	.20	.22
				Farming	-.45	-.15	-.21
				South	.11	.27	.13
		$R^2=.35$				$R^2=.63$	

80% Law				I&R		
Variable	r	B	Beta	Variable	r	B	Beta
Soc. Corp. Comm. '14	.51	1.17	.44	West	-.52	-.40	-.41
Mining	.49	.24	.28	Soc. Corp. Comm. '14	.47	.73	.31
West	-.41	-.26	-.24	Mining	.55	.19	.26
Dem. Corp. Comm. '14	.02	.31	.17	East	-.23	-.70	-.24
		$R^2=.46$				$R^2=.55$	

Note: The western variable is highly correlated with the Mormon variable, and the European-born variable is highly correlated with the mining variable. Votes on blacklisting, railroad rate regulation, the 80 percent employment law, and the old, age pension were highly intercorrelated.

1916 GENERAL ELECTIONS (CORRELATIONS)
(N=140)

Variable	Gubernatorial			Presidential		
	Dem.	Rep.	Soc.	Dem.	Rep.	Soc.
Rep. Corp. Comm. '14	-.33**	.41**	-.29**	-.30**	.48**	-.31**
Dem. Corp. Comm. '14	.36**	-.28	-.26**	.54**	-.38**	-.20*
Pro. Corp. Comm. '14	-.41**	.38**	.07	-.32**	.28**	-.11
Soc. Corp. Comm. '14	.37**	-.52**	.60*	-.02	-.36**	.75**
Rep. Regis. '16	-.54**	.59**	-.21*	-.47**	.60**	-.33**
Dem. Regis. '16	.53**	-.50**	-.05	.46**	-.43**	.12
Soc. Regis. '16	.12	-.33**	.75**	-.07	-.31**	.66**
Mis. Regis. '16	-.28**	.26**	.05	-.21*	.15	-.06
East	-.14	.12	.04	-.25*	.21*	-.01
West	-.26*	.26**	-.06	.23*	-.12	-.15
Midwest	-.24*	.22*	.04	-.29**	.26**	-.07
South	.11	-.24*	.46**	.01	-.28**	.46**
Europe	.24*	-.21*	-.04	.09	-.14	.23*
Hispanic	.21*	-.14	-.19	.01	.09	-.17
Mormon	-.26**	.29**	-.14	.30**	-.17	-.17
Mining	.40**	-.36**	-.06	.15	-.17	.23*
Farming	-.35**	.26**	.25*	.02	-.12	.04
Mixed	-.09	.18	-.33**	-.22*	.38**	-.34**

1916 GENERAL ELECTIONS (*cont.*)

Variable	Gubernatorial			Presidential		
	Dem.	Rep.	Soc.	Dem.	Rep.	Soc.
Female	-.38**	-.43**	-.24*	.05	.07	-.32**
I&R	-.19	.18	.01	-.22*	.26*	-.07
Tax. Exemp.	.32**	-.33**	.07	-.11	.06	.19
Prohib.	-.25	.22*	.11	.22*	-.23*	-.02
Local Option	.40*	-.37**	-.07	-.20*	.19	.09
Unicameral	.52**	-.59**	.33**	.00	-.25*	.55*
Death Pen.	.50**	-.57**	.32**	-.01	-.23*	.39**
Dept. of Labor	.64**	-.64**	.08	.13	-.26*	.40**
St. Architect	.59**	-.58**	.08	.04	-.18	.45**

1916 GENERAL ELECTIONS(*cont.*)

			Proposition Voting			
Variable	I&R	Local Option	Unicam. Leg.	Death Pen.	Dept. Labor	State Architect
Rep. Regis. '16	.17	-.08	-.37**	-.34**	-.44**	-.35**
Dem. Regis. '16	-.19	.10	.29**	.19	.43**	.40**
Soc. Regis. '16	.05	-.14	.31**	.14	.14	.08
Mis. Regis. '16	.10	.03	-.15	-.01	-.24*	-.31*
East	.17	.09	.06	.19	-.03	-.02
West	-.10	-.47**	-.44**	-.40**	-.36**	-.29**
Midwest	-.02	-.10	-.12	.15	-.22**	-.27**
South	.15	-.11	.16	.22*	.04	.01
Europe	-.26*	.31**	.34**	.08	.36**	.43**
Hispanic	.14	.29**	.18	.01	.22*	.18
Mormon	-.13	-.47**	-.38**	-.44**	-.30**	-.24*
Mining	-.08	.35**	.51**	.16	.61**	.65**
Farming	.05	-.53**	-.42**	-.10	-.53**	-.52**
Mixed	.28**	-.07	-.06	-.00	-.02	-.02
Female	-.03	-.21*	-.46**	-.33**	-.38**	-.45**

Note: 1-tailed significant: * -.01; ** -.001.

1916 ELECTIONS (REGRESSIONS)
Gubernatorial Election

Democrat				Republican			
Variable	r	B	Beta	Variable	r	B	Beta
Dept. Labor	.64	.32	.49	Dept. Labor	-.64	-.27	-.40
Dem. Corp. Comm. '14	.36	.40	.29	Death Pen.	-.57	-.39	-.36
Death Pen.	.50	.28	.26	Rep. Corp. Comm '14	.41	.40	.24
				Midwest	.22	.20	.18
		$R^2=.55$				$R^2=.59$	

Socialist

Variable	r	B	Beta
Soc. Corp. Comm. '14	.60	.36	.64
South	.46	.12	.28
Dept. Labor	.08	-.07	-.34
Death Pen.	.32	.06	.18
		$R^2=.54$	

Presidential Election

Democrat				Republican			
Variable	r	B	Beta	Variable	r	B	Beta
Dem. Corp. Comm. '14	.54	.49	.51	Rep. Corp. Comm. '14	.48	.40	.35
Mixed	-.22	-.12	-.28	Midwest	.26	.23	.30
Mormon	.30	.13	.17	Dept. Labor	-.26	-.13	-.28
I&R	-.22	-.12	-.16	Local Option	.19	.16	.24
				Mixed	.38	.08	.19
				Hispanic	.09	.10	.18
				I&R	.26	.12	.15
		$R^2=.42$				$R^2=.49$	

1916 ELECTIONS (cont.)

Socialist

Variable	r	B	Beta
Soc. Corp. Comm. '14	.75	.46	.63
South	.46	.20	.35
Europe	.23	.08	.17
	R^2=.67		

Propositions

Initiatives and Referenda				Local Option			
Variable	r	B	Beta	Variable	r	B	Beta
Europe	-.26	-.33	-.29	Farming	-.53	-.20	-.42
Mormon	-.13	-.19	-.19	Mormon	-.47	-.36	-.33
	R^2=.10				R^2=.38		

Unicameralism				Death Penalty			
Variable	r	B	Beta	Variable	r	B	Beta
Farming	-.42	-.20	-.33	Rep. Regis.	-.34	-.40	-.37
Soc. Regis.	.31	1.16	.26	Mormon	-.44	-.30	-.30
Rep. Regis.	-.08	-.37	-.25	Female	-.33	-.31	-.20
West	-.44	-.25	-.24	Soc. Regis.	.14	.54	.16
Female	-.46	-.48	-.23				
	R^2=.52				R^2=.41		

Dept. of Labor				State Architect			
Variable	r	B	Beta	Variable	r	B	Beta
Farming	-.53	-.28	-.39	Mining	.65	.38	.47
Mining	.61	.31	.34	Farming	-.52	-.17	-.27
Dem. Regis.	.43	.34	.26	South	.01	.36	.18
Soc. Regis.	.14	1.15	.22	Mis. Regis.	.10	-.46	-.18
South	.04	.32	.15	Female	-.02	-.40	-.18
	R^2=.56				R^2=.58		

Note: The western variable is highly correlated with the Mormon variable, and the European-born variable is highly correlated with the Mining variable.

1916 VOTING RECORDS OF PARTISANS REGISTERED IN 1916 COMPARED TO PAST PARTISAN SUPPORTERS OF 1914[1]
(SIMPLE CORRELATIONS)

	Democrats		Republicans		Socialists	
	Current	Past	Current	Past	Current	Past
I&R	-.19	-.09	.17	.08	.05	-.16
Tax. Exp.	.30**	.06	-.26**	-.05	.03	.18
Prohib.	.04	-.00	-.10	-.04	.21*	-.05
Local Option	.10	.05	-.07	-.02	-.14	.12
Unicam.	.29**	-.07	-.38**	-.07	.31**	.57**
Death Pen.	.19	.04	-.33**	-.27**	.33**	.36**
Dept. Labor	.44**	.11	-.44**	-.17	.14	.51**
St. Architect	.40**	.08	-.35**	-.07	.08	.52**
Female	-.17	-.12	.16	.15	-.29**	-.33**
East	-.27**	-.29**	.21*	.17	.04	-.01
West	.01	.16	.08	.18	-.06	-.21*
Midwest	-.49**	-.36**	.43**	.04	.12	-.04
South	.21*	.07	-.34**	-.35**	.27**	.24*
Europe	.08	.07	-.11	-.05	.01	.24*
Hispanic	.20	.08	-.16	.01	-.18	-.04
Mormon	.06	.16	.03	.13	-.08	-.20*
Mining	.30**	.10	-.36**	-.15	.04	.29**
Farming	-.21*	-.16	.08	-.12	.22*	-.11
Mixed	-.02	.05	.22*	.32**	-.39**	-.26**

Note: 1-tailed significant: * -.01; ** -.001.

[1] Based on 1914 vote for corporation commission.

APPENDIX E

POLITICAL TRENDS

TRENDS IN GROUP PARTISANSHIP: 1892–1916
(SIMPLE CORRELATIONS)

	Democrats				
Year	East	West	Mid-W	South	Eur.
1892	-.39★	.07	.01	.32★	-.02
1894	-.25	.40	-.05	.22★	-.15
1896	-.27	.20	-.11	.06★	-.13
1898	.12	-.10	.14	.30★	.06
1900	-.27	.04	-.09	.02	.16
1906	-.06	.14	-.06	.42★	-.04
1908	-.12	.11	-.17	.40★	-.16
1910	-.10	.15	.09	.23	-.35★
1911	.12	.05	-.00	.37★	-.27★
1912	-.05	.17	-.13★	.17	-.40★
1914	-.34★	.16	-.36★	.07	.05
1916	-.27	.01	-.49★	.21★	.08

Year	Hisp.	Morm.	Farm.	Min.	Mix.
1892	-.04	.24★	.35	-.04	-.33
1894	-.20	.46★	.45	-.54★	-.12
1896	.12★	.39★	.24	-.28★	-.06
1898	-.28★	.12	.07	.12	-.16
1900	.09	.18	.04	.21★	-.23
1906	-.24	.32★	.47★	-.12	-.36
1908	-.03	.24★	.34	-.08	-.30★
1910	-.09	.23	.40★	-.34	-.15
1911	-.12	.10	.27★	-.19★	-.14
1912	.11	.18	.33★	-.33	-.09
1914	.09	.16	.12	.08	.07
1916	.20	.06	-.21	.30★	-.02

TRENDS IN GROUP PARTISANSHIP (cont.)

Republicans

Year	East	West	Mid-W	South	Eur.	Hisp.	Morm.	Farm.	Min.	Mix.
1892	.39*	-.06	-.01	-.32*	.02	.04	-.24*	-.36	.04	.33
1894	.01	-.19	-.22	-.31	.08	.48*	-.26	-.40*	-.16*	.50
1896	-.14	.19	-.07	-.19	-.01	.14	-.08*	-.08*	-.38*	.32
1898	-.12	.10	-.15*	-.33*	-.06	.30*	-.12	-.07	-.19	.20
1900	.27*	-.04	.09	-.02	-.16	-.09	-.18	-.05	-.21*	.23
1906	.03	-.00	-.03	-.42*	-.20*	.31	-.25*	-.28	-.16	.41*
1908	.07	.00	.14	-.40*	.05	.04	-.17	-.22	-.08	.31*
1910	.08	.06	-.04	-.45*	.04	.12	-.14	-.14	-.06	.34*
1911	-.12	-.05	.00	-.37*	.27	.12	-.10	-.27*	.19	.14
1912	.32*	.19*	.07	-.24	-.01	-.20	.05	-.17*	-.20	.32
1914	.17	.19	.04	-.37*	-.05	.01	.13	-.10	-.15*	.32*
1916	.21	.08	.43*	-.34*	-.11	-.16	.03	.08	-.36*	.22

Populists

Year	East	West	Mid-W	South	Eur.	Hisp.	Morm.	Farm.	Min.	Mix.
1894	.16	-.10	.22	.11	.03	-.27*	-.08	.04	.49*	-.35
1896	.34	-.32*	.15	.10	.11	-.21*	-.26	-.14	.54*	-.20

TRENDS IN GROUP PARTISANSHIP (cont.)

Socialists

Year	East	West	Mid-W.	South	Eur.	His.	Morn.	Farm.	Min.	Mix.
1906	.05	-.23	.15	.05	.43	-.15★	-.09	-.28	.48★	-.13
1908	.09	-.18	.11	.02	.15	-.04	-.11	-.11	.22★	-.08
1910	-.11	-.25	-.11	.15★	.39	.07	-.13	-.26	.53★	-.19
1912	-.07	-.21	.03	.18★	.46★	-.17	-.19	-.13	.37	-.20
1914	-.02	-.22	-.03	.23★	.23	-.02	-.20	-.15	.25★	-.25
1916	.04	-.06	.12	.27★	.01	-.18	-.08	.22	.04	-.39★

Progressives

Year	East	West	Mid-W.	South	Eur.	Hisp.	Morn.	Farm.	Min.	Mix.
1912	-.18	-.11	-.05	-.00	-.06	.22★	-.04	.06	.16	.14
1914	.25	-.19★	.42★	.08	-.22	-.10	-.16	.37★	-.16	-.18

Note: From 1892 to 1908, elections covered are for territorial delegate to Congress. Elections covered in 1910 are for delegates to the constitutional convention, in 1911 and 1912 for single seat in the U.S. House of Representatives, and in 1914 for Corporation Commission. In 1916 party registration figures are used. Figures reported are simple correlations.

★ Refers to variables that were significant at .05 level or beyond when all variables were entered into the same equation.

GROUPS, PARTIES AND, ISSUES: 1912, 1914, 1916

Yr./Iss.	East	West	Mid-W.	South	Eur.	Hisp.	Morm.	Farm.	Min.	Mix.
(1912)										
Recall	-.21	-.15	.03	.23	.13	-.02	-.11	.22	-.19	-.44*
Ind. Pur.	-.10	-.39*	.04	.22	.15	.21	-.21	.06	.28	-.37*
Suff.	-.09	.37	-.04	.10	.15*	-.34	.40*	.41*	-.14	-.30
R. Lth.	-.10	-.39	-.08	-.02	.38	.25	-.38*	-.35*	.52*	-.15
R. Rate	-.30	-.12	-.18	.11	.22	.17*	-.03	.05	.42*	-.38
Tax	-.23	-.20	-.03	.17	.06	.20*	-.10	.13	.18	-.30*
(1914)										
Prohib.	-.18*	.51	.08	.11	-.40	-.24	.58*	.66	-.45*	-.34
R. Rate.	-.15*	-.52	-.07	.06	.38	.30	-.49*	-.33	.55*	-.13
Cap. Pun.	.07	-.46	.34*	.08	.19	-.02	-.47*	-.10	.03	-.18
Blacklist	-.18*	-.53*	-.11	.11*	.41	.30	-.46	-.45*	.57*	-.10
80% Law	-.10	-.41*	-.10	.15	.42	.15	-.33	-.40	.49*	-.07
I&R	-.20*	-.52*	-.07	.13	.48	.22	-.35	-.33	.55*	-.21
(1916)										
I&R	.17	-.10	-.02	.15	-.26*	.14	-.13*	.05	-.08	.28
Local Option	.09	-.47	-.10	-.11	.31	.29	.35	-.53*	.35	-.07
Unicam. Leg.	.06	-.44	-.12*	.16	.34	.18	-.38	-.42*	.51	-.06
Death Pen.	.19	-.40	.15	.22	.08	.01	-.44*	-.10	.16	.19
Dept. Lab.	-.03	-.36	-.22	.04*	.36	.22	-.30	-.53*	.61*	-.02
St. Architect	-.02	-.29	-.27	.01*	.43	.18	-.24	-.52*	.65*	-.02

GROUPS, PARTIES, AND ISSUES (*cont.*)

Yr./Iss.	Dem.	Rep.	Soc.	Farm.
(1912)				
Recall	-.03	-.54★	.39★	
Ind. Pur.	-.18★	-.48★	.42	
Suff.	-.12	-.13	.26★	
R. Lth.	-.33	-.19	.42★	
R. Rate	-.12	-.38	.39	
Tax	-.09	-.47★	.32	
(1914)				
Prohib.	-.09	-.04	-.18	.35★
R. Rate	-.07	-.23	.41★	-.34
Cap. Pun.	-.18	-.19	.28★	-.15
Blacklist	-.05	-.24	.53★	-.39
80% Law	.02	-.29	.51★	-.33
I&R	-.06	-.32	.47★	-.23
(1916)				
I&R	-.19	.17	.05	-.03
Local Option	.10	-.08	-.14	-.21
Unicam. Leg.	.29	-.37★	.31★	-.46★
Death Pen.	.19	-.34★	.14★	-.33★
Dept. Lab.	.43★	-.44	.14★	-.38
St. Architect	.40	-.35	.08	-.45★

Note: Elections covered are for single seat in the U.S. House of Representatives in 1912, for Corporation Commission in 1914. In 1916 party registration figures are used. Figures reported are simple correlations.

★ Refers to variables that were significant at .05 level or beyond when all variables were entered into the same equation.

REGRESSION OF PARTISANSHIP BY ETHNOCULTURAL, ECONOMIC, AND ISSUE VARIABLES: 1912, 1914, 1916

1912
(Congressional Election)

Variable	Democrat r	B	Beta	Variable	Republican r	B	Beta
R. Lth.	-.33	-.16	-.26	Recall	-.54	-.51	-.47
Midwest	-.13	-.24	-.30	Hispanic	-.20	-.11	-.19
Mixed	-.09	-.11	-.25	South	-.24	-.17	-.17
Suff.	-.12	-.30	-.35	East	.32	.27	.17
Mining	-.33	-.19	-.43				
Recall	-.03	.22	.19				
	$R^2=.33$				$R^2=.38$		

Variable	Progressive r	B	Beta	Variable	Socialist r	B	Beta
Ind. Pur.	.31	.32	.31	Europe	.46	.40	.48
				Ind. Pur.	.42	.27	.26
				South	.18	.24	.24
				Suff.	.26	.13	.15
	$R^2=.10$				$R^2=.41$		

1914
(Corporation Commission Election)

Variable	Democrat r	B	Beta	Variable	Republican r	B	Beta
Midwest	-.36	-.22	-.26	South	-.37	.31	-.35
East	-.34	-.38	-.22	Mining	-.15	-.07	-.20
				Mixed	.32	.07	.19
				Cap. Pun.	-.19	-.11	-.16
	$R^2=.17$				$R^2=.25$		

REGRESSION OF PARTISANSHIP (*cont.*)

Progressive				Socialist		
Variable	r	B	Beta	Variable	r	B	Beta
Midwest	.42	.16	.24	Blacklist	.54	.20	.57
Farming	.37	.08	.27	Mixed	-.25	-.06	-.18
West	-.19	-.18	-.36	Hispanic	-.02	-.07	-.17
Prohib.	.30	.15	.28				
		$R^2=.36$				$R^2=.35$	

1916
(Party Registration)

Democrat				Republican		
Variable	r	B	Beta	Variable	r	B	Beta
Midwest	-.49	-.52	-.41	Midwest	.43	.37	.38
Dept. Lab.	.43	.23	.31	South	-.34	-.43	-.34
South	.21	.32	.20	I&R	.17	.14	.16
I&R	-.19	-.24	-.20	Mining	-.36	-.14	-.28
				Death Pen.	-.33	-.22	-.23
		$R^2=.41$				$R^2=.48$	

Socialist			
Variable	r	B	Beta
Mixed	-.39	-.06	-.33
Death Pen.	.33	.08	.26
Female	-.29	-.09	-.18
Hispanic	-.18	-.04	-.18
		$R^2=.29$	

VOTING TURNOUT: 1890–1920

Election Year	Voting Pop.	Turnout Cong.	Percent Voting
1890	26,472	11,078	42
1892	29,994	11,641	39
1894	33,516	13,427	40
1896	37,038	14,050	38
1898	40,566	15,595	38
1900	44,081	16,330	37
1902	50,075	18,955	38
1904	56,069	21,220	38
1906	62,063	22,088	36
1908	68,057	26,074	38
1911	77,882	21,381	27
1912	81,113	23,545	29
1914	151,775	44,665	29
1916	163,827	52,344	32
1918	175,878	44,381	25
1920	187,929	61,238	33

Note: The estimated voting population is based on census figures on males of voting age for 1890 to 1912 and males and females of voting age for 1914 to 1920. Elections are for single seat in the U.S. House of Representatives. Based on the few total turnout figures available, total turnout was from 3 to 4 percent higher than the percentages given in the table.

NOTES

INTRODUCTION

1. See literature review by Arthur S. Link and Richard L. McCormick, *Progressivism* (Arlington Heights, Ill.: Harlan Davidson, 1983).

2. Political reform efforts differ little from social or protest movements. The terms "political" and "reform" were chosen to more directly focus attention on the goals of the movement rather than its source (society) or methods of attaining goals (protest). The term "effort" was chosen to indicate more diverse and decentralized activity than suggested by the term "movement."

    For a discussion of collective behavior, see Neil J. Smelser, *Theory of Collective Behavior* (New York: Free Press, 1962); and Roberta Ash, *Social Movements in America* (Chicago: Markham Publishing Co., 1972). On protest movements, see Michael Unseem, *Protest Movements in America* (Indianapolis: Bobbs-Merrill, 1975). For reviews of the large body of relevant literature, see Frances Fox Piven and Richard A. Cloward, *Poor People's Movements: Why They Succeed, How They Fail* (New York: Vintage Books, 1979), 1–40; and Norman I. Fainstein and Susan S. Fainstein, *Urban Political Movements* (Englewood Cliffs, N.J.: Prentice-Hall, 1974), appendix. Particularly relevant on mobilization theory are Donna A. Barnes, *Farmers in Rebellion: The Rise and Fall of the Southern Farmers Alliance and People's Party in Texas* (Austin: University of Texas Press, 1984), who generally reviews the literature and examines structural strain and mobilization theories in light of the history of the Texas Alliance organization; Scott G. McNall, *The Road to Rebellion: Class Formation and Kansas Populism, 1865–1900* (Chicago: University of Chicago Press, 1988); and John McCarthy and Mayer Zald, "Resource Mobilization and Social Movements: A Partial Theory," *American Journal of Sociology* 82 (1977): 1212–1241.

3. See, for example, Martin J. Sklar, *The Corporate Reconstruction of American Capitalism, 1890–1916* (Cambridge: Cambridge University Press, 1988). The term "anti-monopoly reform effort" is appropriate to describe the type of reform activity at the heart of the Populist crusade in the Mountain West. See Robert W. Larson, *Populism in the Mountain West* (Albuquerque: University of New Mexico Press, 1986). In the longer reform effort, one in which Socialists and non-Socialist progressives as well as Populists participated, however, the central link among

reformers was the focus on the abuses of corporations rather than on corporate size or market power.

4. On states as "meeting places," see Lorrin Kennamer, introduction to D. W. Meinig, *Imperial Texas: An Interpretive Essay in Cultural Geography* (Austin: University of Texas Press, 1969).

5. See Rodman W. Paul, *Mining Frontiers of the Far West, 1848–1880* (New York: Holt, Rinehart, and Winston, 1963).

6. On "first effective settlement," see Wilbur Zelinsky, *The Cultural Geography of the United States* (Englewood Cliffs, N.J.: Prentice-Hall, 1973), 23; and Raymond D. Gastil, *Cultural Regions of the United States* (Seattle: University of Washington Press, 1975), 27–28.

7. Charles F. Willis, *Arizona State Bureau of Mines Bulletin* 3 (1915–1916): 6.

8. *Ibid.*

CHAPTER 1

1. James Buchanan, second annual message, December 6, 1858, in *Messages and Papers of the Presidents, 1789–1897,* ed. James D. Richardson (Washington, D.C.: GPO, 1899), 5: 514.

2. Quoted material is from documents attached as appendix material to B. Sacks, *Be it Enacted: The Creation of the Territory of Arizona* (Phoenix Arizona Historical Foundation, 1964), 134.

3. John A. Gurley, speech presented in the House of Representatives, May 8, 1862, in the George W.P. Hunt Collection, Arizona Collection, Arizona State University.

4. Manuel P. Servin, *An Awakened Minority: The Mexican-Americans,* 2d ed. (Beverly Hills: Glencoe Press, 1974), 28–30.

5. George H. Kelly, ed., *Legislative History of Arizona, 1864–1912* (Phoenix, Ariz.: Manufacturing Stationers, Inc., 1926), 81.

6. Charles D. Poston, *Building a State in Apache Land* (Tempe, Ariz.: Aztec Press, 1963), 122.

7. *Arizona Miner,* May 1, 1869, p. 2.

8. *Ibid.,* February 20, 1869, p. 2.

9. See Rufus K. Wyllys, *Arizona: The History of a Frontier State* (Phoenix Arizona Historical Foundation, 1950), 183.

10. *Arizona Miner,* September 24, 1870, p. 1.

11. See, for example, an account by Representative Selim M. Franklin in Kelly, *op. cit.,* 305–307.

12. John Nicholson, ed., *The Arizona of Joseph Pratt Allyn* (Tucson University of Arizona Press, 1974), 70.

13. Kelly, *op. cit.,* 9.

14. Poston, *op. cit.*, 121.

15. Samuel P. Hays, *The Response to Industrialization, 1885–1914* (Chicago: University of Chicago Press, 1957), 17.

16. *Arizona Citizen*, October 15, 1870, p. 2.

17. William H. Lyon, "The Corporate Frontier in Arizona," *Journal of Arizona History* 9 (1968): 1–17.

18. *Arizona Silver Belt*, January 19, 1884, p. 2.

19. *Ibid.*, May 2, 1879, p. 1.

20. See Clark C. Spence, *British Investments and the American Mining Frontier, 1860–1901* (Ithaca: Cornell University Press, 1958).

21. For background on mining entrepreneurs in Arizona, see Robert Glass Cleland, *A History of Phelps Dodge, 1834–1950* (New York: Knopf, 1952); and Herbert V. Young, *Ghosts of Cleopatra Hill* (Jerome, Ariz.: Jerome Historical Society, 1964).

22. Rodman W. Paul, *California Gold: The Beginning of Mining in the Far West* (Cambridge, Mass.: Harvard University Press, 1947), 332–333.

23. Servin, *op. cit.*, 28–30, 34.

24. Victor S. Clark, "Mexican Labor in the United States," *Bulletin of the Bureau of Labor* (September 1908): 466–522.

25. See David J. Weber, ed., *Foreigners in Their Native Land: Historical Roots of the Mexican Americans* (Albuquerque: University of New Mexico Press, 1973), 204–260.

26. James D. McBride, "The Development of Labor Unions in Arizona Mining 1884 to 1919" (M.A. Thesis, Arizona State University, 1974), 35. See also John Rowe, *The Hard-Rock Men: Cornish Immigrants and the North American Mining Frontier* (New York: Harper and Row Publishers, Inc., Barnes and Nobel Import Division, 1974), 215–227.

27. *Report of the Territorial Governor*, 1905.

28. Vernon H. Jensen, *Heritage of Conflict: Labor Relations in the Nonferrous Metals Industry Up to 1930* (Ithaca: Cornell University Press, 1950), 355.

29. *Report of the Territorial Governor*, 1893, 53.

30. Jay Wagoner, *Arizona Territory: 1863–1912* (Tucson: University of Arizona Press, 1990), 205.

31. *Report of the Territorial Governor*, 1897, 8.

32. See Rodolfo Acuna, *Occupied America: The Chicano's Struggle Toward Liberation* (San Francisco: Canfield Press, 1972), 89–93.

33. Rowe, *op. cit.*, 215.

34. Maurice Duverger, *Political Parties: Their Organization and Activity in the Modern State* (New York: Wiley, 1954), 278.

35. "Home Makers to the Front," editorial in the *Prescott Courier*, quoted in the *Arizona*

Republican, October 9, 1897, p. 2.

36. See, for example, letter from W. K. Meade, member of the Democratic National Committee for Arizona, to Lucius Q.C. Lamar, secretary of interior, August 4, 1885, in the National Archives and Records Service, *General Records of the Department of the Interior, Appointment Papers: Arizona Territory, 1857–1907,* Record Group 48. See also John Myers, *The Last Chance: Tombstone's Early Years* (New York: Dutton, 1950), 102–103.

37. H. A. Hubbard, "The Arizona Enabling Act and President Taft's Veto," *Pacific Historical Review* 3 (1934): 307–322.

38. *Ibid.,* 308.

39. As an 1889 editorial in the *Globe Silver Belt* put it: "Nevada had a greater population when admitted into the union than Arizona has today, and in other respects was better fitted to support a state government, and yet as a state has been a conspicuous failure. There is no indication for self government within the next five years, and in order to be eligible then, the boom will have to come soon" (quoted in the *Arizona Journal Miner,* July 13, 1889).

40. Proceedings as recorded in the *Phoenix Herald,* September 24, 1891, pp. 6–9.

41. Quote from Hubbard, *op. cit.,* 308.

42. James H. McClintock, *Arizona: The Youngest State* (Chicago: S. J. Clarke, 1916), 388–389.

43. Quoted by Arthur Schlesinger, *Political and Social History of the United States, 1829–1925* (New York: The Macmillan Company, 1925), 393.

44. Governor Kibbey, quoted in Kelly, *op. cit.,* 248.

45. Message of Governor Louis C. Hughes to the eighteenth legislative assembly, January 23, 1895.

46. *Territorial Report of the Governor,* 1895, 53.

47. Kelly, *op. cit.,* 78.

48. See articles on the convention in the *Phoenix Herald,* September 24, 1891, and the *Daily Arizona Journal Miner,* September 28, 1891.

49. Letter from Mrs. L. C. Hughes to Morris Goldwater, December 14, 1898, in the Morris Goldwater Collection, Arizona Foundation.

50. Carrie Chapman Catt and Nettie Rogers Shuler, *Woman Suffrage and Politics* (New York: Charles Scribner's Sons, 1923), 128–129.

51. Editorial, *Phoenix Republican,* quoted in the *Daily Arizona Journal Miner,* October 19, 1891, p. 2.

52. Annual report of Governor N. O. Murphy, quoted in the *Graham County Guardian,* October 19, 1894, p. 1.

53. *The Oasis,* October 25, 1894, p. 2.

54. See discussion by Keith J. Melville, "Political Conflict and Accommodation in Utah since Statehood," in *"Soul-Butter and Hog Wash,"* ed. Thomas G. Alexander,

Notes

Charles Redd Monographs (Provo, Utah: Brigham Young University Press, 1978), 139–141.

55. Editorial, *Phoenix Herald*, December 27, 1884, p. 1.

56 *Prescott Journal Miner*, July 25, 1889.

57. *Daily Arizona Journal Miner*, September 11, 1891, p. 2.

58. See Eugene E. Williams, "The Territorial Governors of Arizona," *Arizona Historical Review* 7 (January 1936): 69–84.

59. McClintock, *op. cit.*, 38.

60. Peter Lyon, *To Hell in a Day Coach* (Philadelphia: Lippincott, 1968), 66. A contemporary account of the free pass evil is found in George W. Berge, *The Free Pass Bribery System* (Lincoln, Nebr.: Independent Publishing Company, 1905; New York: Arno Press, 1974).

61. *Ibid.*, 31.

62. *Message to the Legislature*, 1895, 14.

63. McClintock, *op. cit.*, 333.

64. *Message to the Legislature*, 1893, 10.

65. *Arizona: A State Guide* (New York: Hastings House Publishers, 1940), 96.

66. McBride, *op. cit.*

67. Will Robinson, *The Story of Arizona* (Phoenix, Ariz.: The Berryhill Company, 1919), 287.

68. See, for example, *Report of the President's Mediation Commission to the President of the United States* (Washington, D.C.: GPO, 1918), 4.

69. Duane A. Smith, *Rocky Mountain Mining Camps: The Urban Frontier* (Bloomington: Indiana University Press, 1967), 39.

70. A. Blake Brophy, *Foundlings on the Frontier* (Tucson: University of Arizona Press, 1972), xi–xii.

71. See Smith, *op. cit.*, 202–203.

72. Patrick Hamilton, *The Resources of Arizona* (San Francisco: Bancroft Co., 1884), 156.

73. *Arizona: A State Guide, op. cit.*, 97.

74. Smith, *op. cit.*, 202–203.

75. Servin, *op. cit.*, 36.

76. *Mohave County Miner*, August 12, 1893, p. 3.

77. *Ibid.*

78. *Ibid.*, August 26, 1893, p. 2.

79. *Report of the Governor of Arizona*, 1889, 4–5.

80. Charles F. Willis, "Arizona," *Arizona State Bureau of Mines Bulletin* (1915–1916): 5.

81. *Phoenix Herald,* October 18, 1895, pp. 1, 3.

82. *Governor's Message,* 1895, 18.

83. Lawrence Goodwyn, *Democratic Promise: The Populist Movement in America* (New York: Oxford University Press, 1976), 173, 226.

84. Bert Haskett, "History of the Sheep Industry in Arizona," *Arizona Historical Review* 8 (1936): 3–49.

85. Colin Cameron, "Report of Colin Cameron," in *Report of the Territorial Governor to the Secretary of the Interior,* 1896, 20–25.

86. James A. Wilson, "Cattle and Politics in Arizona, 1886–1941" (Ph.D. Dissertation, University of Arizona, 1967), 72.

CHAPTER 2

1. Joseph H. Kibbey, "Republican Outlook," *Rita* 2 (February 23, 1896): 11–12.

2. William O'Neill, "Populist Outlook," *Rita* 2 (February 23, 1896): 13.

3. *Report of the Governor,* 1893, 54.

4. Will Robinson, *The Story of Arizona* (Phoenix, Ariz.: The Berryhill Company, 1919), 170.

5. On campaigning in the territorial period, see the Barnes Manuscript Collection, Arizona Collection, Arizona State University; and Odie B. Faulk, *Tombstone: Myth and Reality* (New York: Oxford University Press, 1972), 193.

6. See David R. Berman, *Parties and Elections in Arizona, 1863–1984* (Tempe: Morrison Institute, Arizona State University, 1985).

7. *Report of the Governor of Arizona,* 1889, 4.

8. See petition to Benjamin Harrison from Mexican citizens on behalf of Safford, National Archives and Records Service, Washington, D.C., Interior Department, *Appointment Papers: Arizona Territory, Governors, 1857–1907,* Record Group 48 (n.d.).

9. See E. B. Fincher, *Spanish-Americans as a Political Factor in New Mexico, 1912–1950* (New York: Arno Press, 1974), 102–103.

10. See letter from John M. Fair to Grover Cleveland regarding Hughes' appointment, *Appointment Papers, op. cit.*

11. On the Hughes affair, see newspaper article from the *Douglas Democrat,* Tucson (n.d.), in *Appointment Papers, op. cit.;* and O'Neill's defense of Hughes in a letter to President Cleveland on July 28, 1895, in the Cleveland Papers (Library of Congress, microfilm). See also letter from Hughes to Hon. Henry T. Thuber, June 15, 1895, in the Cleveland Papers.

12. On goldbugs, see letter from J.L.B. Alexander, president, and Frank Baxter, secretary, of the Cleveland Club to President Cleveland, April 10, 1895, in *Appointment Papers, op. cit.*

13. See Howard Lamar, *The Far Southwest: 1846–1912* (New York: Norton, 1970), 501.

14. See Majorie Haines Wilson, "The Gubernatorial Career of George W.P. Hunt" (Ph.D. Dissertation, Arizona State University, 1973).

15. Peter Clark McFarlane, "The Galahad of Arizona: Governor Hunt," *Colliers* (April 15, 1916): 21–27.

16. *Report to the Secretary of Interior*, 1881, 918.

17. *Arizona Journal Miner*, May 21, 1892, p. 2.

18. *Arizona Silver Belt*, January 18, 1896, p. 2.

19. *Arizona Journal Miner*, October 17, 1894, p. 2.

20. *Arizona Silver Belt*, September 13, 1890, p. 1.

21. See Jay Wagoner, *Arizona Territory: 1863–1912* (Tucson: University of Arizona Press, 1970), 94–95.

22. See J. W. Spear, *"Uncle Billy" Remembers* (Phoenix, Arizona Republic and Gazette, 1940), 3–4.

23. Letter from John H. Carpenter, member of the territorial council and nineteenth legislature and speaker of the House of Representatives, to Hon. George C. Perkings, U.S. senator, December 15, 1896, in *Appointment Papers, op. cit.*

24. *Alta Arizona*, June 17, 1882, p. 2.

25. *Mohave County Miner*, July 23, 1892, p. 2.

26. *Ibid.*

27. John D. Hicks, *The Populist Revolt: A History of the Farmer's Alliance and the People's Party* (Minneapolis: University of Minnesota Press, 1931), 301.

28. Paul W. Glad, *McKinley, Bryan, and the People* (Philadelphia: Lippincott, 1964), 67.

29. Hicks, *op. cit.*

30. Glad, *op. cit.,* 197.

31. *Weekly Phoenix Herald*, October, 11, 1894, p. 1. For other commentary on the People's party in Arizona, see letters to George W.P. Hunt from Frank L. Gates, September 28, 1892, and from Henry C. Roemer, July 7, 1892. Gates contended the People's party had no following outside of Globe. Roemer, having attended a meeting of the People's party, concluded that it would have a short life. Both letters are in the George W.P. Hunt Collection, Arizona Collection, Arizona State University.

32. *Arizona Daily Gazette*, October 7, 1892, p. 1.

33. *Arizona Silver Belt*, November 15, 1890, p. 1.

34. *Ibid.,* October 15, 1892, p. 1.

35. See generally Ralph Keithly, *Buckey O'Neill* (Caldwell, Idaho: The Caxton Press, 1949).

36. James H. McClintock, *Arizona: The Youngest State* (Chicago: S. J. Clarke, 1916), 523.

37. Keithly, *op. cit.*, 174.

38. Buckey O'Neill, *An Open Letter to Hon. N. O. Murphy and John C. Herndon*, October 12, 1894, in the Buckey O'Neill Collection, Sharlot Hall Museum, Prescott, Arizona.

39. *Ibid.*

40. *Arizona Populist*, September 29, 1894, p. 2; *Tombstone Epitaph*, November 2, 1896.

41. Statement of the People's party of Maricopa County, *Arizona Republican*, August 19, 1896, p. 1. See also statement of principles in the *Arizona Populist*, September 29, 1894, p. 1; and the platform of the People's party of Cochise County in the *Tombstone Epitaph*, November 2, 1896.

42. *Arizona Populist*, September, 24, 1894, p. 2.

43. *Ibid.*

44. *Open Letter, op. cit.*

45. *Ibid.*

46. *Ibid.*

47. *Ibid.*

48. *Ibid.*

49. *Ibid.*

50. Platform of the People's party of Maricopa County, September 29, 1894.

51. *Arizona Republican*, August 19, 1896, p. 1.

52. *Open letter, op. cit.*

53. *Ibid.*

54. *Ibid.*

55. *Ibid.*

56. See *Arizona Weekly Journal Miner*, September 19, 1894.

57. Editorial, *Phoenix Herald*, quoted in the *Arizona Journal Miner*, November 28, 1894, p. 2.

58. *Prescott Weekly Courier*, November 16, 1894, p. 1.

59. *Arizona Gazette*, November 17, 1894, in the Buckey O'Neill Scrapbook, Sharlot Hall Museum, Prescott, Arizona, 47.

60. *Tucson Star*, October 13, 1894, in the Buckey O'Neill Scrapbook, *ibid.*

61. "Another Open Letter," from A. A. Long to William O'Neill, October 19, 1896, in the Buckey O'Neill Collection, Sharlot Hall Museum.

62. *Mohave County Miner*, July 7, 1894, p. 2; October 27, 1894, p. 4; and December 27, 1894, p. 2.

63. O'Neill, "Populist Outlook," *op. cit.*, 12.

64. *Our Mineral Wealth,* November 15, 1897, p. 2; and August 24, 1900, p. 2.

65. *Arizona Republican,* August 19, 1896, p. 4.

66 *Ibid.,* September 23, 1896, p. 1.

67. Spear, *op. cit.,* p. 15.

68. *Arizona Republican,* September 25, 1896, p. 1.

69. *Mohave County Miner,* October 31, 1896, n.p.

70. Will C. Barnes, "Autobiography of a Pioneer," in Barnes Manuscript Collection, Arizona Collection, Arizona State University, 238.

71. See appendix material; and David R. Berman, "Electoral Support for Populism in the Mountain States: Some Evidence from Arizona" *Social Science Journal* 24 (January 1987): 43–52.

72. See *Report of the Governor,* 1895, 81.

73. *Arizona Daily Gazette,* October 8, 1892, p. 2.

74. Berman, "Electoral Support for Populism," *op. cit.*

75. Vernon H. Jensen, *Heritage of Conflict: Labor Relations in the Nonferrous Metals Industry Up to 1930* (Ithaca: Cornell University Press, 1950), 256–259.

76. See Stanley B. Parsons, *The Populist Context: Rural Versus Urban Power on a Great Plains Frontier* (Westport, Conn.: Greenwood Press, 1973).

77. Robert W. Cherny, *Populism, Progressivism, and the Transformation of Nebraska Politics, 1885–1915* (Lincoln: University of Nebraska Press, 1981), 62.

78. *Arizona Silver Belt,* October 15, 1892, p. 1.

79. *Arizona Populist,* September 22, 1894, p. 2.

80. *Arizona Silver Belt,* November 3, 1894, p. 2.

81. See William J. Gaboury, "From State House to Bull Pen: Idaho Populism and the Coeur d'Alene Troubles of the 1890's," *Pacific Northwest Quarterly* (January 1967): 16.

82. J. S. Hilizinger, "The People's Party," *Arizona Magazine* 1 (1893): 22.

83. On class radicalism among workers, see Melvin Dubofsky, "The Origins of Western Working Class Radicalism, 1890–1905," *Labor History* 7 (1966): 131–154.

84. Letter from O'Neill to James McClintock, November 7, 1897, in the McClintock Collection, Phoenix Public Library.

85. Letter from O'Neill to James McClintock, July 14, 1897, in the McClintock Collection, Phoenix Public Library.

86. Letter from Frances W. Munds to James McClintock, April 4, 1915, in the McClintock collection, Phoenix Public Library.

87. Letter from Harry Nash to G. W. Hunt, August 21, 1898, in the Hunt Collection, Arizona Collection.

88. Cherny makes the same point in regard to Nebraska Populists (*op. cit.*, 51).
89. *Arizona Silver Belt,* September 17, 1896, p. 3.
90. *Arizona Republican,* August 19, 1898, p. 1.
91. *Arizona Silver Belt,* October 13, 1898, p. 2.
92. *Arizona Silver Belt,* November 17, 1898, p. 1.
93. O'Neill, *Open Letter, op. cit.*

CHAPTER 3

1. See Richard E. Sloan, *Memories of an Arizona Judge* (Stanford: Stanford University Press, 1932), 205.
2. See, for example, *Mohave County Miner,* August 17, 1901, p. 1.
3. Quoted material from a statement by delegate Marcus A. Smith before the Committee on Territories, U.S. Senate, *Senate Documents,* Vol. 5, 57th Cong., 2d sess., 1902–1903, 320.
4. See H. A. Hubbard, "The Arizona Enabling Act and President Taft's Veto," *Pacific Historical Review* 3 (1934): 307–322.
5. See John E. Braeman, *Albert J. Beveridge : American Nationalist* (Chicago: University of Chicago Press, 1971), 82–83.
6. The letters are discussed by Claude G. Bowers, *Beveridge and the Progressive Era* (Cambridge: Houghton Mifflin Company, The Riverside Press, 1932), 183.
7. Braeman, *op. cit.,* 84.
8. See H. A. Hubbard, "Arizona's Struggle Against Joint Statehood," *Pacific Historical Review* 11 (1942): 415–423.
9. Hubbard, "Arizona Enabling Act," *op. cit.,* 315.
10. Braeman, *op. cit.,* 96.
11. Quoted by George H. Kelly, ed., *Legislative History of Arizona, 1864–1912* (Phoenix, Ariz.: Manufacturing Stationers, Inc., 1926), 240.
12. Braeman, *op. cit.,* 91.
13. See *The Statehood Bill,* speech of Hon. Albert J. Beveridge of Indiana, Senate of the United States, Thursday, March 8, 1906, in the George W.P. Hunt Collection, Arizona Collection, Arizona State University.
14. Smith's account of the matter is found in a letter reprinted by Kelly, *op. cit.,* 287–289.
15. Letter to the editor of the *Democrat and Chronicle* (n.d), sent after the 1906 vote on jointure.
16. Braeman, *op. cit.,* 97.
17. A. Blake Brophy, *Foundlings on the Frontier* (Tucson: University of Arizona Press, 1972), 21.

18. *Mohave County Miner,* April 30, 1898, p. 2.

19. Brophy, *op. cit.*

20. *Arizona Silver Belt,* February 21, 1901, p. 2.

21. Jay Wagoner, *Arizona Territory: 1863–1912* (Tucson: University of Arizona Press, 1970), 406.

22. *Arizona Silver Belt,* October 18, 1900.

23. *Ibid.*

24. *Daily Enterprise,* July 3, 1900, p. 2. See also *Mohave County Miner,* October 27, 1900.

25. Mary E. Gill and John S. Goff, "Joseph H. Kibbey and School Segregation in Arizona," *Journal of Arizona History* (Spring 1980): 411–421.

26. See, for example, Peter Clark MacFarlane, "The Galahad of Arizona: Governor Hunt," *Colliers* (April 15, 1916): 21–27.

27. *Mohave County Miner,* February 9, 1901, p. 2.

28. *Report of the Governor of Arizona,* 1905, 53.

29. *The Statehood Bill,* speech of Hon. Albert J. Beveridge, Senate of the United States, March 8, 1906, 22.

30. Data from Interstate Commerce Commission, *Statistics of Railways* (Washington, D.C.: GPO, 1901), 97; *ibid.,* 1912, 81.

31. Letter from William Brooks to his mother, April 24, 1904, in the William E. Brooks Collection, Arizona Collection, Arizona State University.

32. *Phoenix Enterprise,* February 3, 1904, p. 3.

33. Letter from attorney Frank Baxter to Hunt, February 1, 1907, in the Hunt Collection, Arizona Collection.

34. See Victor S. Griffith, Jr., "State Regulation of Railroad and Electric Rates in Arizona to 1925" (M.A. Thesis, University of Arizona, 1931).

35. McFarlane, *op. cit.*

36. *Arizona Silver Belt,* August 24, 1905, p. 1.

37. Wagoner, *op. cit.,* 330.

38. Letter from L. D. Ricketts to Hunt, February, 18, 1907, in the Hunt Collection, Arizona Collection.

39. *Report to Secretary of Interior,* 1907.

40. Eliot Jones, *Principles of Railway Transportation* (New York: Macmillan, 1929), 413.

41. Eugene V. Debs, "Railroad Employees and Socialism," *International Socialist Review* 9 (October 1908): 241–249, 242.

42. *Ibid.*

43. *Adair* v. *United States,* 208 U.S. 161 (1908).

44. Joseph R. Conlin, *Big Bill Haywood and the Radical Union Movement* (Syracuse:

Syracuse University Press, 1969), 31.

45. *Miners Magazine* 1 (January 1900): 17.

46. *Ibid.*, 17–18.

47. *Ibid.*, 2 (1902): 3.

48. John Fahey, "Ed Boyce and the Western Federation of Miners," *Idaho Yesterdays* 25 (Fall 1981): 19.

49. *Ibid.*, 28. In 1902 the WFM resolved to follow a course of independent political action and urged "the adoption of the Socialist Party of America by the locals of the Federation in conjunction with a vigorous policy of education along the lines of political economy." See Ronald C. Brown, *Hard-Rock Miners: The Intermountain West, 1860–1920* (College Station: Texas A&M University Press, 1979), 159–160.

50. Fahey, *op. cit.*, 23.

51. Committee on President's Report, *Proceedings of the Western Federation of Miners,* 1911, 317.

52. *Ibid.*

53. From 1896 to 1900 the WFM affiliated with the American Federation of Labor. In 1900 the WFM, unhappy with the amount of attention and financial support it had received from the AFL, joined the Western Federation of Labor that, in 1902, changed its name to the American Labor Union (ALU). This organization adopted the platform of the Socialist party of America as its political platform. In 1905 it merged into the Industrial Workers of the World. In 1908, following ideological differences with IWW, the Western Federation of Miners severed its ties with the international organization. Later, the WFM became the International Union of Mine, Mill, and Smelter Workers affiliated with the AFL.

54. Fahey, *op. cit.*, 19.

55. *Proceedings of the Western Federation of Miners,* 1903, 95.

56. Report of Marion W. Moor, *Proceedings of the Western Federation of Miners,* 1906, 222.

57. *Arizona Silver Belt,* May 2, 1902, p. 2.

58. Quoted in David J. Weber, ed., *Foreigners in Their Native Land: Historical Roots of the Mexican Americans* (Albuquerque: University of New Mexico Press, 1973), 253.

59. Testimony of Joseph D. Cannon before the President's Mediation Commission, sessions held in Globe, Arizona, October 9–16, 1917. Proceedings reported by E. W. Powers, Phoenix, Arizona (typewritten), in the Arizona Collection.

60. See "Labor Conditions in the Southwest," *Engineering and Mining Journal* (March 31, 1904): 510.

61. Brophy, *op. cit.*, 18.

62. Manuel P. Servin, *An Awakened Minority: The Mexican-Americans,* 2d ed. (Beverly Hills: Glencoe Press, 1974), 36.

63. *Report to Secretary of Interior,* 1903, 190.

64. *Engineering and Mining Journal* (March 31, 1904): 510.

65. Will Robinson, *The Story of Arizona* (Phoenix, Ariz.: The Berryhill Company, 1919), 208.

66. Remarks by delegate P. C. Rawlings from the Bisbee local, *Proceedings of the Convention of the Western Federation of Miners,* 1907, 197, 202.

67. Remarks of Joseph D. Cannon, *Proceedings of the Convention of the Western Federation of Miners,* 1907, 389.

68. H. S. McCluskey, *Absentee Capitalists Menace Popular Government in Arizona.* Bound reprint of articles appearing in the *Miami Daily Silver Belt,* August 27–October 21, 1921, 8, in the H. S. McCluskey Collection, Arizona Collection.

69. *Report of the Industrial Commission — Agriculture* (Washington, D.C.: GPO, 1901), 106.

70. *Arizona Silver Belt,* September 27, 1906, p. 4.

71. See, for example, *ibid.,* September 4, 1902, p. 1.

72. *Mohave County Miner,* September 28, 1902, p. 2.

73. *Arizona Silver Belt,* October 2, 1902, p. 2.

74. *Ibid.,* March 21, 1901, p. 4.

75. *Mohave County Miner,* March 23, 1901, p. 2. See also *Arizona Silver Belt,* July 19, 1902, p. 2.

76. Before the formation of the Socialist party of America, the principal Socialist political party was the Socialist-Labor party. See Nathan Fine, *Labor and Farmer Parties in the United States, 1828–1928* (New York: Russell and Russell, 1961); Ira Kipnis, *The American Socialist Movement, 1897–1912* (New York: Columbia University Press, 1952); David A. Shannon, *The Socialist Party of America* (Chicago: Quadrangle Books, 1967); and James Weinstein, *The Decline of Socialism in America, 1912–1919* (New York: Monthly Review Press, 1967).

77. *International Socialist Review* 5 (1904–1905): 207.

78. See generally James David McBride, "Henry S. McCluskey: Workingman's Advocate" (Ph.D. Dissertation, Arizona State University, 1982).

79. See, for example, *Arizona Socialist Bulletin* (December 27, 1912), which was devoted to municipal reform in Prescott.

80. George Williams, Jr., quoted in Betty Graham Lee, ed., *Cornerstones of the 1908 LDS Academy: A Research Guide* (Thatcher: Eastern Arizona College, 1981), 43. Williams, from Safford, ran as a Socialist candidate for the state legislature in 1904 and city council in 1905.

81. Editorial, *Arizona Daily Star,* August 18, 1904, p. 4.

82. John S. McCormick, "Hornets in the Hive: Socialists in Early Twentieth-Century Utah," *Utah Historical Quarterly* 50 (Summer 1982): 240.

83. A. M. Simons, "The Socialist Outlook," *International Socialist Review* 5 (1904–1905): 203–207.

84. McAllister Coleman, *Eugene V. Debs: A Man Unafraid* (New York: Greenberg, 1930), 225–227.

85. Wayne H. Morgan, *Eugene V. Debs: Socialist for President* (Syracuse: Syracuse University Press, 1962), 65.

86. John Curtis Kennedy, "Socialist Tendencies in American Trade Unions," *International Socialist Review* 8 (1907–1908): 338.

87. See report of Marion Moor, *Proceedings of the Western Federation of Miners, 1906*, 220.

88. *Miner's Magazine* 2 (1902): 12.

89. *Arizona Silver Belt*, September 4, 1902, p. 1.

90. *Globe Times*, April 25, 1901, p. 1.

91. *Arizona Silver Belt*, October 2, 1902, p. 1.

92. *Ibid.*, October 1, 1903, p. 2.

93. Letter from Brooks to his mother, August 7, 1904, in the Brooks Collection, Arizona Collection.

94. Letter from Brooks to his mother, September 18, 1904, in the Brooks Collection, Arizona Collection.

95. *Arizona Republic*, October 28, 1911. Cited by J. Morris Richards, *The Birth of Arizona: The Baby State* (Phoenix, Ariz.: State Department of Education, 1940), 46.

96. Kipnis, *op. cit.*, 366.

97. *Arizona Star*, August 25, 1904, p. 4. The same theme was pursued in the *Star* on August 28, 1904, p. 4.

98. *Ibid.*, August 28, 1904, p. 4.

99. Pamphlet, "The First Step in National Progress is Direct Legislation," A. A. Worsley, Lawyer, Tucson, Arizona Star Job Rooms, Particular Printing, n.d., 1 in the Hunt Collection, Arizona Collection.

100. *Ibid.*, 2.

101. From article by "Marxist," "The Referendum Movement and the Socialist Movement in America," *International Socialist Review* 4 (1903–1904): 202–212.

102. H. F. Kane in *Graham County Advocate*, September 1908, reproduced in *Cornerstones, op. cit.*, 49.

103. *Ibid.*

104. Robert F. Hoxie, "The Rising Tide of Socialism," *Journal of Political Economy* 19 (October 1911): 621.

105. *Ibid.*, 624.

106. See Appendix D. For a comparative analysis of Arizona and Nevada on this point, see David R. Berman, "Environment, Culture, and Radical Third Parties: Electoral Support for the Socialists in Arizona and Nevada, 1912–1916," *Social Science*

Notes

Journal 27 (1990): 147–158.

107. Hoxie, *op. cit.*

CHAPTER 4

1. Letter from Theodore Roosevelt to Edward Kent, November 9, 1908, in *The Letters of Theodore Roosevelt,* ed. Elting E. Morrison, et al. (Cambridge, Mass.: Harvard University Press, 1954), 6: 1338.

2. Letter from Theodore Roosevelt to Albert Beveridge, November 19, 1908, in *Letters of Theodore Roosevelt,* 6: 1367.

3. H. A. Hubbard, "The Arizona Enabling Act and President Taft's Veto," *Pacific Historical Review* 3 (1934): 317.

4. *Presidential Addresses and State Papers of William Howard Taft, From March 4, 1909 to March 4, 1910* (New York: Doubleday, Page & Company, 1910), 1: 353–359.

5. W. H. Taft, address at City Hall, Phoenix, Arizona, October 13, 1909, in *ibid.,* 354.

6. W. H. Taft, address at Prescott, Arizona, October 13, 1909, in *ibid.,* 356–359.

7. Peter Clarke MacFarlane, "The Galahad of Arizona: Governor Hunt," *Colliers* (April 15, 1916): 21–27.

8. Letter from Mulford Winsor to Hunt, September 22, 1910, in the George W.P. Hunt Collection, Arizona Collection, Arizona State University.

9. Letter from William Cleary to Hunt, June 30, 1910, in the Hunt Collection.

10. Charles Foster Todd, "The Initiative and Referendum in Arizona" (M.A. Thesis, University of Arizona, 1931), 15.

11. See A. A. Lassich, "Something The Western Federation of Miners Has Accomplished In The State of Arizona," letter in *Miner's Magazine* (November 27, 1913): 11.

12. See *Arizona Gazette,* July 13, 1910, p. 2; and Todd, *op. cit.,* 15.

13. *Jerome News,* July 16, 1910, p. 1.

14. Letter from Ernest Liebel to Hunt, December 13, 1911, in the Hunt Collection.

15. *Arizona Gazette,* July 13, 1910, p. 2.

16. *Ibid.*

17. See items in Microfilming Corporation of America, *The Papers of the Socialist Party of America, 1897–1963,* Ser. 3, Pt. C, Arizona, 1912–1960 (New York, 1975).

18. Letter from Mulford Winsor to Hunt, July 26, 1910, in the Hunt Collection.

19. Todd, *op. cit.,* 17. Todd's sources for the "deal" were interviews with H. S. McCluskey, Arizona labor organizer, on April 21, 1931, and labor leader J. C. Provost, on April 20, 1931.

20. Cannon's remarks are taken from an article he wrote, "Arizona Socialists Forced

Constitution on the Old Line Politicians," reproduced from the *California Social Democrat* (January 27, 1912) in *Papers of the Socialist Party, op. cit.*

21. *Arizona Republican,* June 19, 1910, p. 2.

22. See letter from labor attorney William B. Cleary to Hunt, June 30, 1910, in the Hunt Collection; and *Voice of the People,* September 30, 1910.

23. *Arizona Republican,* September 13, 1910, p. 1.

24. *Ibid.*

25. *Ibid.*

26. Hubbard, "Arizona Enabling Act," *op. cit.,* 320.

27. Calvin N. Brice, "The Constitutional Convention of Arizona" (M.A. Thesis, Arizona State College, 1953), 37.

28. For annotated references to provisions of the Arizona constitution, see Bruce B. Mason, John P. White, and Russell B. Roush, *A Guide to the Arizona Constitution* (Scottsdale, Ariz.: Cross Plains Publishers, 1982).

29. Requirements were set at a number equal to 10 percent of the votes cast at the last election for the initiative, 5 percent for the referendum, and 25 percent for the recall. Writing to Hunt on November 5, 1910, an official of the Globe miners' union, W. M. Wills, noted: "If we can get the initiative on a ten per cent basis and the referendum on a five or six percent basis . . . it will be as good as anyone, no matter how radical, would desire at this time knowing as we do that the constitution has to pass muster at Washington" (letter in the Hunt Collection). On the severity of the requirements, see comments made by William J. Bryan, reprinted in *Commoner* (February 24, 1911): 2, from a speech he made in Tucson on February 7, 1911, on behalf of the proposed constitution.

30. Todd, *op. cit.,* 29–31.

31. J. Morris Richards, *The Birth of Arizona: The Baby State* (Phoenix, Ariz.: State Department of Education, 1940), 16.

32. Letter from J. H. Briggs, Jr., superintendent, Immigration Restriction League of Arizona, to Hunt, November 14, 1910, in the Hunt Collection.

33. *Ibid.*

34. Quoted in Richards, *op. cit.,* 19.

35. See Manuel P. Servin, *An Awakened Minority: The Mexican-Americans,* 2d ed. (Beverly Hills: Glencoe Press, 1974), 40.

36. Letter from Frances Munds to Hunt, August 20, 1910, in the Hunt Collection.

37. Letter from Hunt to W. A. Moody, July 15, 1916, in the Hunt Collection.

38. Richards, *op. cit.,* 26.

39. Richard E. Sloan, *Memories of an Arizona Judge* (Stanford: Stanford University Press, 1932), 234.

40. *Ibid.,* 238.

41. See J. N. Morrison, "Joseph D. Cannon and the Arizona Movement," in *Papers of the Socialist Party, op. cit.,* n.p.

42. Record of proceedings, report of the executive board of the Western Federation of Miners, January 14, 1911, 68.

43. Joseph D. Cannon, "What Has the Western Federation of Miners or President Moyer Ever Done?" Speech presented at the Twenty-second Consecutive and the Second Biennial Convention of the Western Federation of Miners, Great Falls, Montana, July 1916. Reprinted in *Miner's Magazine* (August 17, 1916): 7.

44. *Proceedings of the Western Federation of Miners,* 1911, 318–319.

45. Letter from Hunt to Wilson, January 2, 1911, in *The Papers of Woodrow Wilson,* ed. Arthur S. Link (Princeton: Princeton University Press, 1983), 22: 291.

46. "The Arizona Constitution," *Commoner* (February 24, 1911): 2.

47. *Ibid.*

48. *Ibid.*

49. Letter from Weldon B. Heyburn to L. W. Coggins, May 15, 1911, in the L.C. Coggins Collection, Arizona Collection.

50. Richards, *op. cit.*

51. Letter from Jonathan Bourne to Hunt, December 29, 1910, reprinted in the *Daily Globe,* n.d., in the Hunt Collection.

52. See Donald F. Anderson, *William Howard Taft: A Conservative's Conception of the Presidency* (Ithaca: Cornell University Press, 1973).

53. Democratic platform, in the *Arizona Gazette,* November 11, 1911, p. 1.

54. *Los Angeles Examiner,* November 12, 1911, p. 1, in the Hunt Collection.

55. *Daily Arizona Silver Belt,* September 15, 1910, p. 5.

56. See letter from W. B. Kelly, editor of *The Copper Era,* to Reese Ling, August 3, 1912, in the Reese Ling Collection, Special Collections, Northern Arizona University.

57. Newspaper article, "Candidates Return to Phoenix," unidentified source and date, in the Hayden Collection, Arizona Collection.

58. Richards, *op. cit.,* 37.

59. Letter from Brady O'Neill to Hunt, September 8, 1911, in the Hunt Collection.

60. This view was also shared by newspapers. See Steven A. Fazio, "Marcus A. Smith, Arizona Politician" (M.A. Thesis, University of Arizona, 1968), 141.

61. Letter from Brady O'Neill to Hunt, September 8, 1911, in the Hunt Collection.

62. Menzo E. Hatter, "The Major Issues in Arizona's Gubernatorial Campaigns" (M.A. Thesis, Arizona State University, 1951), 7.

63. Letter from Eugene W. Miller to Jacob Weinberger, November 2, 1911, in the Jacob Weinberger Collection, Special Collections, Northern Arizona University.

64. George Hunter, "John C. Greenway and the Bull Moose Movement in Arizona" (M.A. Thesis, University of Arizona, 1966), 29.

65. Joseph W. Folk, former governor of Missouri, quoted by Hatter, *op. cit.*, 16.

66. Quote from *ibid.*, 14.

67. *Arizona Gazette,* October 10, 1911, p. 1.

68. *Observer* (St. Johns, Arizona), November 18, 1911, p. 2.

69. Attachment to letter from J. W. Stimson to Carl Hayden, November 15, 1911, in the Hayden Collection.

70. Letter from the secretary of the Bisbee miners union to the McCabe miners union, reprinted in *Miners Magazine* (December 7, 1914): 10.

71. Richards, *op. cit.*, 57.

72. *Ibid.*, 58.

73. Sloan, *op. cit.*, 245.

74. *Ibid.*, 246.

75. Letter from Ernest Libel to Hunt, December 13, 1911, in the Hunt Collection.

76. *Compiled Messages of Geo. W.P. Hunt and Thos. E. Campbell, Governors of Arizona From 1912 to 1923 Inclusive.* Compiled by H. S. McCluskey, Secretary to Governor Hunt, 1924, 3.

77. *Ibid.*, 4.

78. *Ibid.*

79. *Ibid.*

80. *Ibid.*, 22.

81. Message of the governor of Arizona to the first state legislature, 3d sess., February 3, 1913, 7.

82. "The Oration of Governor Hunt, Delivered July 4th at Bisbee, Arizona," *Miner's Magazine* (July 17, 1913): 8.

83. *Ibid.*

84. Letter from Hunt to Rosa McKay, September 18, 1919, in the Hunt Collection.

85. Messages, *op. cit.*, 11.

86. *Tucson Citizen,* June 20, 1912, p. 4.

87. Letter to Reese Ling, August 30, 1912, in the Reese Ling Collection.

88. *Tucson Citizen,* November 2, 1914, p. 1.

89. *Arizona Gazette,* April 8, 1912, p. 1; April 9, 1912, p. 1.

90. Letter from M. M. Kelly, editor and publisher of *The Copper Era,* to Reese Ling, August 3, 1912, in the Reese Ling Collection.

91. *Ibid.* See also *Tucson Citizen,* September 6, 1912, p. 1.

92. *Coconino Sun,* September 27, 1912, p. 4.

93. See David R. Berman, "Male Support for Woman Suffrage: An Analysis of Voting Patterns in the Mountain West," *Social Science History* 11 (Fall 1987): 281–294.

94. Messages, *op. cit.,* 13.

95. Testimony of J. Tom Lewis before the President's Mediation Commission, sessions held in Globe, Arizona, October 9–16, 1917. Proceedings reported by E. W. Powers, Phoenix, Arizona, 554–560, in the Arizona Collection.

96. *Coconino Sun,* June 28, 1912, p. 4.

97. Letter from William Brooks to J. H. Gray, June 4, 1915, in the William Brooks Collection, Arizona Collection.

98. *Coconino Sun,* April 19, 1912, p. 1.

99. Messages, *op. cit.,* 28.

100. Howard Caleb, "The Labor Movement in Arizona," manuscript, Arizona State Library, n.d.

101. Cannon, "What Has the Western Federation of Miners or President Moyer Ever Done," *op. cit.*

102. *Tucson Citizen,* August 26, 1914, p. 8.

103. *Arizona Gazette,* April 16, 1912, p. 1.

104. *Ibid.,* May 29, 1912, p. 4.

105. *Ibid.,* May 31, 1912, p. 4.

106. *Miner's Magazine* (May 15, 1913): 10.

107. *Coconino Sun,* August 30, 1912, p. 4.

108. Figures from Interstate Commerce Commission, *Statistics of Railways* (Washington, D.C.: GPO, 1918), 97–98.

109. Address, March 18, 1912, 27.

110. *Coconino Sun,* September 20, 1912, p. 4.

111. Letter from J. B. Breathitt to Frank J. Duffy, October 16, 1914, in the Hunt Collection.

112. *First Annual Report of the State Auditor of Arizona,* Phoenix, December 2, 1912.

113. Hunt, message to the third state legislature, February 3, 1913, 33.

114. *Ibid.,* 34.

115. *Coconino Sun,* June 13, 1913, p. 4.

116. Pamphlet, "Distrust of States' Legislatures," address by George W.P. Hunt at the governor's conference, Colorado Springs, Colorado, August 28, 1913, in the Hunt Collection.

117. *Ibid.*

118. J. L. Loveless, "Democratic Disruptions in Arizona Deplored," *Arizona Democrat,* April 23, 1913, pp. 1, 5.

119. Letter from Reese Ling to Major George H. Kelly, August 2, 1912, in the Reese

Ling Collection.

120. *Tucson Citizen,* May 31, 1912, p. 3; *Coconino Sun,* March 29, 1912, p. 4.

CHAPTER 5

1. *Tucson Citizen,* July 20, 1912, p. 3.

2. Francis L. Broderick, *Progressivism at Risk: Electing a President in 1912* (Westport, Conn.: Greenwood Press, 1989), 1. A useful summary of the platforms of the various candidates is found in Arthur S. Link and Richard L. McCormick, *Progressivism* (Arlington Heights, Ill.: Harlan Davidson, 1983). An analysis of the 1912 contest in Arizona is found in David R. Berman, "Voters, Candidates, and Issues in the Progressive Era: An Analysis of the 1912 Presidential Election in Arizona," *Social Science Quarterly* 67 (June 1986): 255–266.

3. Roosevelt as a Rough Rider in the Spanish-American War became well known to Arizonans and intimate with a number of future territorial politicians. In 1903 he made a well-publicized trip to the Grand Canyon. Eight years later he returned to dedicate a large irrigation dam that bore his name. Debs too was well known in Arizona, especially in mining areas where he had toured on several occasions prior to 1912. See generally Wayne H. Morgan, *Eugene V. Debs: Socialist for President* (Syracuse: Syracuse University Press, 1962).

4. Donald F. Anderson, *William Howard Taft: A Conservative's Conception of the Presidency* (Ithaca: Cornell University Press, 1973), 232.

5. One newspaper article quoted Mormon leader Joseph Smith as having written in a church publication: "If he, Taft, is once again called to the presidential chair it is not likely the people will regret it." Smith continued: "No reasonable citizen can in any way find fault with the present administration. Taft has met the just needs of the people and economic demands of the country with steadfastness and wisdom" (*Prescott Journal Miner,* September 27, 1912, p. 1).

6. Theodore Roosevelt, *An Autobiography* (New York: Charles Scribner's Sons, 1925), 484.

7. *Tombstone Epitaph,* September 22, 1912, n.p., found in the Hunt Collection, Arizona Collection, Arizona State University.

8. On finance, see the letter from J.L.B. Alexander to John C. Greenway, October 21, 1912, in the J.L.B. Alexander Collection, Arizona Collection.

9. "The Principles of the National Progressive Party of Arizona," adopted at the state convention of the Progressive party held in Phoenix, July 30, 1912, in the Alexander Collection.

10. *Arizona Republic,* October 17, 1912, p. 1.

11. *Ibid.*

12. *Coconino Sun,* October 11, 1912, p. 1.

13. See Bernard J. Brommel, *Eugene V. Debs: Spokesman for Labor and Socialism*

(Chicago: Charles H. Kerr, 1978), p. 137.

14. See generally Brommel, *op. cit.;* and Morgan, *op. cit.*

15. Quoted by Broderick, *op. cit.,* 173.

16. J. N. Morrison, "Joseph D. Cannon and the Arizona Movement," in Microfilming Corporation of America, *The Papers of the Socialist Party of America, 1897–1963,* Ser. 3, Pt. C, Arizona (New York, 1975), n.p.

17. On the national party, see McAllister Coleman, *Eugene V. Debs: A Man Unafraid* (New York: Greenberg 1930), 261–263.

18. *Coconino Sun,* October 18, 1912, p. 1.

19. *Arizona Republic,* November 1, 1912, p. 5.

20. Quoted by Morgan, *op. cit.,* 130.

21. *The Master Method of The Great Reform: Speeches of Eugene W. Chafin, Prohibition Candidate for President 1908–1912* (Chicago, Ill.: Lincoln Temperance Press, 1913), 1, 27.

22. Broderick, *op. cit.,* 174.

23. *Arizona Bulletin* (December 1912).

24. *Arizona Gazette,* November 21, 1912, p. 4.

25. *Coconino Sun,* March 29, 1912, p. 4.

26. Letter from Theodore Roosevelt to Benjamin Ide Wheeler, December 21, 1911, in *The Letters of Theodore Roosevelt,* ed. Elting E. Morrison, et al. (Cambridge, Mass.: Harvard University Press, 1954), 7: 461–462.

27. Hunt, message to the first state legislature, 3d sess., February 3, 1913, 22.

28. Letter from Hunt to E.H.M. Wilson, June 1, 1911, in the Hunt Collection.

29. See Carrie Chapman Catt and Nettie Rogers Shuler, *Woman Suffrage and Politics* (New York: Charles Scribner's Sons, 1912), 176–177.

30. See *Tucson Citizen,* November 2, 1914, p. 1.

31. Philip S. Foner, *Women and the American Labor Movement* (New York: The Free Press, 1979), 270–277.

32. *Yuma Morning Sun,* October 14, 1914, n.p.

33. See, for example, articles in the *Tucson Citizen,* November 3, 1912, p. 4.

34. Nancy K. Tisdale, "The Prohibition Crusade in Arizona" (M.A. Thesis, University of Arizona, 1965), p. 137.

35. Quoted in *ibid.,* 141–142.

36. See generally Lee Benson, *Merchants, Farmers, and Railroads: Railroad Regulation and New York Politics, 1850–1877* (Cambridge, Mass.: Harvard University Press, 1955); and George H. Miller, *Railroads and the Granger Laws* (Madison: University of Wisconsin Press, 1971). A brief discussion of the Arizona situation is found in Richard C. Cortner, *The Arizona Train Limit Case: Southern Pacific vs. Arizona*

(Tucson: Institute of Government Research, University of Arizona Press, 1970). An analysis of the links between constituents and representatives on these issues is found in David R. Berman, "State Legislators and Their Constituents: Regulating Arizona Railroads in the Progressive Era," *Social Science Quarterly* 71 (December 1990): 812–823.

37. *Arizona Gazette,* November 6, 1912, p. 1.

38. Keith L. Bryant, *History of the Atchison, Topeka and Santa Fe* (New York: Macmillan, 1974), 207–208.

39. *Tucson Citizen,* August 21, 1912, p. 4.

40. *Arizona Gazette,* June 17, 1912, p. 1; *Tucson Citizen,* August 27, 1914, p. 4.

41. Pamphlet, *What Every Voter in the State Should Know — And Why,* n.d., 3.

42. *Ibid.*

43. *Arizona Gazette,* November 6, 1912, p. 8.

44. *Ibid.,* 15.

45. On the perception of Wilson, see Berman, "Voters, Candidates, and Issues," *op. cit.*

46. Gains in Hispanic areas may have been due to some extent to implementation of the literacy test passed by the first legislature. These gains, however, also appear to reflect a shift of support in the Hispanic community to the Democratic party, a shift that, as the following chapter indicates, was even more manifest in 1916.

47. *Arizona Gazette,* November 8, 1912, p. 1.

48. See David R. Berman, "Male Support for Woman Suffrage: An Analysis of Voting Patterns in the Mountain West," *Social Science History* 11 (Fall 1987): 281–294.

49. Hunt, message to the legislature, 3d sess., February 3, 1913.

50. Hunt, address, February 14, 1914.

51. Letter from Theodore Roosevelt to Dwight Heard, June 26, 1914, in *Letters of Theodore Roosvelt, op. cit.,* 767.

52. George Hunter, "John C. Greenway and the Bull Moose Movement in Arizona" (M.A. Thesis, University of Arizona, 1966), 73.

53. *Coconino Sun,* August 22, 1913, p. 4.

54. *Ibid.,* October 9, 1914, p. 3.

55. *Ibid.*

56. *Tucson Citizen,* August 21, 1914, p. 4.

57. See, for example, *Platform of the Republican Party Council,* September 29, 1914.

58. *Coconino Sun,* October 16, 1914, p. 2.

59. Declaration of the principles of the Progressive party, adopted September 29, 1914, in the Alexander Collection.

60. Copy of published advertisement: "Don't Throw Your Vote Away," n.d., in the

George Y. Young Collection, Arizona Collection.

61. *Arizona Gazette,* November 7, 1914, p. 12.

62. *Ibid.*

63. *Bisbee Daily Review,* September 19, 1914, p. 4.

64. *Pamphlet Containing Measures To Be Submitted To The Electors of Arizona,* November 3, 1914, 4–5.

65. *Ibid.,* 7.

66. Tisdale, *op. cit.,* 154.

67. *Ibid.,* 162.

68. "Is Hunt for Prohibition?" *Arizona Gazette,* undated clipping on file under "prohibition," in the James H. McClintock Collection, Phoenix Public Library.

69. Speaking about workers in various parts of the state, labor leader Henry S. McCluskey noted: "Previous to the prohibition law going into force it was almost impossible to do anything toward organizing these men. They were unable to read the literature given them, and when they had money they were under the influence of booze. We were unable to reason with them or to do anything to try to improve their condition," (interview, "Labor Unions Take Notice," in the H. S. McCluskey Collection, Arizona Collection).

70. See "What is Labor's Debt to Prohibition?" *Miner's Magazine* (April 2, 1914): 9; and "Prohibition a Menace to the Workers," *Miner's Magazine* (July 9, 1914): 7.

71. *Arizona Socialist Bulletin* (December 27, 1912): 3.

72. Will Robinson, *The Story of Arizona* (Phoenix, Ariz.: The Berryhill Company, 1919), 356.

73. *Ibid.,* 358–359.

74. Tisdale, *op. cit.,* 166.

75. *Miner's Magazine* (December 18, 1913): 17.

76. Letter from John P. Stiegel to Earnest Mills, August 2, 1914, in the WFM Archives, University of Colorado.

77. Publicity Pamphlet, 1914, *op. cit.,* 70.

78. *Ibid.*

79. *Ibid.,* 72.

80. *Ibid.,* 83.

81. See Michael E. Parrish, *Mexican Workers, Progressives, and Copper: The Failure of Industrial Democracy in Arizona During the Wilson Years* (La Jolla, Calif.: Chicano Research, University of California, 1979), 6.

82. For the case against the 80 percent law, see editorial in the *Tucson Citizen,* August 27, 1914, p. 4.

83. As the regression of the Hunt vote for 1914 in Appendix D indicates, the extent

of Mormon support for Hunt is magnified when one controls for the vote on capital punishment.

84. See generally Meredith A. Snapp, "Defeat the Democrats: The Congressional Union for Women Suffrage in Arizona, 1914 and 1916," *Journal of the West* 14 (October 1975): 131–139.

85. Letter from Frances Munds to George Hunt, November 18, 1914, in the Hunt Collection.

CHAPTER 6

1. *Coconino Sun*, January 22, 1915, p. 4.

2. *Ibid.*, August 25, 1916, p. 6.

3. *Truax* v. *Raich*, 239 U.S. 33 (1916).

4. Argument by B. T. Wilkinson, president of Arizona State Federation of Labor, *Pamphlet Containing Measures to be Submitted to the Electors of Arizona, November 7, 1916* (Phoenix: Secretary of State of Arizona, 1916), 4.

5. *Arizona Labor Journal* (March 30, 1916): 2.

6. *Pamphlet Containing Measures, op. cit.*

7. See Gerald D. Nash, *The American West in the Twentieth Century* (Englewood Cliffs, N.J.: Prentice-Hall, 1973), 11–14.

8. See Robert Kim Nimmons, "Arizona's Forgotten Past: The Negro in Arizona, 1539–1965" (M.A. Thesis, Northern Arizona University, 1971), 89, 118.

9. *Ibid.*

10. See Shirley J. Roberts, "Minority-Group Poverty in Phoenix: A Socio-Economic Survey," *Journal of Arizona History* 19 (1973): 347–362.

11. *Arizona Republic,* November 17, 1911, p. 9.

12. Nimmons, *op. cit.,* 117.

13. See report from the *Arizona Republic,* September 18, 1933, in the Labor file, Arizona State Library.

14. These developments are discussed by Michael E. Parrish, *Mexican Workers, Progressives, and Copper: The Failure of Industrial Democracy in Arizona During the Wilson Years* (La Jolla, Calif.: Chicano Research, University of California, 1979).

15. Letter from Guy Miller to Charles H. Moyer, July 15, 1915, WFM Executive Board Report, 1915, 3, in the WFM Collection, University of Colorado.

16. *Ibid.,* letter of September 2, 1915.

17. James R. Kluger, *The Clifton-Morenci Strike* (Tucson: University of Arizona Press, 1970), 23–24.

18. *Coconino Sun*, October 22, 1915, p. 7.

19. James Lord, president of the Mining Department, *Annual Report, 1916, Submitted*

to Baltimore Convention of the American Federation of Labor, 5.

20.   Mary Field Parton, ed., *Autobiography of Mother Jones* (Chicago: Charles H. Kerr, 1925), 172–177.

21.   Lord, *op. cit.*

22.   Parton, *op. cit.,* 174.

23.   James W. Byrkit, *Forging the Copper Collar* (Tucson: University of Arizona Press, 1982), 55–62.

24.   See analysis by James M. Patton, *History of Clifton* (Greenlee County, Ariz.: Chamber of Commerce, 1977), 40–42.

25.   *Ibid.,* 37.

26.   *Tombstone Epitaph,* October 31, 1915, p. 4.

27.   *Coconino Sun,* October 29, 1915, p. 4.

28.   Letter from Hunt to Mulford Winsor, December 9, 1915, in the Hunt Collection, Arizona Collection, Arizona State University.

29.   Letter from Winsor to Hunt, December 27, 1915, in the Hunt Collection.

30.   Letter from Mother Jones to Hunt, June 12, 1916, in the Hunt Collection.

31.   *Ibid.*

32.   "Is Hunt for Prohibition?" *Arizona Gazette,* n.d., n.p., in the McClintock Collection, Phoenix Public Library.

33.   *Tucson Citizen,* August 14, 1916, in the Hayden Collection.

34.   Bert M. Fireman, *Arizona: Historic Land* (New York: Knopf, 1982), 206.

35.   This position was taken by Hayden in a series of letters in August 1916 to labor union officials who were strong supporters of Hunt. These letters are found in the Hayden Collection.

36.   Letter from William E. Beck to Hayden, August 4, 1916, in the Hayden Collection.

37.   Letter from Leon Jacobs to Hayden, August 9, 1916, in the Hayden Collection.

38.   Letter from Hayden to Arthur Davis, August 28, 1916, in the Hayden Collection.

39.   Letter from W. B. Kelly to Hayden, August 13, 1916, in the Hayden Collection.

40.   *Coconino Sun,* September 22, 1916, p. 6.

41.   *Ibid.,* June 30, 1916, p. 6.

42.   Menzo E. Hatter, "The Major Issues in Arizona's Gubernatorial Campaigns" (M.A. Thesis, Arizona State University, 1951), 28–29.

43.   "Texas Day in Arizona," address by George W.P. Hunt, governor of Arizona, April 22, 1916 (Phoenix: R.A. Watkins, n.d), n.p., in the Hunt Collection.

44.   "The Best Man Loses," unidentified clipping in the Hunt Collection.

45.   Letter from J.L.B. Alexander to the Progressives of Arizona, August 25, 1916, in the J.L.B. Alexander Collection, Arizona Collection.

46. "State Party Directory," *Arizona Socialist Bulletin* (October 11, 1916): 4.

47. W. S. Bradford, "Is Hunt for the Workers?" *Arizona Socialist Bulletin* (October 11, 1916): 1.

48. *Ibid.,* 4.

49. *Ibid.*

50. Allen Campbell, "Republican Politics in Democratic Arizona," *Journal of Arizona History* (Summer 1981): 177–196.

51. *Coconino Sun,* January 5, 1917, p. 2.

52. *Ibid.,* 1.

53. *Ibid.,* January 12, 1917, p. 4.

54. Letter from Alfred Maddern to Hunt, June 2, 1918, in the Hunt Collection.

55. Letter from Charles A. Stauffer to Dwight Heard, July 11, 1916, in the Charles A. Stauffer Collection, Arizona Historical Foundation.

56. Nash, *op. cit.,* 11.

57. David Sarasohn, "The Election of 1916: Realigning the Rockies," *Western Historical Quarterly* (July 1980): 285–305.

58. *Ibid.*

59. See Hunter, *op. cit.*

60. Letter from Leon Jacobs to Hayden, August 9, 1916, in the Hayden Collection.

61. Charles Foster Todd, "The Initiative and Referendum in Arizona" (M.A. Thesis, University of Arizona, 1931), 54.

62. See *Arizona Labor Journal, op. cit.;* and George W.P. Hunt, "The Single Legislative Branch," *Welfare* (October 1913): 11.

63. *Arizona Gazette,* November 2, 1916, p. 3.

64. *Ibid.*

65. *Ibid.*

66. See generally S. D. Lovell, *The Presidential Election of 1916* (Carbondale and Edwardsville: Southern Illinois University Press, 1980); Christine A. Lunardini and Thomas J. Knock, "Woodrow Wilson and Woman Suffrage: A New Look," *Political Science Quarterly* 95 (Winter 1980–1981): 655–671; and Meredith A. Snapp, "Defeat the Democrats: The Congressional Union for Women Suffrage in Arizona, 1914 and 1916," *Journal of the West* 14 (October 1975): 131–139.

67. Letter from George Powell to H. S. McCluskey, February 8, 1917, in the McCluskey Collection, Arizona Collection.

68. Will Robinson, *The Story of Arizona* (Phoenix, Ariz.: The Berryhill Company, 1919), 299.

69. Robert W. Bruere, *Following the Trail of The IWW* (New York: New York Evening Post, 1918), 3.

70. *Ibid.*, 7.

71. *Ibid.*

72. Letter from Eugene Semmes Ives to Wilson, June 29, 1917, in *The Papers of Woodrow Wilson*, ed. Arthur S. Link (Princeton: Princeton University Press, 1966–1988), 43: 53.

73. Memorandum from Joseph Tumulty to the President, July 5, 1917, *Papers of Woodrow Wilson*, 43: 104.

74. Enclosure in a letter from Smith to Woodrow Wilson, July 8, 1917, *Papers of Woodrow Wilson*, 43: 127.

75. Campbell's sentiments are attached to a note from Joseph Patrick Tumulty with enclosure to Wilson, July 12, 1917, *Papers of Woodrow Wilson*, 43: 156–158.

76. Letter from Wilson to Thomas Edward Campbell, July 12, 1917, *Papers of Woodrow Wilson*, 43: 158.

77. Letters from J. L. Donnelly and Thomas A. French to Wilson, August 6, 1917, *Papers of Woodrow Wilson*, 43: 373. See also letter from Samuel Gompers, July 20, 1917, 43: 230–231.

78. Wilson's feelings are referred to in a letter from Samuel Gompers to Wilson, August 10, 1917, *Papers of Woodrow Wilson*, 43: 416–417.

79. George Hunt writing to Wilson, September 3, 1917, *Papers of Woodrow Wilson*, 44: 134–139.

80. *Ibid.*, 137.

81. *Ibid.*, 139.

82. Department of Labor, Office of the Secretary, *Report on the Bisbee Deportations, Made by the President's Mediation Commission to the President of the United States, November 6, 1917* (Washington, D.C.: GPO, 1918), 6.

83. Letter from Roosevelt to Felix Frankfurter, December 19, 1917, in *The Letters of Theodore Roosevelt*, ed. Elting E. Morrison, et al. (Cambridge, Mass.: Harvard University Press, 1951–1954), 8: 1262.

84. Letter from Frances Munds to Hunt, September 12, 1918, in the Hunt Collection.

85. Bruere, *op. cit.*, 5.

86. *Ibid.*, 5.

87. "Governor Hunt's Farewell Address," *Dunbar's Weekly*, January, 4, 1919, in the Hunt Collection.

88. Letter from Munds to Hunt, September 17, 1918, in the Hunt Collection.

89. *Ibid.*

90. George F. Sparks, ed., *A Many-Colored Toga: The Diary of Henry Fountain Ashurst* (Tucson: University of Arizona Press, 1962), 132.

91. See generally David R. Berman, *Parties and Elections in Arizona, 1863–1984* (Tempe: Morrison Institute, Arizona State University, 1985), 13–29.

CHAPTER 7

1. Letter from Theodore Roosevelt to Benajmin Ide Wheeler, December 21, 1911, in *The Letters of Theodore Roosevelt*, ed. Elting E. Morrison, et al. (Cambridge, Mass.: Harvard University Press, 1954), 7: 462.

2. When regressed, mining alone accounts for nearly 30 percent of the variance for the Populists in 1896 and the Socialist-Labor candidates in 1910, better than 20 percent for the Populists in 1894 and the Socialists in 1906, and 16 percent for the Socialists (Debs in 1912; Hunt in 1916).

3. See, for example, Martin J. Sklar, *The Corporate Reconstruction of American Capitalism, 1890–1916* (Cambridge: Cambridge University Press, 1988), 22–26.

4. As David Sarasohn has noted about what he calls the "political progressives" of the era, they "never expected to replace the emerging corporate system with either a New Jerusalem or an older America, but simply to reduce the power wealth received from the arrangement" (*The Party of Reform: Democrats in the Progressive Era* [Jackson: University of Mississippi Press, 1989], viii).

5. Michael Paul Rogin makes this point about Populism in the United States and Marxism in America. See *The Intellectuals and McCarthy: The Radical Specter* (Cambridge, Mass.: MIT Press, 1967), 169–170.

6. On class consciousness, see E. P. Thompson, *The Making of the English Working Class* (New York: Pantheon Books, 1963), 10, and works cited therein.

7. Relevant statistics are found in the *Daily Arizona Journal*, September 5, 1891, p. 2.

8. F. Chris Garcia and Rudolph O. de la Garza, *The Chicano Political Experience: Three Perspectives* (North Scituate, Mass.: Duxbury Press, 1977). These authors explore an internal colonization model to explain the Chicano's place in the political system. See also Rodolfo Acuna, *Occupied America: The Chicano's Struggle Toward Liberation* (San Francisco: Canfield Press, 1972), especially 80–100.

9. Robert K. Nimmons, "Arizona's Forgotten Past: The Negro in Arizona, 1539–1965" (M.A. Thesis, Northern Arizona University, 1971).

10. Sarasohn, *op. cit.*, 17–21. See also Dewey W. Grantham, *Southern Progressivism: The Reconciliation of Progress and Tradition* (Knoxville: University of Tennessee Press, 1983).

11. See Rogin, *op. cit.*, 9–31.

12. Donna A. Barnes, *Farmers in Rebellion: The Rise and Fall of the Southern Farmers Alliance and People's Party in Texas* (Austin: University of Texas Press, 1984), 5.

13. See, for example, Neil J. Smelser, *Theory of Collective Behavior* (New York: The Free Press, 1962).

14. The literature on the radicalism of the western hardrock miners is voluminous. Among the leading works are Ronald C. Brown, *Hard-Rock Miners: The Intermountain West, 1860–1920* (College Station: Texas A&M University Press, 1979);

Vernon H. Jensen, *Heritage of Conflict: Labor Relations in the Nonferrous Metal Industry Up to 1930* (Ithaca: Cornell University Press, 1950); Joseph R. Conlin, *Big Bill Haywood and the Radical Union Movement* (Syracuse: Syracuse University Press, 1969); Melvin Dubofsky, *We Shall Be All: A History of the Industrial Workers of the World*, 2d ed. (Urbana: University of Illinois Press, 1988); and Mark W. Wyman, *Hard Rock Epic: Western Miners and the Industrial Revolution* (Berkeley: University of California Press, 1979).

15. These points are developed in David R. Berman, "Environment, Culture, and Radical Third Parties: Electoral Support for the Socialists in Arizona and Nevada, 1912–16," *Social Science Journal* 27 (1990): 147–158.

16. On the desire of Irish miners for safe and steady employment, see David M. Emmons, *The Butte Irish: Class and Ethnicity in an American Mining Town* (Urbana and Chicago: University of Illinois Press, 1989).

17. Frances Fox Piven and Richard A. Cloward, *Poor People's Movements: Why They Succeed, How They Fail* (New York: Vintage Books, 1979), 20.

18. See, for example, Donald G. Sofchalk, "Organized Labor and the Iron Ore Miners of Northern Minnesota, 1907–1936," *Labor History* 12 (Spring 1971): 214–242.

19. See Richard H. Peterson, *The Bonanza Kings: The Social Origins and Business Behavior of Western Mining Entrepreneurs, 1870–1900* (Lincoln: University of Nebraska Press, 1977).

20. A useful overview of the literature is found in D. Stephen Rockwood, et al., *American Third Parties Since the Civil War: An Annotated Bibliography* (New York: Garland Publishing, 1985).

21. See generally Steven J. Rosenstone, Roy L. Behr, and Edward H. Lazarus, *Third Parties in America: Citizen Response to Major Party Failure* (Princeton: Princeton University Press, 1984).

22. Daniel A. Mazmanian, *Third Parties in Presidential Elections* (Washington, D.C.: The Brookings Institution, 1974), 5.

23. See, for example, Paul Kleppner, "Voters and Parties in the Western States, 1876–1900," *Western Historical Quarterly* (January 1983): 49–68.

24. Roy E. Brown, "Colorful Colorado: State of Varied Industries," in *Rocky Mountain Politics*, ed. Thomas C. Donnelly (Albuquerque: University of New Mexico Press, 1940), 70.

25. Rogin, *op. cit.*, 37.

26. Rosenstone, et al., *op. cit.*, 89.

27. Milton Cantor, *The Divided Left: American Radicalism, 1900–1975* (New York: Hill and Wang, 1978), 26.

28. Berman, "Environment, Culture," *op. cit.* On how conditions reinforced the inclinations of Finnish miners toward radicalism, see Sofchalk, *op. cit.*

29. James R. Green, *Grass-Roots Socialism: Radical Movements in the Southwest, 1895–1943* (Baton Rouge: Louisiana State University Press, 1978).

30. Remarks of P. W. Galentine, *Proceedings of the Western Federation of Miners,* 1907, 409.

31. See generally on this pattern Robert Wiebe, *Businessmen and Reform* (Cambridge, Mass.: Harvard University Press, 1962), 173.

32. See, for example, John H. Laslett and Seymour Martin Lipset, *Failure of a Dream? Essays in the History of American Soialism* (New York: Doubleday and Company, 1974).

33. Testimony before the President's Mediation Commission, sessions held in Globe, Arizona, October 9–16, 1917. Proceedings reported by E. W. Powers, Phoenix, Arizona (typewritten), 219, in the Arizona Collection, Arizona State University.

34. Letter from George Hunt to P. W. Doyle, June 29, 1918, in the Hunt Collection, Arizona Collection.

35. See Eric N. Moody, "Nevada's Bull Moose Progressives: The Formation and Function of a State Political Party in 1912," *Nevada Historical Society Quarterly* 16 (Fall 1973): 157–180; and Robert W. Cherny, *Populism, Progressivism and the Transformation of Nebraska Politics, 1885–1915* (Lincoln: University of Nebraska Press, 1981), 121.

36. George Hunter, "John C. Greenway and the Bull Moose Movement in Arizona" (M.A. Thesis, University of Arizona, 1966), 123.

37. James Edward Wright, *The Politics of Populism: Dissent in Colorado* (New Haven: Yale University Press, 1974), 260–261.

38. For a contemporary assessment of the reform era along these lines, see, for example, Fred E. Haynes, *Third Party Movements Since the Civil War: With Special Reference to Iowa* (New York: Russell and Russell, 1966).

39. See, for example, Gabriel Kolko, *Railroads and Regulation, 1877–1916* (Princeton: Princeton University Press, 1965).

40. William Letwin, "The Past and Future of the American Businessman," *Daedalus* 98 (Winter 1969): 12.

41. See, for example, Sarasohn, *op. cit.*

42. See, for example, Michael Paul Rogin and John L. Shover, *Political Change in California: Critical Elections and Social Movements, 1890–1966* (Westport, Conn.: Greenwood Press, 1970).

43. These factors helped account for the success reformers enjoyed in Wisconsin with the voters. See David P. Thelen, "Social Tensions and the Origins of Progressivism," *Journal of American History* 56 (1969): 323–341.

44. In this respect, the framers of the Arizona constitution differed, for example, from the framers of the Montana or New Mexico constitutions. See James J. Lopach, et al., *We the People of Montana* (Missoula: Mountain Press Publishing Company, 1983), 10; and James H. Fowler, "Constitutions and Conditions Contrasted: Arizona and New Mexico, 1910," *Journal of the West* 13 (October 1974): 51–58.

45. On permissive consensus, see V. O. Key, Jr., *Public Opinion and American Democracy* (New York: Knopf, 1961).

46. Views of Socialists on Hunt are found in a letter from Earnest Libel to Hunt, December 13, 1911, in the Hunt Collection, and in the *Arizona Socialist Bulletin* (October 11, 1916): 4.

47. See J. Morris Richards, *The Birth of Arizona: The Baby State* (Phoenix, Ariz.: State Department of Education, 1940).

48. On California, see R. Hall Williams, *The Democratic Party and California Politics, 1880–1896* (Stanford: Stanford University Press, 1973). See also William R. Brock, *Investigation and Responsibility: Public Responsibility in the United States, 1865–1900* (London: Cambridge University Press, 1984); and compare with Kolko, *op. cit.*

49. David R. Berman, "State Legislators and Their Constituents: Regulating Arizona Railroads in the Progressive Era," *Social Science Quarterly* 71 (December 1990): 812–823.

50. One finds a comparable process in the notion of an "issue attention cycle." See Anthony Downs, "Up and Down With Ecology — the Issue-Attention Cycle," *Public Interest* 28 (1972): 38–50.

51. On attitudes of this nature growing out of the statehood process, see Alan G. Bogue, Thomas D. Phillips, and James E. Wright, eds., *The West of the American People* (Itasca, Ill.: F. E. Peacock, 1970), 151.

52. James W. Byrkit, *Forging the Copper Collar* (Tucson: University of Arizona Press, 1982), 72.

53. Letter from Hunt to Upton Sinclair, July 23, 1919, in the Hunt Collection.

54. H. S. McCluskey, *Absentee Capitalists Menace Popular Government in Arizona,* bound reprint of articles appearing in the *Miami Daily Silver Belt,* August 27–October 21, 1921, n.p., in the McCluskey Collection, Arizona Collection.

55. See Rogin and Shover, *op. cit.,* 3–65.

56. See, for example, Beverly Beeton, *Women Vote in the West: The Woman Suffrage Movement, 1869–1896* (New York: Garland Publishing, 1986); and Alan Grimes, *The Puritan Ethic and Woman Suffrage* (New York: Oxford University Press, 1967). The empirical work referred to is William F. Ogburn and Inez Goltra, "How Women Vote: A Study of an Election in Portland Oregon," *Political Science Quarterly* 34 (September 1919): 413–433.

57. See, for example, Wright, *op. cit.,* 252.

58. See Stanley B. Parsons, *The Populist Context: Rural Versus Urban Power on a Great Plains Frontier* (Westport, Conn.: Greenwood Press, 1973).

59. See, for example, Wyman, *op. cit.* and John D. Buenker, *Urban Liberalism and Progressive Reform* (New York: Charles Scribner's Sons, 1973).

CONCLUDING NOTE

1. This category normally includes the noncoastal Western states of Arizona, Colorado, Idaho, Montana, New Mexico, Nevada, Utah, and Wyoming.

2. On the latter point, see Mark W. Wyman, *Hard-Rock Epic: Western Miners and the Industrial Revolution* (Berkeley: University of California Press, 1979), 202.

3. On the limited scope of Mountain State populism, see John D. Hicks, *The Populist Revolt: A History of the Farmer's Alliance and the People's Party* (Minneapolis: University of Minnesota Press, 1931), 268; Richard Hofstadter, *The Age of Reform* (New York: Vintage, 1955), 50, 106; and Lawrence Goodwyn, *Democratic Promise: The Populist Movement in America* (New York: Oxford University Press, 1976).

4. See review by Robert W. Larson, *Populism in the Mountain West* (Albuquerque: University of New Mexico Press, 1986).

5. See *ibid.*

6. Gerald D. Nash, *The American West in the Twentieth Century* (Englewood Cliffs, N.J.: Prentice-Hall, 1973), 11.

7. Loren B. Chan, *Sagebrush Statesman: Tasker L. Oddie of Nevada* (Reno: University of Nevada Press, 1973), 66.

8. For more on the relationship among party, issues, and background (ethnocultural or economic) factors, see Appendix A. See also David R. Berman, "Voters, Candidates, and Issues in the Progressive Era: An Analysis of the 1912 Presidential Election in Arizona," *Social Science Quarterly* 67 (June 1986): 255–266.

NOTES APPENDIX A

1. The classic study on the psychological aspects of party identification is Angus Campbell, Philip E. Converse, Warren Miller, and Donald E. Stokes, *The American Voter* (New York: Wiley, 1960). On an alternative explanation that places more emphasis on party performance, see Morris P. Fiorina, *Retrospective Voting in American National Elections* (New Haven: Yale University Press, 1981).

2. On the topic of realignment, see V. O. Key, Jr., "A Theory of Critical Elections," *Journal of Politics* 17 (1955): 198–210; and Walter Dean Burnham, *Critical Elections and the Mainsprings of American Politics* (New York: Norton, 1970).

3. See general discussion in Joel H. Silbey, Allan G. Bogue, and William H. Flanigan, eds., *The History of American Electoral Behavior* (Princeton: Princeton University Press, 1978), 3–44, 253–262.

4. On the importance of ethnocultural conflict, see Lee Benson, *The Concept of Jacksonian Democracy: New York as a Test Case* (Princeton: Princeton University Press, 1961); Paul Kleppner, *The Cross of Culture: A Social Analysis of Midwestern Politics, 1850–1900* (New York: The Free Press, 1970); Richard Jensen, *The Winning of the Midwest: Social and Political Conflict, 1888–1896* (Chicago: University

of Chicago Press, 1971); and Paul Kleppner, *The Third Electoral System, 1853–1892* (Chapel Hill: University of North Carolina Press, 1979). In regard to the Populists the traditional approach was to give considerable importance to economic variables. See, in particular, John D. Hicks, *The Populist Revolt: A History of the Farmer's Alliance and the People's Party* (Minneapolis: University of Minnesota Press, 1931). Some more recent work suggests the importance of such factors. See, for example, James Edward Wright, *The Politics of Populism: Dissent in Colorado* (New Haven: Yale University Press, 1974). A recent study indicating the importance of economic stress in the Socialist vote is Lee M. Wolfle and Robert W. Hodge, "Radical-Party Politics in Illinois, 1880–1924," *Sociological Inquiry* 53 (1983): 33–60. See also James R. Green, *Grass-Roots Socialism: Radical Movements in the Southwest, 1895–1943* (Baton Rouge: Louisiana State University Press, 1978).

5. The theoretical relation among background, issue, party, and candidate choice are treated in David R. Berman, "Voters, Candidates, and Issues in the Progressive Era: An Analysis of the 1912 Presidential Election in Arizona" *Social Science Quarterly* 67 (June 1986): 255–266.

6. See John Muller, "Ballot Patterns and Historical Trends in California," *American Political Science Review* 63 (1969): 1197–1212; and James H. Kuklinski, Daniel S. Metlay, and W. D. Kay, "Citizen Knowledge and Choices on the Complex Issue of Nuclear Energy," *American Journal of Political Science* 26 (1982): 615–642. For other studies concerning the characteristics of proposition voting, see Carl Lutrin and Allan K. Settle, "The Public and Ecology: The Role of Initiatives in California's Environmental Politics," *Western Political Quarterly* 28 (1975): 352–371; and David B. Magleby, *Direct Legislation: Voting on Ballot Propositions in the United States* (Baltimore: Johns Hopkins University Press, 1984).

7. To avoid distorted percentages caused by a small number of total votes, a cutoff point of thirty-five total votes was employed. This resulted in a loss of less than 10 percent of the statewide vote. To offset disparities caused by using precincts of different sizes, the voting data were weighted in proportion to the total vote in each precinct.

8. Following the selection of a random number to provide a starting point, the author randomly sampled every fifth household head in Arizona.

9. People born in the United States were considered to have come from one of four regions: East (Connecticut, Maine, Massachusetts, New Hampshire, New Jersey, New York, Pennsylvania, Rhode Island, and Vermont); Midwest (Illinois, Indiana, Iowa, Kansas, Michigan, Minnesota, Missouri, Nebraska, North Dakota, Ohio, South Dakota, and Wisconsin); South (Alabama, Arkansas, Delaware, Florida, Georgia, Kentucky, Louisiana, Maryland, Mississippi, North Carolina, Oklahoma, South Carolina, Tennessee, Texas, Virginia, and West Virginia); and West (Arizona, California, Colorado, Idaho, Montana, Nevada, New Mexico, Oregon, Utah, Washington, and Wyoming).

10. See Harvey J. Tucker and Eric B. Herzik, "The Persisting Problem of Region in American State Policy Research," *Social Science Quarterly* 67 (1986): 84–97.

11. Daniel J. Elazar, *American Federalism: A View from the States* (New York: Crowell, 1966, 1972). These theories are operationalized and tested by Ira Sharkansky, "The Utility of Elazar's Political Culture: A Research Note," *Polity* 2 (1969): 66–83. For a critical assessment of Elazar's typology as operationalized by Sharkansky using data similar to that used in this study, see David R. Berman, "Political Culture, Issues and the Electorate," *Western Political Quarterly* 41 (March 1988): 169–180.

12. See Robert S. Erikson, John P. McIver, and Gerald C. Wright, Jr., "State Political Culture and Public Opinion," *American Political Science Review* 81 (September 1987): 798–813.

13. Richard Jensen, "On Modernizing Frederick Jackson Turner: The Historiography of Regionalism," *Western Historical Quarterly* (July 1980): 307–322.

14. Wilbur S. Shepperson, *Restless Strangers: Nevada's Immigrants and Their Interpreters* (Reno: University of Nevada Press, 1970): 8. There was considerable variation in the cultural backgrounds and values of European immigrants, although precisely how these variations relate to support for the reforms of interest here are not altogether clear. See Peter Kivisto, *Immigrant Socialists in the United States: The Case of the Finns and the Left* (Cranbury, N.J.: Associated University Press, 1984). This study could not focus on various nationality units because their numbers were too small to make reliable estimates.

15. See Elazar, *op. cit.;* and Berman, "Political Culture, Issues, and the Electorate," *op. cit.*

16. This measurement, which also provides an index of the larger pietistic population, is discussed more fully in David R. Berman, "Male Support for Woman Suffrage: An Analysis of Voting Patterns in the Mountain West," *Social Science History* 11 (Fall 1987): 281–294.

17. See, for example, Stanley B. Parsons, *The Populist Context: Rural Versus Urban Power on a Great Plains Frontier* (Westport, Conn.: Greenwood Press, 1973).

18. The classic work on the ecological problem is William S. Robinson, "Ecological Correlations and the Behavior of Individuals," *American Sociological Review* 15 (1950): 351–357.

19. See, for example, William H. Flanigan and Nancy H. Zingale, "Alchemist's Gold: Inferring Individual Relationships from Aggregate Data," *Social Science History* 9 (Winter 1985): 71–91.

REFERENCES

ARCHIVAL MATERIALS

Arizona Collection, Arizona State University (collections)
Alexander, J.L.B.
Barnes, William C.
Brooks, William E.
Coggins, L. W.
Hayden, Carl
Hunt, George W.P.
McCluskey, Henry S.
Young, George U.

Arizona Department of Library and Archives, Phoenix
Records of the secretary of state (voting records)

Arizona Historical Foundation, Tempe (collections)
Goldwater, Morris
Stauffer, Charles A.

Arizona Historical Society, Tucson (collections)
Hughes, Louis C.
Rice, M. M.
Smith, Marcus
Trittle, Frederick A.
Wiley, Joseph Lee

Duke University, William R. Perkins Library
The Papers of the Socialist Party of America, 1897–1963, Ser. 3, Pt. C, Arizona, 1912–1960. On microfilm by Microfilming Corporation of America (Reel 94), New York, 1975.

National Archives and Records Service, Washington, D.C.
Interior Department, *Appointment Papers: Arizona Territory, 1857–1907,* Record Group 48.

Northern Arizona University (special collections)
Loveless, J. L.

Ling, Reese

Weinberger, Jacob

Phoenix Public Library (collections)

McClintock, James H.

Presidential Papers

Cleveland, Grover. Papers, Library of Congress (microfilm).

Link, Arthur S., ed. *The Papers of Woodrow Wilson.* 58 vols. Princeton: Princeton University Press, 1966–1988.

Morrison, Elting E., et al., eds. *The Letters of Theodore Roosevelt.* 8 vols. Cambridge, Mass.: Harvard University Press, 1951–1954.

Presidential Addresses and State Papers of William Howard Taft, From March 4, 1909 to March 4, 1910). Vol. 1. New York: Doubleday, Page and Company, 1910.

Richardson, James D., ed. *Messages and Papers of the Presidents, 1789–1897.* Vol. 5. Washington, D.C.: GPO, 1899.

Taft, William Howard. Papers, Library of Congress (microfilm).

Sharlot Hall Museum (Prescott, Arizona)

O'Neill, Buckey. Collection.

O'Neill, Buckey. Scrapbook.

University of Arizona (special collections)

Smith, Marcus. Scrapbook.

University of Colorado (western collection)

Archives of the Western Federation of Miners

NEWSPAPERS, MAGAZINES, AND JOURNALS

Alta Arizona

Argus

Arizona Blade Tribune

Arizona Bulletin

Arizona Citizen

Arizona Daily Gazette

Arizona Daily Orb

Arizona Daily Star

Arizona Gazette

Arizona Journal Miner

Arizona Labor Journal

Arizona Miner

Arizona Populist

Arizona Republic

Arizona Republican

Arizona Silver Belt

Arizona Socialist Bulletin

References

Arizona Star
Arizona, The State Magazine
Arizona Weekly Journal Miner
Bisbee Daily Review
Bisbee Evening Miner
Coconino Sun
Copper Era
Daily Arizona Journal Miner
Daily Arizona Silver Belt
Daily Arizona Star
Daily Enterprise
Douglas Democrat
Dunbar's Weekly
Engineering and Mining Journal
Florence Tribune
Globe Times
Graham County Advocate
Graham County Guardian
Holbrook News
International Socialist Review
Jerome News
Los Angeles Examiner
Miami Daily Silver Belt
The Miner's Magazine
Mohave County Miner
The Oasis
The Observer
Our Mineral Wealth
Proceedings of the Arizona Federation of Labor
Phoenix Enterprise
Phoenix Herald
Phoenix Republican
Prescott Courier
Prescott Journal Miner
Prescott Weekly Courier
Silver Belt
The Tombstone Epitaph
Tucson Citizen
Tucson Star
Voice of the People
Weekly Phoenix Herald
Yuma Morning Sun

GOVERNMENT DOCUMENTS

Adair v. *United States,* 208 U.S. 161 (1908).

Arizona Session Laws (various years).

Arizona State Bureau of Mines, *Bulletins* (various years).

Campbell v. *Hunt,* 18 Ariz. 442 (1917), 162 Pac. 882.

Census of the United States, Arizona (1864, 1870, 1890, 1900, 1910).

First Annual Report of the State Auditor of Arizona. Phoenix: State of Arizona, December 2, 1912.

Hunt v. *Campbell,* 19 Ariz. 254 (1917), 169 Pac. 596.

Journal of the First and Special Legislative Assemblies of the State of Arizona, 1912, 1913.

McCluskey, H. S., comp. *Compiled Messages of Geo. W.P. Hunt and Thoms. E. Campbell, Governors of Arizona From 1912 to 1923 Inclusive,* 1924.

Messages to the Territorial Legislature (file).

Pamphlets Containing Measures to be Submitted to the Electors of Arizona. Phoenix: Secretary of State, 1912, 1914, 1916.

Powers, E. W., reporter. President's Mediation Commission, sessions held at Globe, Arizona, October 9–16, 1917 (typewritten).

Proceedings of the State Board of Equalization, 1916.

Report on the Bisbee Deportations. President's Mediation Commission, November 6, 1917. Washington, D.C.: GPO, 1918.

Report of the Governor of the Territory to the Secretary of Interior. Washington, D.C.: GPO, various years.

Statistics of Railroads. U.S. Interstate Commerce Commission, vols. 13, 23, 29 (1901, 1912, 1918).

Truax v. *Raich,* 239 U.S. 33 (1916).

Yearbook of Agriculture. U.S. Department of Labor, various years.

BOOKS

Acuña, Rodolfo. *Occupied America: The Chicano's Struggle Toward Liberation.* San Francisco: Canfield Press, 1972.

Adams, Ward. *History of Arizona.* Phoenix, Ariz.: Record Publishing Company, 1930.

The American Labor Year Book 1916. New York: Rand School of Social Science, 1916.

Anderson, Donald F. *William Howard Taft: A Conservative's Conception of the Presidency.* Ithaca: Cornell University Press, 1973.

Argersinger, Peter. *Populism and Politics: William Alfred Peffer and the People's Party.* Lexington: University Press of Kentucky, 1974.

Arizona: A State Guide. Writer's Program of the Works Projects Administration, American Guide Series. New York: Hastings House Publishers, 1940.

Ash, Roberta. *Social Movements in America.* Chicago: Markham, 1972.

Asher, Herbert. *Causal Modeling.* Beverly Hills, Calif.: Sage, 1983.

References

Barnes, Donna A. *Farmers in Rebellion: The Rise and Fall of the Southern Farmers Alliance and People's Party in Texas.* Austin: University of Texas Press, 1984.

Beeton, Beverly. *Women Vote in the West: The Woman Suffrage Movement, 1869–1896.* New York: Garland Publishing, 1986.

Bell, Daniel. *Marxian Socialism in the United States.* Princeton: Princeton University Press, 1967.

Benson, Lee. *Merchants, Farmers, and Railroads: Railroad Regulation and New York Politics, 1850–1877.* Cambridge, Mass.: Harvard University Press, 1955.

———. *The Concept of Jacksonian Democracy: New York as a Test Case.* Princeton: Princeton University Press, 1961.

Berge, George W. *The Free Pass Bribery System.* Lincoln, Nebr.: Independent Publishing Company, 1905. Reprint. New York: Arno Press, 1974.

Berman, David R. *Parties and Elections in Arizona, 1863–1984.* Tempe: Morrison Institute, Arizona State University, 1985.

Berthoff, Rowland. *British Immigrants in Industrial America.* Cambridge, Mass.: Harvard University Press, 1953.

Bogue, Allan G., Thomas D. Phillips, and James E. Wright, eds. *The West of the American People.* Itasca, Ill.: F. E. Peacock, 1970.

Bowers, Claude G. *Beveridge and the Progressive Era.* Cambridge: Houghton Mifflin, The Riverside Press, 1932.

Braeman, John E. *Albert J. Beveridge: American Nationalist.* Chicago: University of Chicago Press, 1971.

Brock, William R. *Investigation and Responsibility: Public Responsibility in the United States, 1865–1900.* London: Cambridge University Press, 1984.

Broderick, Francis L. *Progressivism at Risk: Electing a President in 1912.* Westport, Conn.: Greenwood Press, 1989.

Brommel, Bernard J. *Eugene V. Debs: Spokesman for Labor and Socialism.* Chicago: Charles H. Kerr, 1978.

Brophy, A. Blake. *Foundlings on the Frontier.* Tucson: University of Arizona Press, 1972.

Brown, Ronald C. *Hard-Rock Miners: The Intermountain West, 1860–1920.* College Station: Texas A&M University Press, 1979.

Bruere, Robert W. *Following the Trail of the IWW.* New York: New York Evening Post, 1918.

Bryant, Keith L. *History of the Atchison, Topeka and Sante Fe.* New York: Macmillan, 1974.

Buenker, John D. *Urban Liberalism and Progressive Reform.* New York: Charles Scribner's Sons, 1973.

Burnham, Walter Dean. *Critical Elections and the Mainsprings of American Politics.* New York: Norton, 1970.

Byrkit, James W. *Forging the Copper Collar.* Tucson: University of Arizona Press, 1982.

Campbell, Angus, Philip E. Converse, Warren Miller, and Donald E. Stokes. *The American Voter.* New York: Wiley, 1960.

Canovan, Margaret. *Populism.* New York: Harcourt, Brace, and Jovanovich, 1981.

References

Cantor, Milton. *The Divided Left: American Radicalism, 1900–1975*. New York: Hill and Wang, 1978.

Catt, Carrie Chapman, and Nettie Rogers Shuler. *Woman Suffrage and Politics*. New York: Charles Scribner's Sons, 1923.

Chafin, Eugene W. *The Master Method of the Great Reform: Speeches of Eugene W. Chafin, Prohibition Candidate for President 1908–1912*. Chicago: Lincoln Temperance Press, 1913.

Chan, Loren B. *Sagebrush Statesman: Tasker L. Oddie of Nevada*. Reno: University of Nevada Press, 1973.

Cherny, Robert W. *Populism, Progressivism, and the Transformation of Nebraska Politics, 1885–1915*. Lincoln: University of Nebraska Press, 1981.

Cleland, Robert Glass. *A History of Phelps Dodge, 1834–1950*. New York: Knopf, 1952.

Clinch, Thomas A. *Urban Populism and Free Silver in Montana*. Helena: University of Montana Press, 1970.

Coleman, McAllister. *Eugene V. Debs: A Man Unafraid*. New York: Greenberg, 1930.

Conlin, Joseph R. *Big Bill Haywood and the Radical Union Movement*. Syracuse: Syracuse University Press, 1969.

Cortner, Richard C. *The Arizona Train Limit Case: Southern Pacific vs. Arizona*. Tucson: Institute of Government Research, University of Arizona Press, 1970.

Dubofsky, Melvin. *We Shall Be All: A History of the Industrial Workers of the World*. 2d ed. Urbana: University of Illinois Press, 1988.

Duverger, Maurice. *Political Parties: Their Organization and Activity in the Modern State*. New York: Wiley, 1954.

Elazar, Daniel J. *American Federalism: A View From the States*. New York: Crowell, 1966, 1972.

Elben, Jack E. *The First and Second United States Empires*. Pittsburgh: University of Pittsburgh Press, 1968.

Elliott, Russell R. *History of Nevada*. 2nd. rev. ed. Lincoln: University of Nebraska Press, 1987.

Emmons, David M. *The Butte Irish: Ethnicity in an American Mining Town*. Urbana and Chicago: University of Illinois Press, 1989.

Fainstein, Norman I., and Susan S. Fainstein. *Urban Political Movements*. Englewood Cliffs, N.J.: Prentice-Hall, 1974.

Faulk, Odie B. *Arizona: A Short History*. Norman: University of Oklahoma Press, 1970.
———. *Tombstone: Myth and Reality*. New York: Oxford University Press, 1972.

Fincher, E. B. *Spanish-Americans as a Political Factor in New Mexico, 1912–1950*. New York: Arno Press, 1974.

Fine, Nathan. *Labor and Farmer Parties in the United States, 1828–1928*. New York: Russell and Russell, 1961.

Fiorina, Morris P. *Retrospective Voting in American National Elections*. New Haven: Yale University Press, 1981.

Fireman, Bert M. *Arizona: Historic Land*. New York: Knopf, 1982.

References

Flexner, Eleanor. *Century of Struggle: The Woman's Rights Movement in the United States.* Cambridge, Mass.: Harvard University Press, 1959.

Foner, Philip S. *Women and the American Labor Movement.* New York: The Free Press, 1979.

Foster, James C., ed. *American Labor in the Southwest: The First One Hundred Years.* Tucson: University of Arizona Press, 1982.

Gable, John A. *The Bull Moose Years.* Port Washington, N.Y.: Kennikot, 1978.

Garcia, F. Chris, and Rudolph O. de la Garza. *The Chicano Political Experience: Three Perspectives.* North Scituate, Mass.: Duxbury Press, 1977.

Gastil, Raymond D. *Cultural Regions of the United States.* Seattle: University of Washington Press, 1975.

Glad, Paul W. *McKinley, Bryan, and the People.* Philadelphia: Lippincott, 1964.

Glass, Mary Ellen. *Silver and Politics.* Reno: University of Nevada Press, 1969.

Goldman, Eric F. *Rendezvous with Destiny.* New York: Knopf, 1958.

Goff, John S. *Arizona Territorial Officials II: The Governors, 1863–1912.* Cave Creek, Ariz.: Black Mountain Press, 1978.

———. *George W.P. Hunt and His Arizona.* Pasadena, Calif.: Socio-Technical Publications, 1973.

Goodwyn, Lawrence. *Democratic Promise: The Populist Movement in America.* New York: Oxford University Press, 1976.

———. *The Populist Moment: A Short History of the Agrarian Revolt in America.* New York: Oxford University Press, 1978.

Gould, Lewis L. *The Progressive Era.* Syracuse: Syracuse University Press, 1974.

———. *Wyoming: A Political History, 1868–1896.* New Haven: Yale University Press, 1968.

Grantham, Dewey W. *Southern Progressivism: The Reconciliation of Progress and Tradition.* Knoxville: University of Tennessee Press, 1983.

Green, James R. *Grass-Roots Socialism: Radical Movements in the Southwest, 1895–1943.* Baton Rouge: Louisiana State University Press, 1978.

Grimes, Alan. *The Puritan Ethic and Woman Suffrage.* New York: Oxford University Press, 1967.

Hamilton, Patrick. *The Resources of Arizona.* San Francisco: Bancroft Co., 1884.

Haynes, Fred E. *Third Party Movements Since the Civil War: With Special Reference to Iowa.* New York: Russell and Russell, 1966. First published in 1916.

Hays, Samuel P. *The Response to Industrialization, 1885–1914.* Chicago: University of Chicago Press, 1957.

Hesseltine, William. *The Rise and Fall of Third Parties.* Gloucester, Mass: Peter Smith, 1948.

Hicks, John D. *The Populist Revolt: A History of the Farmer's Alliance and the People's Party.* Minneapolis: University of Minnesota Press, 1931.

Hofstadter, Richard. *The Age of Reform.* New York: Vintage Books, 1955.

Howe, Irving. *Socialism and America.* New York: Harcourt, Brace, Jovanovich, 1985.

Jensen, Richard. *The Winning of the Midwest: Social and Political Conflict, 1888–1896.* Chicago: University of Chicago Press, 1971.

Jensen, Vernon H. *Heritage of Conflict: Labor Relations in the Nonferrous Metals Industry Up to 1930.* Ithaca: Cornell University Press, 1950.

Johnpoll, Bernard K., and Lillian Johnpoll. *The Impossible Dream: The Rise and Demise of the American Left.* Westport, Conn.: Greenwood Press, 1981.

Johnson, Donald B., and Kirk H. Porter, comps. *National Party Platforms: 1840–1972.* Urbana: University of Illinois Press, 1974.

Jones, Eliot. *Principles of Railway Transportation.* New York: Macmillan, 1929.

Keithly, Ralph. *Buckey O'Neill.* Caldwell, Idaho: The Caxton Printers, 1949.

Kelly, George H., ed. *Legislative History of Arizona, 1864–1912.* Phoenix, Ariz.: Manufacturing Stationers, Inc., 1926.

Kerlinger, Fred N., and Elazar J. Pedhazur. *Multiple Regression in Behavior Research.* New York: Holt, Rinehart and Winston, 1973.

Key, V. O., Jr. *Public Opinion and American Democracy.* New York: Knopf, 1961.

Kipnis, Ira. *The American Socialist Movement 1897–1912.* New York: Columbia University Press, 1952.

Kivisto, Peter. *Immigrant Socialists in the United States: The Case of Finns and the Left.* Cranbury, N.J.: Associated University Press, 1984.

Kleppner, Paul. *The Cross of Culture: A Social Analysis of Midwestern Politics, 1850–1900.* New York: The Free Press, 1970.

———. *The Third Electoral System, 1853–1892.* Chapel Hill: University of North Carolina Press, 1979.

Kluger, James R. *The Clifton-Morenci Strike.* Tucson: University of Arizona Press, 1970.

Kolko, Gabriel. *Railroads and Regulation, 1877–1916.* Princeton: Princeton University Press, 1965.

———. *The Triumph of Conservatism.* Chicago: Quadrangle, 1963.

Kraditor, Aileen S. *The Ideas of the Woman Suffrage Movement, 1890–1920.* New York: Columbia University Press, 1965.

Lamar, Howard. *Dakota Territory, 1861–1889.* New Haven: Yale University Press, 1956.

———. *The Far Southwest: 1846–1912.* New York: Norton, 1970.

Langbein, Laura Irwin, and Allan J. Lichtman. *Ecological Inference.* Beverly Hills, Calif.: Sage, 1978.

Larson, Robert W. *New Mexico Populism.* Boulder: Colorado Associated University Press, 1974.

———. *Populism in the Mountain West.* Albuquerque: University of New Mexico Press, 1986.

Laslett, John H. *Labor and the Left: A Study of Socialist and Radical Influences in the American Labor Movement, 1881–1924.* New York: Basic Books, 1970.

Laslett, John H., and Seymour Martin Lipset. *Failure of a Dream? Essays in the History of American Socialism.* New York: Doubleday and Co., 1974.

Lee, Betty Graham, ed. *Cornerstones of the 1908 LDS Academy: A Research Guide.* Thatcher: Eastern Arizona College, 1981.

Lingenfelter, Richard E. *The Hardrock Miners: A History of the Mining Labor Movement in the American West, 1863–1893.* Berkeley: University of California Press, 1974.

Link, Arthur S. *Wilson: The Road to the White House.* Princeton: Princeton University Press, 1947.

Link, Arthur S., and Richard L. McCormick. *Progressivism.* Arlington Heights, Ill.: Harlan Davidson, Inc., 1983.

Lopach, James J., et al. *We the People of Montana.* Missoula, Mont.: Mountain Press Publishing Company, 1983.

Lord, James. *Mining Department, Annual Report 1916.* Submitted to the Baltimore Convention of the American Federation of Labor.

Lovell, S. D. *The Presidential Election of 1916.* Carbondale and Edwardsville: Southern Illinois University Press, 1980.

Lyon, Peter. *To Hell in a Day Coach.* Philadelphia: Lippincott, 1968.

McClintock, James H. *Arizona: The Youngest State.* Vol. 2. Chicago: S. J. Clarke Co., 1916.

McConnell, Grant. *Private Power and American Democracy.* New York: Knopf, 1966.

McNall, Scott G. *The Road to Rebellion: Class Formation and Kansas Populism, 1865–1900.* Chicago: University of Chicago Press, 1988.

Magleby, David B. *Direct Legislation: Voting on Ballot Propositions in the United States.* Baltimore: Johns Hopkins University Press, 1984.

Mason, Bruce B., John P. White, and Russell B. Roush. *A Guide to the Arizona Constitution.* Scottsdale, Ariz.: Cross Plains Publishers, 1982.

Mazmanian, Daniel A. *Third Parties in Presidential Elections.* Washington, D.C.: The Brookings Institution, 1974.

Miller, George H. *Railroads and the Granger Laws.* Madison: University of Wisconsin Press, 1971.

Miller, Robert. *Oklahoma Populism.* Norman: University of Oklahoma Press, 1987.

Miller, Sally. *The Radical Immigrant.* New York: Twayne, 1974.

Morais, Herbert M., and William Cahn. *Gene Debs: The Story of a Fighting American.* New York: International Publishers, 1948.

Morgan, Wayne H. *Eugene V. Debs: Socialist for President.* Syracuse: Syracuse University Press, 1962.

Mowry, George E. *The California Progressives.* Berkeley: University of California Press, 1951.

———. *The Era of Theodore Roosevelt and the Birth of Modern America, 1900–1912.* New York: Harper and Row, 1958.

———. *Theodore Roosevelt and the Progressive Movement.* Madison: University of Wisconsin Press, 1946.

Murdock, John R. *Constitutional Development of Arizona.* Phoenix: Arizona Republican, 1927.

Myers, John. *The Last Chance: Tombstone's Early Years.* New York: Dutton, 1950.

Nash, Gerald D. *The American West in the Twentieth Century.* Englewood Cliffs, N.J.: Prentice-Hall, 1973.

Nicholson, John, ed. *The Arizona of Joseph Pratt Allyn.* Tucson: University of Arizona Press, 1974.

Nie, Norman, et al. *Statistical Package for the Social Sciences.* New York: McGraw-Hill, 1975.

Nugent, Walter T.K. *The Tolerant Populists: Kansas Populism and Nativism.* Chicago: University of Chicago Press, 1963.

Parrish, Michael E. *Mexican Workers, Progressives, and Copper: The Failure of Industrial Democracy in Arizona During the Wilson Years.* La Jolla: Chicano Research, University of California 1979.

Parsons, Stanley B. *The Populist Context: Rural Versus Urban Power on a Great Plains Frontier.* Westport, Conn.: Greenwood Press, 1973.

Parton, Mary Field, ed. *Autobiography of Mother Jones.* Chicago: Charles H. Kerr and Company, 1925.

Patton, James M. *History of Clifton.* Greenlee County, Ariz.: Chamber of Commerce, 1977.

Paul, Rodman W. *California Gold: The Beginning of Mining in the Far West.* Cambridge, Mass.: Harvard University Press, 1947.

————. *Mining Frontiers of the Far West, 1848–1890.* New York: Holt, Rinehart, and Winston, 1963.

Peplow, Edward H., Jr. *History of Arizona.* Vol. 2. New York: Lewis Historical Publishing Co., 1958.

Peterson, Richard H. *The Bonanza Kings: The Social Origins and Business Behavior of Western Mining Entrepreneurs, 1870–1900.* Lincoln: University of Nebraska Press, 1977.

Piven, Frances Fox, and Richard A. Cloward. *Poor People's Movements: Why They Succeed, How They Fail.* New York: Vintage Books, 1979.

Pollack, Norman. *The Populist Response to Industrial America.* Cambridge, Mass.: Harvard University Press, 1962.

Pomeroy, Earl S. *The Territories and the United States, 1860–1890.* Philadelphia: University of Pennsylvania Press, 1971.

Poston, Charles D. *Building a State in Apache Land.* Tempe, Ariz.: Aztec Press, 1963.

Proceedings of the Convention of Western Federation of Miners (file).

Quint, Howard. *The Forging of American Socialism.* Columbia: University of South Carolina Press, 1953.

Richards, J. Morris. *The Birth of Arizona: The Baby State.* Phoenix, Ariz.: State Department of Education, 1940.

Robinson, Will. *The Story of Arizona.* Phoenix, Ariz.: The Berryhill Company, 1919.

Rockwood, D. Stephen, et al. *American Third Parties Since the Civil War: An Annotated Bibliography.* New York: Garland Publishing, 1985.

References

Rogin, Michael Paul. *The Intellectuals and McCarthy: The Radical Specter*. Cambridge, Mass.: The MIT Press, 1967.

Rogin, Michael Paul, and John L. Shover. *Political Change in California: Critical Elections and Social Movements, 1890–1966*. Westport, Conn.: Greenwood Press, 1970.

Roosevelt, Theodore. *An Autobiography*. New York: Charles Scribner's Sons, 1925.

Rosenstone, Steven, Roy L. Behr, and Edward H. Lazarus. *Third Parties in America: Citizen Response to Major Party Failure*. Princeton: Princeton University Press, 1984.

Rowe, John. *The Hard-Rock Men: Cornish Immigrants and the North American Mining Frontier*. New York: Harper and Row, Barnes and Nobel Import Division, 1974.

Sacks, B. *Be it Enacted: The Creation of the Territory of Arizona*. Phoenix: Arizona Historical Foundation, 1964.

Salvatore, Nick. *Eugene v. Debs: Citizen and Socialist*. Urbana: University of Illinois Press, 1982.

Sarasohn, David. *The Party of Reform: Democrats in the Progressive Era*. Jackson: University of Mississippi Press, 1989.

Schlesinger, Arthur. *Political and Social History of the United States, 1829–1925*. New York: The Macmillan Company, 1925.

Servin, Manuel P. *An Awakened Minority: The Mexican-Americans*. 2nd ed. Beverly Hills: Glencoe Press, 1974.

Shannon, David A. *The Socialist Party of America*. Chicago: Quadrangle Books, 1967.

Shepperson, Wilbur S. *Restless Strangers: Nevada's Immigrants and Their Interpreters*. Reno: University of Nevada Press, 1970.

———. *Retreat to Nevada: A Socialist Colony of World War I*. Reno: University of Nevada Press, 1966.

Silbey, Joel H., Allan G. Bogue, and William H. Flanigan, eds. *The History of American Electoral Behavior*. Princeton: Princeton University Press, 1978.

Sklar, Martin J. *The Corporate Reconstruction of American Capitalism, 1890–1916*. Cambridge: Cambridge University Press, 1988.

Sloan, Richard E. *Memories of an Arizona Judge*. Stanford: Stanford University Press, 1932.

Sloan, Richard E., and Ward R. Adams. *History of Arizona*. 6 vols. Phoenix, Ariz.: Records Publishing Company, 1930.

Smelser, Neil J. *Theory of Collective Behavior*. New York: Free Press, 1962.

Smith, Duane A. *Rocky Mountain Mining Camps: The Urban Frontier*. Bloomington: Indiana University Press, 1967.

Sparks, George F., ed. *A Many-Colored Toga: The Diary of Henry Fountain Ashurst*. Tucson: University of Arizona Press, 1962.

Spear, J. W. *"Uncle Billy" Remembers*. Phoenix: Arizona Republic and Gazette, 1940.

Spence, Clark C. *British Investments and the American Mining Frontier, 1860–1901*. Ithaca: Cornell University Press, 1958.

Thompson, E. P. *The Making of the English Working Class*. New York: Pantheon Books, 1963.

References

Trimble, William J. *The Mining Advance into the Inland Empire*. New York: Johnson Reprint Corporation, 1972.

Ulam, Adam B. *The Unfinished Revolution*. New York: Random House, 1960.

Unseem, Michael. *Protest Movements in America*. Indianapolis: Bobbs-Merrill, 1975.

Wagoner, Jay. *Arizona Territory: 1863–1912*. Tucson: University of Arizona Press, 1970.

Walker, Henry P., and Don Bufkin. *Historical Atlas of Arizona*. Norman: University of Oklahoma Press, 1979.

Weber, David J., ed. *Foreigners in Their Native Land: Historical Roots of the Mexican Americans*. Albuquerque: University of New Mexico Press, 1973.

Weinstein, James. *The Decline of Socialism in America, 1912–1919*. New York: Monthly Review Press, 1967.

Western Federation of Miners, Executive board reports.

Wiebe, Robert. *Businessmen and Reform*. Cambridge, Mass.: Harvard University Press, 1962.

————. *The Search for Order: 1877–1920*. New York: Hill and Wang, 1967.

Williams, R. Hall. *The Democratic Party and California Politics, 1880–1896*. Stanford: Stanford University Press, 1973.

Wright, James Edward. *The Politics of Populism: Dissent in Colorado*. New Haven: Yale University Press, 1974.

Wyllys, Rufus K. *Arizona: The History of a Frontier State*. Phoenix: Arizona Historical Foundation, 1950.

Wyman, Mark W. *Hard Rock Epic: Western Miners and the Industrial Revolution*. Berkeley: University of California Press, 1979.

Young, Herbert V. *Ghosts of Cleopatra Hill*. Jerome, Ariz: Jerome Historical Society, 1964.

Zelinsky, Wilbur. *The Cultural Geography of the United States*. Englewood Cliffs, N.J.: Prentice-Hall, 1973.

ARTICLES, BOOK CHAPTERS, and MONOGRAPHS

"Arizona." In *The History of Woman's Suffrage*, ed. Ida Husted Harper, 6:10–15. New York: National American Woman Suffrage Association. Printed by J. J. Little & Ives Company, New York.

"Arizona." In *Standard Encyclopedia of the Alcohol Problem*. Westlake, Ohio (1925): 193–195.

Berman, David R. "Electoral Support for Populism in the Mountain States: Some Evidence From Arizona." *Social Science Journal*. 24 (January 1987): 43–52.

————. "Environment, Culture, and Radical Third Parties: *Electoral Support for the Socialists in Arizona and Nevada 1912–16.*"*Social Science Journal* 27 (1990): 147–158.

————. "Male Support for Woman Suffrage: An Analysis of Voting Patterns in the Mountain West." *Social Science History* 11 (Fall 1987): 281–294.

————. "Political Culture, Issues, and the Electorate: Evidence from the Progressive Era." *Western Political Quarterly* 41 (March 1988): 169–180.

———. "State Legislators and Their Constituents: Regulating Arizona Railroads in the Progressive Era." *Social Science Quarterly* 71 (December 1990): 812–823.

———. "Voters, Candidates, and Issues in the Progressive Era: An Analysis of the 1912 Presidential Election in Arizona." *Social Science Quarterly* 67 (June 1986): 255–266.

Bradford, W. S. "Is Hunt for the Workers?" *Arizona Socialist Bulletin* (October 11, 1916): 1, 4.

Brown, Roy E. "Colorful Colorado: State of Varied Industries." In *Rocky Mountain Politics,* ed. Thomas C. Donnelly, 51-87. Albuquerque: University of New Mexico Press, 1940.

Bryan, William J. "The Arizona Constitution." *Commoner* (February 24, 1911): 2.

Cameron, Colin. "Report of Colon Cameron." In *Report of the Territorial Governor to the Secretary of Interior,* 20-25. Washington, D.C.: GPO, 1896.

Campbell, Allen. "Republican Politics in Democratic Arizona." *Journal of Arizona History* (Summer 1981): 177–196.

Clark, Victor S. "Mexican Labor in the United States." *Bulletin of the Bureau of Labor* (September 1908): 466–522.

Debs, Eugene V. "Railroad Employees and Socialism." *International Socialist Review* 9 (October 1908): 241–248.

"Democratic Disruptions in Arizona Deplored." *Arizona Democrat* (April 23, 1913).

Downs, Anthony. "Up and Down With Ecology — the Issue-Attention Cycle." *Public Interest* 28 (1972): 38–50.

Dubofsky, Melvin. "The Origins of Western Working Class Radicalism, 1890–1905." *Labor History* 7 (1966): 131–154.

Erikson, Robert S., John P. McIver, and Gerald C. Wright, Jr. "State Political Culture and Public Opinion." *American Political Science Review* 81 (September 1987): 798–813.

Fahey, John. "Ed Boyce and the Western Federation of Miners." *Idaho Yesterdays* 25 (Fall 1981): 18–30.

Filene, Peter. "An Obituary for 'The Progressive Movement,' " *American Quarterly* 22 (1970): 20–34.

Flanigan, William H., and Nancy H. Zingale. "Alchemist's Gold: Inferring Individual Relationships from Aggregate Data." *Social Science History* 9 (Winter 1985): 71–92.

Fowler, James H. "Constitutions and Conditions Contrasted: Arizona and New Mexico, 1910." *Journal of the West* 13 (October 1974): 51–58.

Gaboury, William J. "From Statehouse to Bull Pen: Idaho Populism and the Coeur d'Alene Troubles of the 1890's." *Pacific Northwest Quarterly* (January 1967): 14–22.

Gill, Mary E., and John S. Goff. "Joseph H. Kibbey and School Segregation in Arizona." *Journal of Arizona History* (Spring 1980): 411–421.

Goodman, L. "Some Alternatives to Ecological Correlation." *American Journal of Sociology* 64 (1959): 610–625.

Haskett, Bert. "History of the Sheep Industry in Arizona." *Arizona Historical Review* 8 (1936): 3–49.

References

Hilzinger, J. S. "The People's Party." *Arizona Magazine* 1 (1893): 20–23.

Hoxie, Robert F. "The Rising Tide of Socialism." *Journal of Political Economy* 19 (October 1911): 609–631.

Hubbard, H. A. "The Arizona Enabling Act and President Taft's Veto." *Pacific Historical Review* 3 (1934): 307–322.

———. "Arizona's Struggle Against Joint Statehood." *Pacific Historical Review* 11 (1942): 415–423.

Hunt, George W.P. "Distrust of State Legislatures." Address delivered at governors' conference, Colorado Springs, Colorado, August 28, 1913 (pamphlet).

———. "The Single Legislative Branch." *Welfare* (October 1913): 11.

———. "Texas Day in Arizona." Address delivered April 22, 1916. Phoenix, Ariz.: R. A. Watkins Printing Co., n.d.

Jensen, Richard. "On Modernizing Frederick Jackson Turner: The Historiography of Regionalism." *Western Historical Quarterly* (July 1980): 307–322.

Kazin, Michael. "Struggling with Class Struggle." *Labor History* 28 (1987): 497–514.

Kennamer, Lorrin. "Introduction." In D. W. Meinig, *Imperial Texas: An Interpretive Essay in Cultural Geography.* Austin: University of Texas Press, 1969.

Kennedy, John Curtis. "Socialist Tendencies in American Trade Unions." *International Socialist Review* 8 (1907–1908): 330–345.

Kerr, William T., Jr. "The Progressives of Washington, 1910–1912." *Pacific Northwest Quarterly* (January 1964): 16–27.

Key, V. O., Jr. "A Theory of Critical Elections." *Journal of Politics* 17 (1955): 198–210.

Kibbey, Joseph H. "Republican Outlook." *Rita* 2 (February 23, 1896): 11–12.

King, Judson. "The Arizona Story in a Nutshell." *Equity Series* 14 (January 1912): 7–8.

Kleppner, Paul. "Voters and Parties in the Western States, 1876–1900." *Western Historical Quarterly* (January 1983): 49–68.

Krenkel, John H. "The Disputed Arizona Gubernatorial Election of 1916." *Journal of the West* 13 (October 1974): 59–67.

Kuklinski, James H., Daniel S. Metlay, and W. D. Kay. "Citizen Knowledge and Choices on the Complex Issue of Nuclear Energy." *American Journal of Political Science* 26 (1982): 615–642.

"Labor Conditions in the Southwest." *Engineering and Mining Journal* (March 31, 1904): 510.

Larson, T. A. "Dolls, Vassals, and Drudges — Pioneer Women in the West." *Western Historical Quarterly* (January 1972): 6–16.

———. "Populism in the Mountain West: A Mainstream Movement." *Western Historical Quarterly* 13 (April 1982): 143–164.

Letwin, William. "The Past and Future of the American Businessman." *Daedalus* 98 (Winter 1969): 1–22.

Lunardini, Christine A., and Thomas J. Knock. "Woodrow Wilson and Woman Suffrage: A New Look." *Political Science Quarterly* 95 (Winter 1980–1981): 655–671.

References

Lutrin, Carl, and Allan K. Settle. "The Public and Ecology: The Role of Initiatives in California's Environmental Politics." *Western Political Quarterly* 28 (1975): 352–371.

Lyon, William H. "The Corporate Frontier in Arizona." *Journal of Arizona History* 9 (1968): 1–17.

McCarthy, John, and Mayer Zald. "Resource Mobilization and Social Movements: A Partial Theory." *American Journal of Sociology* 82 (1977): 1212–1241.

McCluskey, H. S. *Absentee Capitalists Menace Popular Government in Arizona.* Bound reprint of articles appearing in the *Miami Daily Silver Belt,* August 27–October 21, 1921. 30 pp.

McCormick, John S. "Hornets in the Hive: Socialists in Early Twentieth-Century Utah." *Utah Historical Quarterly* 50 (Summer 1982): 225–240.

McCormick, John S., and John R. Sillito. "Socialism and Utah Labor: 1900–1920." *Southwest Economy and Society* 6 (Fall 1983): 15–30.

McDonagh, Eileen L., and H. Douglas Price. "Woman Suffrage in the Progressive Era: Patterns of Opposition and Support in Referenda Voting, 1910–1918." *American Political Science Review* 79 (1985): 415–435.

MacDonald, John. "From Butte to Bisbee." *International Socialist Review* 17 (August 1917): 69–74.

MacFarlane, Peter Clark. "The Galahad of Arizona, Governor Hunt." *Colliers* (April 15, 1916): 21–27.

Melville, Keith J. "Political Conflict and Accommodation in Utah Since Statehood." In *"Soul-Butter and Hog Wash,"* ed. Thomas G. Alexander, 138–155. Charles Redd Monographs. Provo: Brigham Young University Press, 1978.

Moody, Eric N. "Nevada's Bull Moose Progressives: The Formation and Function of a State Political Party in 1912." *Nevada Historical Society Quarterly* 16 (Fall 1973): 157–180.

Muller, John. "Ballot Patterns and Historical Trends in California." *American Political Science Review* 63 (1969): 1197–1212.

Ogburn, William F., and Inez Goltra. "How Women Vote: A Study of an Election in Portland Oregon." *Political Science Quarterly* 34 (September 1919): 413–433.

O'Neill, William O. "Populist Outlook." *Rita* 2 (February 23, 1896): 12–13.

"Replacing the Saloon." *Arizona Mining Journal* (May 1919): 1–2.

Roberts, Shirley J. "Minority-Group Poverty in Phoenix: A Socio-Economic Survey." *Journal of Arizona History* 19 (1973): 347–362.

Robinson, William S. "Ecological Correlations and the Behavior of Individuals." *American Sociological Review* 15 (1950): 351–357.

Rogin, Michael Paul. "Progressivism and the California Electorate." *Journal of American History* 55 (1968): 297–314.

Sarashon, David. "The Election of 1916: Realigning the Rockies." *Western Historical Quarterly* (July 1980): 285–305.

Schneider, Mark. "Ethnic Regions of the United States, 1870–1970." *Polity* 12 (1979): 273–290.

References

Sharkansky, Ira. "The Utility of Elazar's Political Culture: A Research Note." *Polity* 2 (1969): 66–83.

Sillito, John R. "Women and the Socialist Party in Utah, 1900–1920." *Utah Historical Quarterly* 19 (Summer 1981): 220–238.

Simons, A. M. "The Socialist Outlook." *International Socialist Review* 5 (1904–1905): 203–207.

Smith, Marcus A. "Statement before Committee on Territories, United States Senate." *Senate Documents.* Vol. 5, 57th Cong., 2d sess. (1902–1903): 319–327.

Snapp, Meredith A. "Defeat the Democrats: The Congressional Union for Women Suffrage in Arizona, 1914 and 1916." *Journal of the West* 14 (October 1975): 131–139.

Sofchalk, Donald G. "Organized Labor and the Iron Ore Miners of Northern Minnesota, 1907–1936." *Labor History* 12 (Spring 1971): 214–242.

Thelen, David P. "Social Tensions and the Origins of Progressivism." *Journal of American History* 56 (1969): 323–341.

Tucker, Harvey J., and Eric B. Herzik. "The Persisting Problem of Region in American State Policy Research." *Social Science Quarterly* 67 (1986): 84–97.

Vander Hill, Warren C. "Colorado Progressives and the Bull Moose Campaign." *Colorado Magazine* 43 (1966): 93–113.

Waltz, Waldo E. "Arizona: A State of New-Old Frontiers." In *Rocky Mountain Politics,* ed. Thomas C. Donnelly, 252–292. Albuquerque: University of New Mexico Press, 1940.

What Every Voter in the State of Arizona Should Know and Why (pamphlet, n.d.).

Williams, Eugene E. "The Territorial Governors of Arizona." *Arizona Historical Review* 7 (January 1936): 69–84.

Wolfle, Lee M., and Robert W. Hodge. "Radical-Party Politics in Illinois, 1880–1924." *Sociological Inquiry* 53 (1983): 33–60.

UNPUBLISHED MATERIAL

Beveridge, Albert J. "The Statehood Bill." Speech delivered in the U.S. Senate, March 8, 1906.

Brice, Calvin N. "The Constitutional Convention of Arizona." M.A. Thesis, Arizona State University, 1953.

Caleb, Howard. "The Labor Movement in Arizona." Manuscript, Arizona State Library, n.d.

Ellinwood, E. E. "Making a Modern Constitution." Speech delivered in the Opera House, Bisbee, Arizona, August 27, 1910.

Fazio, Steven A. "Marcus A. Smith, Arizona Politician." M.A. Thesis, University of Arizona, 1968.

Griffith, Victor S., Jr. "State Regulation of Railroad and Electric Rates in Arizona to 1925." M.A. Thesis, University of Arizona, 1931.

References

Harrison, Charles Buxton. "The Development of the Arizona Labor Movement." M.A. Thesis, Arizona State University, 1954.

Hatter, Menzo E. "The Major Issues in Arizona's Gubernatorial Campaigns." M.A. Thesis, Arizona State University, 1951.

Haynes, Gene R. "First State Legislature of Arizona." M.A. Thesis, Arizona State University , 1954.

Hunter, George. "John C. Greenway and the Bull Moose Movement in Arizona." M.A. Thesis, University of Arizona, 1966.

Kearney, Sharon F. "Arizona Legislature 1912–1914: A Study of State Progressivism." M.A. Thesis, California State University, 1977.

McBride, James D. "The Development of Labor Unions in Arizona Mining, 1884 to 1919." M.A. Thesis, Arizona State University, 1974.

————. "Henry S. McCluskey: Workingman's Advocate." Ph.D. Dissertation, Arizona State University, 1982.

McGinnis, Tru A. "The Influence of Organized Labor on the Making of the Arizona Constitution." M.A. Thesis, University of Arizona, 1930.

Nimmons, Robert Kim. "Arizona's Forgotten Past: The Negro in Arizona, 1539–1965." M.A. Thesis, Northern Arizona University, 1971.

O'Neill, William O. *An Open Letter to Hon. N. O. Murphy and John C. Herndon,* 1894.

Platform of the Republican Party Council, September 29, 1914.

"The Principles of the National Progressive Party of Arizona." Adopted at the state convention of the Progressive party, Phoenix, Arizona, July 30, 1912.

Tisdale, Nancy K. "The Prohibition Crusade in Arizona." M.A. Thesis, University of Arizona, 1965.

Todd, Charles Foster. "The Initiative and Referendum in Arizona." M.A. Thesis, University of Arizona, 1931.

Wilson, James A. "Cattle and Politics in Arizona, 1886–1941." Ph.D. Dissertation, University of Arizona, 1967.

Wilson, Majorie Haines. "The Gubernatorial Career of George W.P. Hunt." Ph.D. Dissertation, Arizona State University, 1973.

Ziede, Alexander. "The Territorial History of the Globe Mining District." M.A. Thesis, University of Southern California, 1939.

INDEX